THE
MUNDUGUMOR

Smithsonian Series in Ethnographic Inquiry

William L. Merrill and Ivan Karp, series editors

Ethnography as fieldwork, analysis, and literary form is the distinguishing feature of modern anthropology. Guided by the assumption that anthropological theory and ethnography are inextricably linked, this series is devoted to exploring the ethnographic enterprise.

THE
MUNDUGUMOR

From the Field Notes
of Margaret Mead
and Reo Fortune

Nancy McDowell

Smithsonian Institution Press
Washington and London

Editor: Gretchen Smith Mui
Production Editor: Duke Johns
Designer: Janice Wheeler

Library of Congress Cataloging-in-Publication Data

McDowell, Nancy, 1947–
    The Mundugumor : from the field notes of Margaret Mead and Reo
Fortune / by Nancy McDowell.
        p.   cm.
    Includes bibliographical references and index.
    ISBN 1–56098–062–1 (cloth)
    1. Biwat (Papua New Guinea people)—Kinship. 2. Biwat (Papua New
Guinea people)—Social life and customs. 3. Ethnology—Papua New
Guinea—Field work. 4. Mead, Margaret, 1901–1978. 5. Fortune, Reo,
1903–   . I. Mead, Margaret, 1901–1978. II. Fortune, Reo, 1903–   . III.
Title.
DU740.42.M39   1991
306'.0899912—dc20   90–24915

British Library Cataloguing-in-Publication Data is available

Manufactured in the United States of America
98 97 96 95 94 93 92 91   5 4 3 2 1

⊗The paper used in this publication meets the minimum requirements
of the American National Standard for Permanence of Paper for Printed
Library Materials Z39.48–1984

For permission to reproduce illustrations appearing in this book, please
correspond directly with the owners of the works, as listed in the individual captions. The Smithsonian Institution Press does not retain reproduction rights for these illustrations individually, or maintain a file of addresses for photo sources.

FOR RHODA MÉTRAUX

CONTENTS

LIST OF FIGURES, TABLES, GENEALOGIES, AND DIAGRAMS

FIGURES

TABLES

GENEALOGIES

DIAGRAMS

ACKNOWLEDGMENTS

This book would not have been possible without the support and assistance of many people and organizations. I would first like to acknowledge financial assistance from the National Science Foundation (Grant no. BNS-8107287), which gave me the leisure of a year away from the chaos of teaching to work on this project. I also appreciate the grants for more specific purposes from the Institute for Intercultural Studies and Franklin and Marshall College.

I want to express special gratitude to Mary Catherine Bateson and the estate of Margaret Mead as well as Ann McLean and the estate of Reo Fortune for their permission to use the field notes from, respectively, mother and uncle. Their aid goes beyond granting permissions, however; both of them were supportive and encouraging about this project, and I hope the results do not disappoint them.

At the Library of Congress, Manuscripts Division, where Margaret Mead's notes and papers are deposited, I received invaluable assistance from Mary Wolfskill.

A variety of people provided aid during my many trips to Papua New Guinea, all of whom somehow enriched this volume. The Catholic Mission (especially Fathers K. Wand and M. Fiedel, both located at Biwat) and Wirui Air Services were especially helpful. Pat

Townsend, Bill Wormsley, and Louise Morauta, then all at the Institute of Applied Social and Economic Research, gave advice and support. Special thanks go to the East Sepik Provincial Government and its research officer, John Wasori.

Many people either read or listened to part of what can be found within this volume, and I thank them all for their comments: Fitz John Porter Poole, Donald Tuzin, Gilbert Herdt, Paul Gorecki, Pamela Swadling, Linda Cunningham, Richard Scaglion, Ann McLean, Pamela Watson, Abraham Rosman, Paula Rubel, Rhoda Métraux, Deborah Gewertz, Mary Catherine Bateson, and Lora Ware.

I want to thank Bernd Lambert for instilling in me an interest in Mundugumor kinship so many years ago.

Arlene Mimm at Franklin and Marshall College went far beyond expected secretarial duties to see to the ultimate appearance of this volume, and I thank her.

Margaret Mead and I once talked about this project, and she encouraged me to tackle it if she did not finish it before her death. I thank her for that, and I thank both her and Reo Fortune for doing their work in the first place.

On the Yuat River there are so many people who helped me, who gave me their knowledge and friendship, that I cannot name all of them in just a page or two. All the people of Bun deserve thanks for supporting me and befriending me when I was there as well as when I visited their downriver neighbors, the Mundugumor, but I want to give special thanks to my *poroman*, Sapina Apouia.

The peoples of Biwat, Branda, Akuran, and Kinakatem welcomed me during a brief visit and were as hospitable and helpful as any people anywhere in the world. I want to give special thanks to a few individuals: Yesinfop (kaunsilman from Akuran), Wasa Kaitavut, John Sanfome, Thomas Kiniva, Thomas Mongi, Vai, Manung, Fwonga, Mongbareung, Akus, Kwakume, and Unglinda. Many more people were helpful, and I thank them all.

Special thanks must go to two very special people: Yosep Ruova, originally from the Mundugumor village of Kinakatem, and his son,

Abraham Kikisima. They were among my best friends; indeed, Yosep served as my father and Abraham as my brother while I did fieldwork in upriver Bun. When I told them of my Mundugumor project and the proposed two-week visit to Kinakatem, they readily agreed to accompany me, introduce me to their relatives and others, and help me straighten out the differences between the two peoples. I could not have done so without their interest, intelligence, curiosity, and insight.

Finally, Rhoda Métraux has helped me in this project, as well as in many others, more than I can easily acknowledge and certainly more than I can ever repay. Without her deep caring and concern, without her advice and assistance, this volume would not exist. It is to Rhoda, a mentor in the best sense of the word, that this book is dedicated.

INTRODUCTION 1

In 1932 Margaret Mead and Reo Fortune journeyed up the Yuat River, in what is now the nation of Papua New Guinea, to Kinaka-tem, the first of four river villages inhabited by people known then as the Mundugumor.[1] The fieldwork they did there eventually provided one of three case studies in *Sex and Temperament in Three Primitive Societies* (1963; first published in 1935), Mead's classic work about the socialization of female and male. They arrived in the community on October 4 and remained until December 18.[2] Although Mead published a considerable portion of her data in that book and in other works, much never came to print.[3] In this volume I construct an ethnography from Mead's and Fortune's materials on the Mundugumor.

My main motivation in doing so concerns the importance of the data. There is valuable information here: Mead and Fortune visited the Mundugumor soon after pacification and provide a glimpse into a society that no longer exists and will never exist again. I do not necessarily subscribe to the world-as-natural-laboratory vision of anthropological fieldwork nor the pseudoinductive stance that the more information gathered the better off the discipline is, but there is material here to which anthropologists will never again have access.

There is a second reason that these data are important. Anthropologists have long recognized that to understand societies in the Sepik area of Papua New Guinea we must examine patterns of interaction among groups and not rely exclusively or predominantly on community-based microstudies.[4] It was Mead (1970) who, as far back as the 1930s, described the Mountain Arapesh as an "importing culture." Although too much work done by English-speaking anthropologists has been based predominantly on a single culture if not a single village,[5] recently we have we begun to take seriously the regional perspective Schwartz (1963) and Mead (1970) called for.[6] The data here, then, may be important to others working in the region.

In addition, some Mundugumor data have already been used in theoretical debates of significance, and fleshing out the available materials can only enrich these discussions. I am thinking, for example, of Lévi-Strauss's response (1976) to Luc de Heusch's assertion that Lévi-Strauss's theory on the "atom of kinship" cannot work among the Mundugumor. Although the details of this relatively esoteric debate need not detain us here, the material presented in this volume is of interest to those who wish to pursue these and similar issues. It is important to understand the context within which Mead and Fortune gathered and formulated their data if one is to make use of them in further analysis and debate, especially when an examination of the data-gathering context can help us perceive more clearly the issues under consideration.

Although anthropologists who specialize in kinship and social organization are familiar with the Mundugumor because of the controversial "rope" system of descent reported by Mead and Fortune, the topics of ethos and gender relations are the ones by which the Mundugumor are better known to others. The Mundugumor, as well as the Arapesh and Tchambuli, have a central position in the now-burgeoning literature on women, male-female relations, and gender ideology because of Mead's treatment of these topics in *Sex and Temperament.* In that volume she explored the relationship between sex and temperament and in doing so advanced the notion that individual differences of temperament are more significant than biological sex in affecting adult personality. She contrasted typically gentle and unassertive Arapesh women and men with typically assertive and aggressive Mundugumor men and women. Socialization or culture and some sort of innate biological endowment unrelated to biological sex were the two main factors that formed adult personality. This work is seminal in the literature on gender, and whatever information is available in the notes can enrich these discussions. Not only is more information useful; again, an understanding of how Mead formulated her data can illuminate the issues involved as well. In fact, however, the notes include surprisingly little on the subject of gender as well as ethos in general. Most of the information—published and otherwise—is Mead's postfield interpretation and can be found in Mead (1963).

Thus, the main impetus for publishing the materials gathered by Mead and Fortune more than 50 years ago is the need for the data, and Mundugumor society is therefore the major focus of this book. But there are other reasons why these data, as well as the attempt to make something of them, are interesting. One is that they come from Margaret Mead and Reo Fortune and, thus, have a place in the history of anthropology. Looking at the nature of their work will assist in evaluating their contributions to the field and putting their work in a proper perspective. Because it is necessary to examine and evaluate the data in order to assess the reliability of the final description, the quality of the notes and an evaluation of the ethnographers who took them is a subsidiary topic. By examining the work Mead and Fortune did in the early 1930s, we can also gain insight into the nature of anthropology at that time as well as the history of the discipline, for they worked within an intellectual framework deeply set in its own historical context. An examination of this theme reveals a related but more general one: the nature of the ethnographic enterprise itself, the processes of data gathering, analysis, and interpretation. Although these and related epistemological

questions are not the main focus of this book, they are important
issues that need to be confronted.

The main purpose of this introductory chapter is to address some
of these issues and thereby outline the parameters that shape the
description contained in this volume. Every ethnography is molded
by a variety of features, and this one is certainly no different. The
historical context in which the work took place, the theoretical
framework of the ethnographers, the particulars of the people studied, the field situation—all contribute to the final form of the ethnography, and these are described in the first section. And because
one anthropologist is writing from the field notes of others, significant additional considerations pertain here. My own perspective,
how I approached the materials left by Mead and Fortune, the
methodological and epistemological problems of constructing an
ethnography from others' data—all these features too affect the
outcome of this enterprise, and these are the subject of the second
section.

FACTORS SHAPING THE DATA

Many interrelated factors affected the nature of the materials available in reconstituting a Mundugumor ethnography. Here I rather
arbitrarily divide them into two categories: (1) the nature of Mead's
and Fortune's particular fieldwork and (2) the historical context
within which it took place and the theoretical frameworks within
which the data were gathered and formulated.

The Nature of this Fieldwork

Mead (1963:164) went to the Pacific intending to research a particular problem (the reasons that I focus on Mead here rather than
Fortune, whose funding was not tied to the investigation of a specific problem, are stated later): ". . . the underlying purpose of my
field studies in New Guinea was to discover to what degree temper-

amental differences between the sexes were innate and to what extent they were culturally determined, and furthermore to inquire minutely into the educational mechanisms connected with these differences." Mead and Fortune had been working in Alitoa, Mountain Arapesh, for about eight months when they left to seek comparative material, Fortune on various areas of sociocultural life and Mead on the problem she set out to investigate.

In *Sex and Temperament* (1963:164, 165) Mead describes the way in which she and Fortune chose the Mundugumor field site. Little was known about the area, and the choice was necessarily arbitrary and unrelated to her research problem. They wanted a location that was, after the difficulties of transportation and movement among the Mountain Arapesh, easily accessible by water and that had not been heavily influenced by missionaries and colonialists. They also wanted to avoid areas in which other anthropologists had worked; thus, the Iatmul on the Middle Sepik, studied by Bateson, and the Banaro on the Keram River, studied by Thurnwald, were excluded.[7] Finally, they required a group that was under at least minimal government control. The Mundugumor, controlled for just over three years, easily met all these criteria. The year was 1932: the time had not yet come when elaborate research proposals and theoretically sophisticated hypotheses were required for funding. Unlike many anthropologists in her day, Mead did go to the field with problems in mind and did focus her data-collecting activities on particular topics but was free to go where it seemed best. And that is precisely what Fortune and Mead did: they went to the next place, easily reached by water, that would not interfere with the work of another anthropologist.

In 1932 there were four Mundugumor villages along the Yuat, or Biwat, River—Kinakatem, Akuran,[8] Branda, and Biwat—and two additional villages in the bush across the river, Dowaning and Andafugan. The name *Mundugumor* is one Mead and Fortune both recorded in 1932; today, the people along the river do not use that name but refer to themselves as Biwat peoples. In 1981 informants volunteered the name *Mundugumor* ("Mundugama") to me as one which they had previously used but no longer did. However, because the name *Mundugumor* is in the literature, because it is the name the people used in 1932, when the ethnographers were there and the time to which these notes and description refer, and because *Biwat* can refer to a village, a river, and a language (Laycock 1973) as well as a people and its use could be confusing, I retain the name *Mundugumor* here.

Mead noted that although all six of these villages spoke the same language and referred to themselves as Mundugumor, river villagers had begun to differentiate between themselves and the bush villagers. River dwellers had started to eat bush villagers, for example, while they continued to observe a taboo on eating people of one's own group. Mead's and Fortune's data come almost exclusively from these four river villages, and unless otherwise noted all data in this book also pertain only to Biwat, Branda, Akuran, and Kinakatem. Mead and Fortune lived in Kinakatem itself, and therefore most descriptions are relevant especially to this village.

The data available come mostly from less than three months of initial fieldwork, from October 4 to December 18, 1932. However, data were gathered during two other periods. In 1938 Mead and Gregory Bateson were working in the Middle Sepik Iatmul village of Tambunam, and two important Mundugumor informants, Omblean and Afima, came to visit. Mead recorded some myths and other data at that time. Finally, Mead revisited the Mundugumor in 1971. Fortune never returned to or gathered further data on the Mundugumor.

As fieldwork goes, Mead's and Fortune's was exceptionally short. They did not have time to gather data on some topics, and on other topics they did not have the opportunity to revise, correct, expand, and deepen. They were unable to do extended case studies, did not observe an annual cycle, did not have time to sense change and periodicities. Some events just did not occur during their stay. The nuances that one perceives slowly after multiple clues have been recorded are weak here. On some topics, such as kinship, there are elaborate data, but on others, such as the annual cycle of yam planting, relatively few. Even their planned eight-month trip was too short, and surely less than three months constitutes a severe limitation. Mundugumor society and culture were far more complex than anyone could begin to comprehend in three months.

Mead never claimed that she and Fortune did a complete ethnography of the Mundugumor, and she knew very well that her materials were especially limited since they left in the middle of their planned field trip. In the introduction to a volume she began working on in 1972 and 1973 about the Mundugumor, Mead attributes the decision to leave early to three main factors: (1) the culture was "disorganized" and "broken," and studying it rather than a "living culture" seemed unwarranted; (2) the Mundugumor did not seem to be illuminating her field problem beyond what she had learned among the Arapesh, for they too did not elaborate a contrast between male and female temperament—both men and women were aggressive and assertive; and (3) the field conditions were, admittedly, difficult ones; the mosquitoes were ferocious and the village flooded. Mead (1972:204–7) also made it clear in her autobiography that she did not enjoy the culture she was studying; in fact, she wrote that "furthermore, I loathed the Mundugumor culture with its endless aggressive rivalries, exploitation, and rejection of children" (1972:205). She was frequently ill during this period, which only made the experience more unpleasant and exacerbated her growing disaffection with Fortune (see Mead 1972:206–7).

Mead was cognizant especially that they had stopped in the middle of a projected eight-month field trip and never completed many of the things they planned to do. In a 1973 manuscript she wrote that

the material has the incomplete character which is inevitable when a field trip is planned for a longer period and interrupted. It was our habit to follow events as they occurred, and in the intervals between attending events and writing the events up, to work with informants on linguistics and other aspects of the culture. Often a preliminary account of some ceremony would be elicited . . . which we expected to see later, but which did not occur while we were there. Or I would stumble on some woman working on a partly completed object and record its state, postponing until later a record of how it was begun. Our notes are filled with questions which were raised, but which were never answered.

This interrupted fieldwork limited and shaped the ways in which I was able to reconstruct an ethnography. Mead made a note on, for example, a form of sorcery and intended to follow up on it later but never had the opportunity to do so. Many of the lacunae in the material are due to this cause. Unfortunately, it is not possible to be certain whether this or some other reason (e.g., a simple lack of interest) was the cause of all the gaps. Contradictions in the notes would probably have been resolved with later work, but because Mead and Fortune left the field before finishing, the contradictions remain (I attempt to resolve some of these contradictions in various ways). The short and interrupted nature of the fieldwork is the most restraining factor in writing this ethnography and more than anything else shapes what is to follow. This volume necessarily contains speculation, inference, and assertions of probability.

The brief and interrupted fieldwork does constitute a severe limitation on the data, but it is not as serious as it might have been had these been ordinary anthropologists. When Fortune and Mead left at the end of 1932, they went up the main Sepik River and stopped in the village of Kankanamun to visit Bateson. In her autobiography Mead (1972:208–9) describes the scene and includes this anecdote:

> . . . less than an hour after our arrival Gregory brought out a copy of *Growing Up in New Guinea* and challenged my statement that Manus men were ignorant of the fact that girls menstruated between menarche and marriage . . . . This was Gregory's opening gambit. He was later to remark that anthropologists who had read my work but did not know me tended to doubt my conclusions because they could not allow for the speed with which I worked.

I think that Bateson was correct—much skepticism about Mead's ethnographic work comes from the fact that people do not comprehend the speed at which she was able to work (see Schwartz 1983 for similar comments). What she and Fortune managed to record and observe about the Mundugumor in less than three months would put many anthropologists to shame. She was simply an incredibly fast fieldworker, relatively tireless, methodical, and organized. And her insight into the behaviors around her during these initial days and weeks was exemplary.

That someone can go back to her notes and make sense of them at all is ample testimony to her skill. If Mead had not been the organized and methodical fieldworker and excellent observer and chronicler that she was (almost all her notes were typed and labeled), this project would not have been possible. Anthropologists trying to decipher untyped, unlabeled notes 50 years later might throw up their hands in dismay, as I did with most of Fortune's notes and as I suspect they would with most anthropologists' field notes— they are written to be read only by the writer. That this ethnography is possible at all is due to Mead's detailed and careful attention to her notes and to her sense of the history of the discipline and the role of ethnographic data within it.

The Mundugumor were the third Melanesian people among whom Mead and Fortune did fieldwork together; the first was the Manus, the second the Mountain Arapesh. They had devised a method for cooperating by dividing up the work topically. This division was more extreme in Mundugumor than in Arapesh, and Mead recognized that they worked more independently than they had before. In the introduction to her proposed volume on the Mundugumor, she wrote this about the division of labor and nature of cooperation between her and Fortune:

We had set about work with the expectation of doing fieldwork in the style that had been set in Manus, where we had combined the methods that I had developed in Samoa ([Mead 1928, 1930])[9] and the methods that he had developed in Dobu ([Fortune 1932a]): complete mapping of households, a period of initial concentration on the language, an event analysis ([see especially Mead 1971]) in which a diary record was combined with detailed accounts of each event, textual work with good informants, a study of childrearing and children's play groups, and the basic technology illustrated by a collection for the American Museum, children's drawings and detailed study of adult artists at work. However, these methods were complicated in two ways: by the fact that we had set them up with an expectation of a minimum six to eight months work and by the rather arbitrary division of labor. We always specialized in different aspects of the culture, after an initial period on the census and language, but in Arapesh Dr. Fortune had specialized on the language, texts of myths, trade, and the men's sacra. The Mundugumor language proved to be less interesting than Arapesh, and Dr. Fortune decided that I could do the language, the children and the technology while he would specialize on the social organization, kinship, warfare and religion . . . .

This quote tells us about more than the division of labor between Mead and Fortune; it reveals much about the multiplicity of their field methods as well as the conceptual apparatus they carried with them into the field. For example, they conceived of discrete topics to be researched, such as myth and trade, and saw social organization and kinship as somehow separable from children (although Mead seems to recognize elsewhere the artificiality of this distinction). Mead never directly addresses what I consider to be a significant question—the ways in which these diverse topics were eventually to be synthesized into a representation of what she called a "living culture."

If Fortune did indeed decide who was to research which topic, then this quote also reveals something about the relationship between Mead and Fortune as well. Anthropologists frequently talk of the benefits of having two people, especially of opposite sex, in the field together; it seems an ideal situation in which, because of the constant cross-checking with each other, a greater amount of reliable data can be gathered. Indeed, Mead was a strong proponent of the advantages of such teams, especially in Melanesia, where a pronounced male-female dichotomy tends to exist and a female-male team would facilitate the acquisition of data from both women and men. I think the assignment of topics in Arapesh and Mundugumor reflects a sexual division of labor between Mead and Fortune, a division that shaped the data that they gathered and that are available for reanalysis. Something other than Mead's preexisting field problem led her to investigate the topics that she did.[10]

Although anthropologists often talk of this ideal of male-female field teams, the reality, which is rarely noted in print, is sometimes more problematic: with such an extreme division of labor, full sharing and intercommunication are required, and these are not always easily achieved. A few passages in *Blackberry Winter* (1972:206–7) indicate that all was not well with Mead and Fortune's professional marriage, and one must wonder about the communication between them (see also Howard 1984). *Blackberry Winter* (1972:205) contains an explicit reference to the problem:

In the middle of our stay I discovered that Reo, who had insisted that he alone would work on the kinship system, had missed a clue. The clue had come from the children's terminology, on which I was working. I felt that if he had not drawn so rigid a dividing line between his work and mine, we would have been able to put the material together much sooner. As it was, we might have missed the clue altogether. . . .

There are other indications that one was not aware of what the other was doing and learning. Mead noted that it was "some time" before they realized that their main informant, Omblean, had on his own decided to tell Fortune the realities and Mead the ideals. They could not have been carefully comparing materials, for surely this would have come to their attention quickly. Furthermore, Mead thought that Fortune was recording the mythology, but he did not. She recorded some myths in 1938 from Omblean, but when she began to prepare her monograph she wrote and asked Fortune where the myths were and why neither of them had recorded them.[11] Again, if they had been discussing issues according to the ideal of cooperation anthropologists hold dear, they would have been aware of this lack in their data. Of course, communication between them existed on some levels and in some contexts, but their joint fieldwork fell below the ideal situation.

This division of labor and the weaknesses of the fieldworkers created another problem. According to Mead, Fortune was supposed to cover kinship and social organization, warfare, and religion, the framework of any ethnographic description. Unfortunately, although Fortune was a superb analyst and theoretician, he was not the methodical and organized fieldworker that Mead was. Perhaps someone can make sense of his handwritten notes; I cannot, or at least I can make little sense of most of them. Even Mead, who should have been able to do so, noted while she was preparing her monograph that his notes were with a few exceptions "virtually unusable." I certainly found this to be true. Where Mead's notes are labeled, typed, and clear, his are handwritten fragments in no particular order. It is unfortunate that most of these notes were never typed and organized; possibly someone more familiar with Fortune's handwriting and style of thought might make more of them than I did, but this would be a monumental task if even Mead could not do so. There are more gaps in the data than there need be because Fortune's notes are not usable and, I am also fairly sure, simply not as thorough and complete as Mead's might have been. Luckily, Mead made notes on kinship and religion (and apparently typed some of Fortune's notes herself) and surely got information from Fortune on these topics. I relied on Mead's notes and therefore do not, in the chapters that follow, attribute every fact or quote to Mead; all material comes from her notes unless I specify otherwise.

That Mead was to gather data on the language presents another limitation on the information available, for she was not much of a linguist. Her ear for hearing sounds and pronunciation was less than keen, and despite her consistency and methodical nature in other areas, her attempts at consistent spellings were inadequate. This problem may, of course, have something to do with the speed with which she worked. And why should she worry about consistency in her personal notes as long as she remembered and was cognizant of the alternatives she may have used? Apart from the obvious problems linguists might have with her materials, I found her data especially difficult in this context because of the inconsistent spelling of personal names. As any anthropologist on the scene might do, I tried to familiarize myself with all the inhabitants but was frequently confused by who was who and even by how many people there were. It is a problem I never completely resolved.

For Mead one of the most interesting methodological aspects of this particular fieldwork concerned the employment of a specific informant, a man named Omblean, whom Mead described in some detail in *Sex and Temperament* (1963:228–30) as a deviant. Although they did have other informants, particularly the young boy Afima, Omblean was undoubtedly their main and often exclusive source of information. He worked alternately with Mead and Fortune—he was, according to Mead (1972:204), the only "very good informant" available. Although he was a remarkable man, having only one good informant for two anthropologists was bound to cause problems and to some extent affect the range of data obtainable. In her manuscript Mead wrote about their fieldwork that

a . . . special problem arising from this material is the extraordinary performance of our best, and almost our only systematic informant, Omblean. He was so far superior in intellectual capacity, fluency in Neo-Melanesian, and understanding of his own culture, that [both] Dr. Fortune and I worked with him as a formal informant. We were working at high speed, and Dr. Fortune's notes were handwritten, so it was some time before we realized that he had made his own decision as to the way in which he would present the culture to each [of us], telling Dr. Fortune all the disastrous events of quarrels, failures to "back" [reciprocate] a woman given in marriage, warfare, etc., and by telling me the formal things about the way the culture should ideally be enacted.

After discussing the nature and role of informants, Mead concludes the section by saying that her monograph would include all of Omblean's statements given to Fortune and Mead, side by side for comparison.

There are no references to Omblean's actions in the actual field notes. The only place in which Mead refers to his tendency to tell her the ideal but Fortune the real is in the introductions to her proposed monograph. Fortune's notes are not sufficiently usable to compare with Mead's to determine whether this assertion is true or not. I am somewhat skeptical and wonder if the kinds of questions asked might not have influenced the answers given. Mead may have missed an opportunity to examine how individual anthropologists' questions, interests, and style influence the response from informants. (Furthermore, in a letter to Boas dated January 29, 1933, Mead intimates that she and Fortune may have split their labors with Omblean in that way and that the division was not necessarily or clearly instigated by the informant himself.)

Both anthropologists relied on observation and questioning, but in the less than three months they were there almost all work was done in Neo-Melanesian or pidgin English, not the local language. The relatively few speakers of pidgin must have restricted the informant pool considerably and in particular ways. It is unlikely that any women spoke pidgin, and it is probable that only younger men who had been away working as laborers on the coast were anywhere near fluent in it. And working almost exclusively in a lingua franca never yields the rich data that working in a native tongue does. Subtle and complex concepts are sometimes difficult to express in pidgin, especially the pidgin prevalent in the early 1930s. And because indigenous concepts and pidgin words are not coterminous, the fact that most of the notes were in pidgin or English made interpreting the precise meaning of many especially difficult. For example, two terms in the local language, *kamain* and *wareun*, are both translated into pidgin as *pren* (friend). In recording Mead often just wrote *pren* and did not specify if the reference was to a *kamain* or a *wareun*, and the two are considerably different. Similarly, Mead used the pidgin word *masalai* (spirit) to mean both *maindjimi* (bush spirit) and *saki* (water spirit), and sometimes it was difficult to discern which spirit she or her informants meant.

Historical Context and Theoretical Framework

All field research is conducted and written up within a specific historical context and an explicit or implicit theoretical framework, and these paradigms significantly shape the research by influencing the questions asked, topics investigated, and the events and behavior perceived. Recording only what occurs is impossible. What did or did not get in the notebooks is another aspect of the problem. Different anthropologists might perceive the same event in different ways, and how are we to know how an individual anthropologist's version compares with his or her informants' versions, which may be different from one another? How what is written gets written is important as well—the connotations of words, the selectivity and filtering. These are basic issues and problems in the discipline of anthropology, and although the solutions (if any exist) are beyond the scope of this book, the problems do pertain to what I have tried to do here and should be kept in mind in examining the data presented.

Mead worked within a particular context, which affected and limited—as any such framework must—how the data were gathered and construed. Some questions were never asked, some topics never investigated, some behaviors, words, or gestures never recorded; events were perceived and recorded in some particular ways rather than others. The uneven coverage of topics in the notes is partly the result of what anthropology at the time considered important as well as what Mead herself thought of interest. The particular problem she went to research also affected her vision and what made its way into her notebook. Her goal was to study the extent to which temperamental differences between women and men were innate or learned, and one can hardly chastise her for not recording data on, say, caloric consumption and its relation to yam gardens and marsupial hunting.

The fact that Fortune and Mead came to the Mundugumor from Arapesh also explains some of the emphases in their Mundugumor material and is itself of contextual relevance. Coming from one Melanesian group—indeed, one Sepik people—to another very different one must have highlighted the contrasts between the two considerably. In fact, as Mead (1963:1950 edition preface) recognizes, many people believed the contrasts to be too fortuitous to be true. After living with the materially poor Arapesh, Mundugumor relative richness and "carelessness" with material goods must, for example, have been striking. Perhaps the juxtaposition of the two did contribute to some muting of similarities and overemphasis on the differences. (Surely Mead's desire to communicate with a general audience rather than professional anthropologists alone also led to some exaggeration of the differences.)

American anthropology, in which Mead was firmly grounded, was a young discipline in the early 1930s. Boas had assumed his position at Columbia only in 1896, and 1901 saw the production of the first Ph.D. dissertation, Kroeber's, under his guidance (de Waal Malefijt 1974:225, 233). Anthropology lacked many of the conceptual tools that have been developed and sharpened in the past 50 years; ideas now recognized as crucial then lacked conceptual precision. The refinements of these core concepts constitute a significant part of anthropological work in the past 50 years. Mead and Fortune worked without benefit of these advances, and not surprisingly a lack of conceptual precision appears in their notes. Anthropologists have learned that "ownership," for example, is not a single, unitary conception—people have substantially different kinds of rights in objects and resources. Mead did not have the benefit of the sharpened concept of ownership that we have today and included all kinds of things under the rubric; now it is difficult to tease apart the diverse kinds of rights in her notes. If anyone had any rights at all to an object or its use, she tended to identify that person as the owner.

This limitation is particularly true for what is still the central concept in anthropology—culture. Tylor had delineated his definition of culture only in 1871 (Tylor 1883; first published 1871), and Kroeber and Kluckhohn did not publish their study of the definition of culture until 1952 (Kroeber and Kluckhohn 1952). Stocking (1968:230) gives considerable credit to Boas for developing the modern concept of culture as something with "historicity, plurality, behavioral determinism, integration, and relativism," but he (1968:202) notes that Boas seemed slow because he did not publish his thoughts on this issue until 1930. He also depicts Boas as a transitional figure in the evolution of a contemporary definition of culture (1968:230). Although Mead, as a student of Boas, must have been exposed to his thinking long before 1930, it is no wonder that she operated in the early 1930s with a simple and somewhat rudimentary concept of culture.

For Mead culture possessed all those attributes identified by Stocking as elements in Boas's definition—"historicity, plurality, behavioral determinism, integration, and relativism"—and she tended to embed it in the socialization process, the place where individuals learned culture and where they were shaped both by it and to it. She seemed to operate with a concept of culture as something that existed outside individuals, separate and apart from them. In doing this, she saw culture as a concrete body of abstractions that existed in one relatively simple and coherent form, something that individuals learned more or less of, that they learned well or not so well. Simple cultures were something that anthropologists too could learn and be done with. One acquired cultures as if they were bodies of literature to be learned or mastered. She wrote of her 1938 encounter with Omblean: "We [Mead and Bateson] also had a chance to do a little work with Omblean in the light of knowledge of Tchambuli [Chambri] and Iatmul culture, neither of which were part of my repertoire in my 1932 trip." The quote reveals the importance of comparison to Mead's anthropology, but it also brings to light something about her view on the nature of cultures—these were challenges to master and add to one's repertoire. Today, of course, we recognize that it is unlikely that a culture could ever be completely, fully "mastered" by any outsider, but it is important to remember that she was writing from the perspective of American cultural anthropology of the 1930s, when human cultural phenomena seemed much simpler than they do today.

All of Mead's work is characterized by a distinctly positivist cast, a presumption that there are facts out there just waiting to be discovered. The ethnographer's task is to gather these empirical nuggets of truth. Mead assumed that one could construct the reality of another society if one worked hard enough, that there was one single reality. Her extremely positivist stance makes me uncomfortable, a discomfort that undoubtedly colors the pages to follow. The description contained herein is far less positivist than would have pleased Mead, yet it is far too positivist to please me. It is not the book either of us would have chosen to write.[12]

Working with one "good" informant posed no significant problem for Mead because if that informant knew the culture well, there was no problem of sampling or perspective. Informants' views were relatively uniform; some simply knew the culture better than others. The more sophisticated notion of a distributive model of culture (see Keesing 1981:71–72) did not exist at this time, and Mead never explicitly recognized the theoretical and methodological problems resulting when individuals and segments of a population differ. I think that she was very much ahead of her time, however, in recognizing that male and female could vary significantly, but because of her view of culture as a single coherent entity she never articulated gender differences as cultural or subcultural differences per se.

Mead was also influenced considerably by Benedict as well as Boas, and it is from Benedict that she takes some of her ideas about culture. The two were in frequent communication while Mead was in the field, and they shared ideas, concepts, and data freely (see, for example, Mead 1972). In some ways Mead's core approach to the nature of culture was Benedict's view that culture was "personality writ large." In fact, it was Mead (1959:vii–viii) who used that phrase in describing Benedict's work:

. . . she [Benedict] developed her own special contribution, her view of human cultures as "personality writ large," her view that it was possible to see each culture, no matter how small and primitive or how large and complex, as having selected from the great arc of human potentialities certain characteristics and then having elaborated them with greater strength and intensity than any single individual could ever do in one lifetime.

As did many other American anthropologists before World War II, Mead saw culture as a pattern or a configuration of integrated elements, perhaps all tied together by a single theme. Benedict (1934:46) wrote that "the significance of cultural behavior is not exhausted when we have clearly understood that it is local and man-made and hugely variable. It tends also to be integrated. A culture, like an individual, is a more or less consistent pattern of thought and action."

Elements were supposed to fit together, according to the prevailing wisdom, and when Mead went to the field she went with that assumption in mind. It is no surprise that she did find themes and patterns that fit together; she had a *theoretical* predilection to mute conflict and a distrust of lack of integration, and the theoretical paradigm or mindset inevitably inhibited the perception of contradiction and led to some simplification. A culture—especially a "simple, homogeneous" (1963:vi) one—was uniform and integrated. Mead operated with a concept of culture that lacked two significant understandings that we have today: (1) culture is not a uniform set of beliefs or practices but rather a complex set of diversities, and (2) culture is not perfectly integrated but contains contradictions, oppositions, and conflicts.

Although Mead worked with a relatively simple idea about what constituted culture, she was an extraordinary observer of human phenomena. Her theory led her to suspect contradictions and deny their existence, but she could not help seeing and perceiving them while she was in the field. The materials available on the Mundugumor are replete with examples of Mead's theory saying one thing and yet Mead seeing more than the theory allowed. In *Sex and Temperament* she highlights the people who do not fit and shows how and why they do not; she goes further, however, to assert that it is those who do not fit the ideal who allow the system to continue. Mead saw and recorded the oppositions and contradictions even if in her writing she stresses one side or one aspect; a close reading of her work illustrates this disjunction between observation and theory. She clearly saw complexities her theory was not prepared to incorporate, and she struggled considerably with these. Eventually she structured them in terms of a dichotomy between the ideal and those who deviated from it—that is, her organizational framework incorporated conflict and contradiction (and to some extent intra-cultural diversity as well) as a form of deviation from the single, stated integrated ideal. For example, in her proposed monograph she planned to underscore the significance of the fact that although the Mundugumor had an ideal scheme in their minds about kinship and marriage, it was so elaborate, cumbersome, and demographically unworkable that they never achieved or even tried to accomplish the ideal—they merely felt guilty when they failed to live up to it. Moreover, she believed, the ideal eventually contributed to what she thought was the "breakdown of the culture." As part of the introduction to her monograph, she wrote that

one of the theoretical points which arose from [Lévi-Strauss's] discussion of the Mundugumor material, and which very much interested the late Radcliffe-Brown, was my contention that it was the members of the society who stuck to a system which had been elaborated to a point of unworkability who did harm by preventing the developing of [a] new and viable system. Prof. Lévi-Strauss is delighted at the elegance with which the Mundugumor had pursued logical relationships to a conclusion which was socially nonviable, while I am stimulated by the even more elaborately revealed relationship between dogmatism and destructive forms of social organization or religion. The Mundugumor had developed a system in which not one single person was correctly married, and everyone who was incorrectly [married]—which was the entire community—was ashamed of their anomalous status.

A variety of factors, then, shapes and structures the corpus of data available for depicting the Mundugumor of 1932, factors that range from the length of fieldwork to the nature of American cultural anthropology at the time. But there is another aspect of the shape of this ethnography, and that is the fact that the ethnographers are not its author. And it is this factor that we must now examine.

RECONSTITUTING MUNDUGUMOR ETHNOGRAPHY

When Fortune and Mead left Kinakatem, they moved on to study the peoples of Chambri Lake and from there to other interests. They both used the data in various contexts, but neither ever wrote a Mundugumor monograph.[13] According to a draft manuscript that Mead wrote in 1972, there had been plans to publish:

When we left the Mundugumor . . . we had no definite plans for how our truncated material would ultimately be written up. However, when our next field choice, the Tchambuli [Chambri], provided genuinely contrastive material on culturally patterned personalities of the two sexes, we decided that I would write up most of the Arapesh ethnography, and Dr. Fortune would take the Mundugumor and Tchambuli ethnography, while I would use only as much Mundugumor and Tchambuli material as was necessary for my report on my field problem of culturally established sex differences, which I did. . . .

Thus, according to Mead, Fortune was to write up the Mundugumor data they acquired together for publication, but unfortunately he never did. Both went on to other projects and did not, until Mead's resurgence of interest in the 1970s, seem to pay much attention to the notes or the ethnography.

Mead's interest was piqued in the early 1970s by three events. One was a revisit to Kinakatem. The second was the interest of another anthropologist—myself—in doing further research on the Yuat River. The final goad was an article, published in 1973 but of which Mead received an early copy, by Lévi-Strauss (Lévi-Strauss 1976). It concerned, in part, the debate between Lévi-Strauss and Luc de Heusch, a debate using Mundugumor data. Correspondence between Mead and Lévi-Strauss indicates that she referred to her original notes to answer his questions about kinship. Because of Lévi-Strauss's theoretical interest in unpublished Mundugumor data, Mead decided that the time had come to go back and consider publication of the materials.

Mead intended to publish these materials in a monograph for the

American Museum of Natural History entitled *The Biwat: Notes on the Ethnography of the Mundugumor People of the Yuat River, Sepik District, Papua New Guinea.* She herself was the sole author but added "including material collected by Reo Fortune." Her notes include two rough outlines and two separate but similar introductions, both of which indicate that the volume would include data, her analysis, and a theoretical response to Lévi-Strauss. In both versions of the introduction Mead indicated that she would discuss Lévi-Strauss's analysis, but in the second version the informant Omblean had taken on a more central position. From both outlines and introductions it is clear that Mead intended to incorporate as much ethnographic detail as possible, even if it was necessary to add a "miscellaneous detail" section.[14]

Unfortunately, despite spending some time organizing and beginning to write up the materials in 1972 and 1973, she did not finish before her death in 1978. She and I talked once about the Mundugumor data, and it was her idea that I write it up as best I could if she never did. I am sure I seemed the logical choice: I never worked or studied with Mead, but I did my own fieldwork in the village of Bun, the first group of people upriver from the Mundugumor and very similar to them. The similarities, especially the complex exchanges that went on, led Mead to believe—rightfully so, I think—that if anyone could make sense of her field notes, I could. And that is what I have tried to do.

When I first discussed the possibility of writing up these materials with Mead, I did not immediately think of the problems, only the exciting possibilities. After working with this material for as long as I have, however, I am keenly aware of the shortcomings of these data and of any attempt to use another person's notes, and it is important to be aware of these problems in order to assess the materials that follow. I divide the discussion here into two general areas: (1) the procedures and methods used to write this ethnographic description and (2) the problems related to working with someone else's field notes and data.[15]

Mead had acquired Fortune's notes and begun to organize them with the intention of writing her monograph. When I made copies of these notes (the originals are with Mead's other notes in the Library of Congress), she had already sorted them into categories. I kept these categories by putting the pages into folders and labeling each piece of paper according to where Mead had placed it. Mead had typed 17 pages of Fortune's notes on individual biographies and 17 other pages of narrative text while in the field, but the remaining 157 pages from Fortune are handwritten and difficult to decipher.[16] (It is possible that sections of the linguistic notes are also Fortune's, but I do not deal with these here.)

I began the process of writing the ethnography as an anthropologist might begin work in a community: by reading over the notes many times in order to become generally familiar with the "place and the people." Then I started a more detailed analysis of the population and tried to become familiar with specific individuals, their households, personalities, and histories. I went through the notes several times and made a census card for each individual. I also made an index of where to find basic information on a variety of topics, so that when writing up the actual narrative text I could be assured of covering the topic reasonably well. I translated a variety of texts and data from pidgin into English and puzzled out meanings from the abbreviations Mead used. Only after this preliminary work did I begin to put the pieces of information together. Whenever I was away from the project for any length of time, I reread all the notes and my materials to regain familiarity with the material. The categories of analysis are mine and not necessarily those of Mead or Fortune; nor are they necessarily meaningful categories in the conceptual world of the Mundugumor.

I faced several practical problems and made some arbitrary decisions. A large proportion of the data is on the language, and I am linguistically naive and untrained. My problem was whether to try to make something of these linguistic notes or leave them for others, and I decided on the latter course. Despite the relatively large amount of linguistic data in the notes, in this study I focus on ethnographic rather than linguistic description.

Another problem was that some of the material from these notes had already been published, especially in *Sex and Temperament.* I pondered the extent to which I should rely on or even use these published materials. In one way it was unfortunate that I was familiar with *Sex and Temperament:* it might have been better if I had never read it and only used the field notes. The notes themselves were set in the particular historical and theoretical context discussed above and shaped profoundly by Mead's own frameworks, and published materials are the ethnographer's further interpretations of these notes. For me to reinterpret them once again seemed to compound the possibility of distortion, and so I tried to ignore my familiarity with the published data:[18] I worked only with the notes until I had written a basic outline for a topic and narrative text. Then and only then did I check published sources for information pertaining to that topic; doing so was necessary in the event that in writing up materials Mead added information from memory that was not included in her original field notes. If the published data merely substantiated what I had already written, I ignored these works and did not cite them, although sometimes I quote from them if the phrasings explain something especially well. When my interpretation did not agree with the published interpretation, I note this in the text, and although I do not necessarily agree with Mead's emphases, in only one instance—that of kinship—is my disagreement substantial enough to warrant special treatment (see chapter 5).

An additional procedure was involved in organizing these materials for publication. When I was in Papua New Guinea in 1981 (for an unrelated reason), I went to Mundugumor for a short time (slightly less than two weeks). My purpose was to gather data on change so that I could add a small section describing what the people's lives are like now, in contrast to what they were like in 1932. I make no pretense of having done fieldwork among the Mundugumor, but while there I did ask a few questions related to gaps or puzzles in the notes. In most cases I found that people simply did not remember. I did, however, update the census materials as best I could and gather some genealogical information as well as my impressions, especially on change.

No matter what the nature of the field notes or theoretical framework, no anthropologist can ever take the notes of another and make of them what the original author might have. Some of what we learn never even comes to consciousness but remains implicit as context and background. Furthermore, no matter how often we tell students to write everything down, never to trust to memory, the truth is that making note of everything is impossible, as is not being selective or emphasizing one aspect of what is observed more than another. More remains in our heads than we ever suspect, and decisions about what to write and how to write it are rarely examined. Mead was thorough in her ethnographic observations, but even she left much unsaid. The process of using someone else's field notes made me keenly aware of what never enters the notebooks—the contexts, the connections and associations, the sensations, and even the obvious, most of which the original researcher probably could recall, probably does know, or at least would use as framework in writing. These are not available later on, and whatever is written from the notes is inevitably impoverished.

A related problem is that even in published works it is sometimes difficult to tell whether the author-ethnographer is reporting actual observed behavior or informants' statements about behavior. This problem also plagued my use of the Mundugumor notes. If I encountered a note stating that "the Mundugumor do X," how was I to interpret it? Did one person tell Mead that he or she did X, did one person tell Mead that most of the Mundugumor did X, did Mead *see* one person or many people doing X, did 10 people tell her that they did X (or perhaps that others did X)? For example, in one place Mead noted that mortuary cannibalism was practiced, but whether she actually observed the practice is uncertain. The issues here are complex; they are not limited to reconstructing descriptions from other people's notes but pervade all ethnography, including the use of illustrative example. Mead was aware of some of these problems when she wrote that "the kinship system would have been fleshed out by observation of actual usage to a far greater extent than it was" when describing what would have occurred during a longer field trip. Although one cannot make too much of this single sentence, it does indicate that Mead relied more on informants' reports of behavior than on observation of actual behavior.

The fact that I was familiar with the peoples of the Yuat River was both positive and negative. I did extensive fieldwork in Bun, the first group of people upriver from the Mundugumor, in 1973–74 and 1977 and during another short trip in 1981. I could make sense of and understand Mead's notes when others might have had far more difficulties doing so. I was able to use Bun material analogically to enrich the vision we have about the Mundugumor, and the role of controlled inference is apparent in the chapters to follow. But there is a problem here as well: although the Bun and the Mundugumor are similar, intermarry today (formerly they were enemies), and assert that they have the same customs, there is plenty of evidence that they are not identical.[19] How and where they are alike and how and where they are different are empirical questions. The difficulty I had in working with these notes is that whenever there was a gap in the data or an interpretation, I was almost unconsciously tempted to fill in with my knowledge of the Bun. I tried, of course, to avoid doing this, or I did it consciously and therefore explicitly, but I may not always have succeeded.[20]

THE PLAN OF THE ETHNOGRAPHY

The substance of this study is predominantly ethnographic. Only in this introduction and again in the conclusion do I directly address these broader epistemological, historical, and methodological questions. Chapter 2 is an introduction to the ecology and demography of the Mundugumor in 1932. It includes a description of the environment and how people extracted their livelihood from it, the village of Kinakatem and its population, the nature of hamlet and household. I also include the data on political organization and warfare here, as well as a section on the nature of change, both from Mead's own perspectives of 1932 and 1971 and my views from 1981.

Chapter 3 contains information on religion, belief, and ritual. There was more information on these topics in the notes than on any other except perhaps kinship. I have tried to present the material in logical sections containing relatively straightforward description.

In some ways chapter 4, on kinship and marriage, is the heart of this book. Mead and Fortune collected much data on the topic, and of all aspects of Mundugumor culture the kinship system has received more discussion in the theoretical literature and more skepticism in the folklore of anthropology than any other. I begin with descriptions of kin terms and behavior and then go on to provide data on marriage and marriage rules and process. The chapter ends with descriptions of clans and the phenomenon of ropes.

Chapter 5 is my own analysis of and commentary on the data provided in chapter 4 and to some extent in chapter 3. In this chapter I re-present Mead's and Fortune's data on the rope in a different way and interpret it from an alternative perspective. Briefly, I argue that ropes were not descent groups at all but metaphors for a very important intergenerational exchange pattern at the heart of the Mundugumor social and cultural system. But the interpretation is mine, not Mead's or Fortune's.

Chapter 6 is a brief conclusion that, once again, asks questions that are more general and less ethnographic.

THE MUNDUGUMOR IN CONTEXT |2|

Societies can best be understood within the environmental, social, and historical contexts in which they exist and which they help create. I begin this chapter by placing the Mundugumor in their physical environment and describing how they exploited the resources around them: their subsistence techniques, diet, and material culture. Demographic considerations are included here as well—how the population was distributed in villages, hamlets, and households. The social environment includes relationships with other groups in the area, predominantly relations of trade, warfare, and alliance. Because much political activity was concerned with war, alliance, and extravillage relations, I describe leadership and political organization here as well. The last part of the chapter is devoted to change and to viewing the Mundugumor in a historical context.

Many American cultural anthropologists of Mead's time were prone to what Keesing (1981:112–13) labels a "mosaic" view of human cultures—each culture was a separate little piece, a unique creation adapted to its environment yet unconnected to the cultures around it. Mead herself certainly exhibited this assumption in much of her work; for example, a major tenet in *Sex and Temperament* is that each of the three separate cultures constituted a unique human creation. However, there are moments in Mead's Sepik ethnography when a more sophisticated view of the complex systemic relations among groups is evident. Such a view is particularly apparent in her materials on the Arapesh, whom she describes as an "importing culture" (see, for example, Mead 1970), and it appears in the Mundugumor ethnography as well, especially in her attempt to locate Mundugumor variants of some general Sepik themes. Whether Mead's tentative gropings for a more systemic approach are the result of theoretical prescience, the special characteristics of the Sepik region and its ethnography, or a combination of both cannot be determined, but surely the last possibility—that it was a combination of Mead's insight and the ethnographic area—is most likely. Anthropology at the historical moments in which Mead wrote did not have a theoretical framework and vocabulary for dealing with these concerns, and Mead structured much of her discussion in terms of the conceptual apparatus available to her, such as diffusion and culture areas. She assumed pattern and configuration and therefore looked for elements that fit together and tended to diminish the significance of those that did not. Her theoretical framework was not adequate to contain her ethnographic insights, and it is possible to catch glimpses of a systemic vision more sophisticated than the simple "mosaic" one.

ENVIRONMENTAL CONTEXT AND DEMOGRAPHY

Although Mead certainly did not subscribe to a simple cultural materialism, she did recognize that the environment in which a society lives, including neighbors, exerts a significant influence on the people's lives, and she especially recognized that the relative richness of the Mundugumor environment allowed them advantages over poorer groups nearby. She intended to begin her monograph as I begin this one, with geographical setting, population and demographic concerns, and trade and relations with other groups.

The Environment and Its Exploitation

"In the mind of the most suburban Rabaulite and in the mind of the wildest bush native, the Sepik stands for mosquitoes, crocodiles, cannibals and floating corpses—and I can assure you we have seen them all" (Mead 1977:130). Thus begins Mead's first published letter written from Kinakatem, a candid description of what appeared to be an unappealing place. Although Mead surely used more poetic license (and exaggeration) in letters to friends and relatives than might be warranted, nevertheless that mosquitoes were a ferocious plague and malaria was a severe health problem. Crocodile attacks made it dangerous to get water from the river at night. Ten-year-olds had eaten human flesh, and Mead and Fortune possibly saw the corpse of at least one infant discarded in the river. Despite these seemingly undesirable aspects, she (1977:132) wrote in the same letter that "it's a pretty enough place, a swift-flowing river about two blocks wide with high grassy banks and a few palms" (see fig. 1). These descriptions encapsulate the salient characteristic of Mead's writing: she saw and wrote about opposites and contradictions but stressed one element in such a way that the other was diminished—indeed, this area contained crocodiles and mosquitoes and cannibals, but it was also a pretty place.[1]

The river was the Yuat, now locally known as the Biwat. It is the second lowest significant tributary of the Sepik (only the Keram River is closer to the mouth of the Sepik); it flows down from the Western Highlands and is fed by, among others, the Jimi River. Mead and Fortune visited Kinakatem during the beginning and approaching the peak of the rainy season, and Mead (1963:168) stresses that the Yuat is a turbulent river with a strong current and unpredictable and dramatic rises. Although this description of the Yuat is appropriate for that time and although the river is certainly never as sleepy as the main Sepik itself, it is considerably lower and calmer during other times of the year.

The environment was more than a "pretty enough place"—it was rich and fertile with ample resources for exploitation. In one sense

Figure 1. The village of Kinakatem, 1972. Photograph by N. McDowell.

the environment's richness was a key to Mundugumor life, for subsistence was a relatively easy task, accomplished predominantly by
women, which Mead believed left the men both time and energy
for other pursuits such as warfare. Mead's view that the Mundugumor were freed from the labor of manufacturing items implies a
value judgment about such manufacture—that it had little prestige
and was of little interest. There is no direct evidence that the Mundugumor shared this valuation, but when given the opportunity they
clearly preferred to trade rather than make things themselves. The
contempt in which they held their neighbors substantiates the possibility that Mead's perspective was shared by those she studied.
Surplus crops, such as the tobacco that grew easily on the high and
fertile ground, were traded with less well-endowed neighbors for
manufactured items.[2]

The relative abundance of resources allowed the people the freedom to defend and even expand their territory (see Mead

1949:135). Their neighbors feared them, and despite an acute shortage of good land, particularly in groups away from the river who lived in swamp- and grassland, no one dared to inhabit the 20 or so miles of prime land below their first hamlet. They had exclusive access to the best land in the area as well as river resources, extensive sago palm swamps, and products of the primary forest. There is, of course, no way to reconstruct the historical process by which the Mundugumor came to hold their predominant place on the riverbank, but one clue does exist. Possibly the ecological changes occasioned by a change in the Yuat River's course provided adaptive opportunities unavailable to less fortunate neighbors. When Mead and Fortune first visited Kinakatem in 1932, the people told them that the river had not always run through Mundugumor territory but had changed its course. At the time Mead knew of no evidence to support this assertion (although she later acknowledged it to be true after viewing aerial photographs clearly showing the earlier riverbed), but she noted that the people did not seem to be river folk. They feared the water and were awkward in their rough dugout canoes (see Mead 1949:n134, 1963:168–69). The river divided the six Mundugumor villages into two groups: Biwat, Branda, Akuran, and Kinakatem on the river bank and Dowaning and Andafugan in the bush. The bush villages had begun to differ from the river ones; as evidence of this differentiation, Mead (e.g., 1963:169, 1970:16) cited linguistic differences and the fact that the river people had begun to cannibalize the bush people. (Laycock [1973:76] calls the language spoken in all six of these villages Biwat and classifies it as a member of the Yuat family, Yuat stock, Ramu subphylum of the large Sepik-Ramu phylum of languages.)

Although their diet was probably more varied, the Mundugumor did resemble most of their neighbors in that they relied on sago as the basic staple. They ate it almost daily, usually in the form of sago pudding. Although sago grew wild in the swamps, men also specifically planted it for their children, and particular sago areas were owned and borders marked. Men cut the trees down, but women did almost all the rest of the processing. By scraping they broke down the trunk's pithy interior into bits and washed these to leach out the sago paste, which was stored with water in large clay pots. The Mundugumor rarely ate sago pudding alone but almost always garnished it with some form of protein or edible green. There had formerly been a taboo on eating any sago that had been processed by one's own child, but few people observed this taboo in 1932. The comment of one old man as to why he continued to observe it illustrates a central symbolic significance of sago: "He has scraped me and washed me; I cannot eat myself. Sago is myself." The absence of further information on this taboo and its decline means that one can only speculate on the possible meanings of an identification between self, child, and sago, but it clearly highlights the importance of sago itself. (See Meigs 1984:106 for an interesting comparison.)

The sago palm was certainly one of the most useful products in the environment. In addition to providing the basic starch, sago was used by hunters to lure wild pigs, the fronds were used to make house thatch, and young shoots were used to make women's grass skirts. Sago supplied the nesting material for grubs, a significant source of protein and a delicacy often included in feasts. Men felled wild palms, and one or two months later women returned to collect the accumulated grubs.

Fish yielded the main source of protein. Women caught most fish using nets they manufactured by attaching bark fibers to a triangular frame. They waded into swamps and *barets*[3] and simply gathered the fish up in the nets. This method was especially effective during the dry season, when waters had receded and fish were concentrated. Sometimes men helped in this activity, and they occasionally used a pronged spear or arrow to shoot fish themselves. At times men built barricades and traps across streams and *barets* to facilitate a larger catch. Mead noted that individual Mundugumor owned each section of a *baret*, and sometimes people constructed new ones to which they claimed ownership. When a man wanted to make a new *baret,* he gathered a large number of people to help, feasted them while they worked, and later was obliged to divide the first catch among them.[4]

Fish were cooked in water, baked in leaves, or fried in broken potsherds. When the catch was abundant, they were smoked. Neither Mead nor Fortune specified the types of fish caught, but today the Yuat and surrounding waters yield groper, perch, tilapia, and others.

In addition to fish, there were other water resources. Women caught prawns by holding their nets in both hands, inserting them into the water, and drawing them in. Fresh water mussels were eaten and their shells used to make lime. Eels and turtles were also caught and eaten. Although, according to Mead, the Mundugumor did not eat crocodile meat, they did eat crocodile eggs. (People in Bun eat crocodile meat and apparently always did.)

Unlike fishing, predominantly a female activity, hunting was a male occupation. However, fish and sago grubs provided the daily intake of protein, and game, especially wild pigs, was important mainly in the context of feasts. Both ceremonially and practically, wild pigs were the most important game animal hunted. Although men tracked pigs alone or with dogs, they usually used a lure baited with sago. A man set out the sago and built a blind for himself; he then returned at night and waited for a pig to eat the sago. It was believed that if no one tampered with the bait, the pig would come tamely and eat the sago much as a domestic pig would, with tail wagging, and the man would have no difficulty shooting it. But if someone with unkind intentions came upon the bait, he or she might pretend to taste the sago and then run away; later, a pig would do the same—it would be wary and run away before the hunter could shoot. The skulls of wild pigs were kept because it was believed that if they were discarded and eventually covered by dirt, the hunter would be unable to shoot additional pigs. Some men purchased pig-killing charms from upriver groups, but the hunter himself could not eat the kill if such magic was used.

Men hunted various other animals also. Bandicoots were hunted at night. The hunter cleared a small patch of ground and then covered it with dry, crackling breadfruit leaves. He placed insects on the leaves as bait and hid and waited nearby. When he heard the scratching sound of the bandicoot on the dried leaves, he reached out and caught it with a long net. The cuscus too was hunted at night. After locating one in a tree, a man broke off the lower branches and surrounded the tree with fire. Then he climbed the tree and shot the cuscus (which had nowhere to go) with bow and arrow. Men used dogs and spears to hunt cassowaries. Flying creatures such as the flying fox and a great variety of birds—for example, the goura pigeon and great hornbill—were killed with bow and arrow.

The Mundugumor usually roasted or boiled meat. They occasionally smoked it in a rattan basket to preserve it, especially if it was earmarked for a feast.

Crocodile, cassowary, and bush hen eggs also provided a source of protein. Both men and women gathered them, although only men possessed charms for finding them. Bush hens were not eaten to ensure a supply of eggs; only people who had ground that included no nesting areas would eat the hens. Eggs were usually poached with yams and salt or baked in the fire. (The people obtained salt— probably potassium chloride—by burning an unspecified kind of leaf and retaining the salty residue of the ashes.)

Because the data are relatively concrete and easily obtained, it is somewhat surprising that information on garden techniques and garden products are not detailed in the notes. One can only speculate on why Mead and Fortune paid so little attention to gardens: Were they uninterested? Were the data, unlike in many other places, especially difficult to obtain? Did they intend to do further work on horticulture but left before they could do so? My guess is that the time of year in the horticultural cycle had something to do with it. Gardens are cleared and planted at the end of the rainy season and beginning of the dry season, and apart from occasional weeding and the final harvest most gardening activity takes place at this time. Mead and Fortune were there only at the beginning of the rainy season when minimal weeding and harvesting occurred.

The Mundugumor practiced a form of slash-and-burn horticulture. Gardens yielded quantities of taro and bananas, and once in the notes Mead refers surprisingly to maize and Fortune to red manioc. Although men did sometimes weed the gardens, probably they cleared the land and left most of the rest of the gardening work to women. The exception was the ritually important long yam garden. Yams and yam gardens of various sorts were a ritual focus in many groups throughout the Sepik and seem to have been so here as well. (For additional examples, see Tuzin 1972, Scaglion and Condon 1979, and Harrison 1982.) Although both long and short yams were grown, the long yam was the ritual focus and under the auspices of the men; the women's only work in these gardens was to train the vines and perhaps to weed occasionally.

Tobacco was a very important crop, and the possession of high fertile land for growing it contributed to what Mead perceived to be the Mundugumor political and economic hegemony in the area. It was tended almost exclusively by women, and the more wives a man had, the more tobacco and therefore wealth he had. It was used as a central item in trade and as a form of payment for labor assistance. When it was mature, the leaves were picked and the ribs removed before being hung to dry. Before the leaves were completely brittle, they were rolled together in a long coil and tied with rattan. Mundugumor of all ages were heavy smokers, rolling several leaves together in the form of a cigar. Tobacco was so abundant that if anyone was dissatisfied with the quality of the tobacco, he or she simply threw it away. It is interesting that Mead thought this fact anomalous enough to note it in writing, the implication being that in other societies she had studied tobacco was more precious and not easily discarded.

Tree crops were also significant. Coconuts were used for a variety of purposes: they were eaten plain or shredded and added as flavoring or garnish to other dishes, and the liquid from green coconuts quenched thirst. In season people ate breadfruit nuts (but not pulp, however). Betel palms also were abundant. As in other places in Melanesia, the nuts were chewed with the catkin or leaf of a pepper plant and lime.

Gathering was only an occasional activity, but Mead did note that the forest yielded wild yams and a variety of edible greens.

In addition to the dogs used for hunting, the Mundugumor also kept a few domestic pigs. Unfortunately, no data exist on customs of pig husbandry or how large the pig herds were. If they were like most other lowland groups, especially in the Sepik area, the pig herds never approached the size frequently found in the highlands, and it is certain that domestic pigs were not a primary focus of interest.

The general outline of the sexual division of labor is embedded in this description of subsistence: Men cleared gardens, grew long yams, and hunted. Women tended the gardens and did most of the fishing. Both sexes processed the sago. It should further be noted that women were also primarily responsible for caring for children, cooking, domestic cleaning, and accumulating firewood, while male activities included planning and conducting warfare and defense, carving and painting, and arranging and staging major rituals. There are no explicit data about the strictness with which the lines between male and female activities were drawn in ideology or practice, but indirect evidence indicates that men did infrequently tend children, and women certainly influenced at least the decision-making process about some public male concerns such as marital arrangements, warfare, and ritual performance. Given Mead's published contention that male and female temperaments among the Mundugumor were alike despite a sexual division of labor, it would be interesting to know if temperamental similarity facilitated more blurring of the lines between assigned tasks than in other Melanesian societies, but there are no data to inform such a determination. One can only speculate, again, that because women were seemingly more assertive here than in many other Melanesian societies, their influence was felt in a variety of political-economic realms.

Both sexes produced items of material culture. Women made the

all-important fishing and bandicoot-catching nets. The most significant item of material culture predominantly produced by men was
the house. Neither Mead nor Fortune notes that women participated in the collecting of any materials for the house, but it seems
unlikely that men gathered all the raw materials. In Bun, although
men did the actual sewing of the thatch, women gathered the leaves
that made the thatch; they also collected the ribs from sago fronds
that comprised the walls of the house. Actual house construction
was a male activity.

All houses were roughly rectangular in shape, but house styles
and forms varied. Mead attributed this diversity to new influences
coming from downriver neighbors, and in one place indicates that
she thought the people ill at ease with these new styles. The old-
style houses were usually about 25 feet long and 15 feet wide; the
newer ones were elongated to 35 or 40 feet long and 10 or 15 feet
wide. All houses were built off the ground on posts and had palm
bark (probably *Kentiopsis archontophoenix*) flooring. Houses varied
in height from 4 feet to 8 or 9 feet. Smaller houses were typically
carefully walled with thatch or mats, whereas larger houses were
more carelessly walled. Rattan was used to fasten the parts together.
Sheltered veranda areas were formed by creating overhanging roofs
or receding floors. There were two kinds of ladders: one consisted
of two sticks or poles with cross rungs; the other was carved from a
single post with notches serving as steps (these single-post ladders
usually had a human face or head carved on the top). Stoves were
built of palm bark covered with sand and either suspended down
through the floor with rattan or built on the ground and elevated up
into the flooring space.

Some houses received decoration on their peaks. Mead observed
the ornamentation placed on the house of Alemi, one of Kinakatem's two most influential men. Mats woven from green and white
palm leaves into a pattern were decorated with strings of red and
green fruit and placed around the house gable. A simple barbed
spear made of hardwood was fastened into the mat. A chain was
also hung from the gable, and on the end of it hung a decorated

enemy skull, a painted coconut, or sometimes a special carving. Mead's notes do not specify whether such decorations were an indication of political power or merely idiosyncratic choice. It does seem probable at least that enemy skull decorations were associated with prowess in warfare and raiding. All these decorations were placed before the final thatch was put on.

Canoes, also made by men, were relatively simple dugouts carved from logs cut in the bush or occasionally cut from logs that floated down the river during the flood season. Men felled the trees with adzes without the use of fire. They shaped the outside of the canoe and hollowed out the inside while the log remained in the bush. When this preliminary cutting and shaping was finished, the canoe was seared with fire. Thwarts were then inserted to ensure that the hull remained open. After clearing a path through the vegetation, a large group of men attached rattan to the canoe and pulled it out of the bush to the riverbank, where a special carver put on the finishing touches, including a carved figurehead, usually a crocodile. Any man could make a canoe paddle or sometimes acquire one in trade from another village. There were no canoe bailers; palm spathes were used to rid the canoe of water.

The construction of slitgong drums was hedged with ceremony and taboo (see chapter 3). The tree was selected carefully. The initial shaping and carving were done in the bush, and then the slitgong was pulled into a village or hamlet, where a fence concealed it from the sight of women and children. The inside was seared with fire, and then it was tested for sound. If the sound was good and carried well, people in other places would respond that they could hear it, and work ceased. The slitgong then was placed in a new house. Mundugumor slitgongs had an ornamented handle at one end, carved by a specialist. Two designs were common—a human face and the head of a crocodile. The tongue always extended deeply into the inside on the beaten side. Slitgongs never accompanied a woman at marriage (as flutes did), nor were small ones ever made for use in a canoe. Breaking the tongue of one was a common means of expressing anger or shame (see fig. 2).

Figure 2. An old and weathered slitgong, 1981. Photograph by
N. McDowell.

For clothing men wore a woven belt to which they attached leaves,
front and back, but Mead thought that big men sometimes wore
skins of flying foxes instead. Although women wore leaves when
fishing, their usual attire (donned at the age of three or four) was a
grass skirt that was short in front and longer in the back (see figs. 3
and 4). Sago frond shoots were used to make skirt fibers. Women
first soaked the shoots in water to blanch the color and then cooked
the shoots with leaves to dye them red or soaked them in mud to
turn them black. Thus three colors (plain, red, and black) were possible, and color patterns and designs were sometimes elaborate.
Both men and women wore woven armbands, sometimes adorned
with shells, and women occasionally wore strings of shells from
their pierced earlobes.

The Mundugumor made a variety of carved wooden objects, including decorated spears, sago-turning sticks, stools (some deco-

Figure 3. Women before a garden house, 1932. Photograph by M. Mead and R. Fortune.

rated, some plain), and digging sticks (made from the wood of the betel nut tree) (see Mead 1970: plate 4 for a photograph of a carved shield). They made fish baskets from cane and rattan and water and cooking containers from bamboo. Women wove strings that were later converted into chest pendants and the nets for fishing and bandicoot catching. Lime gourds were fashioned by rotting out the center of a gourd, wrapping it in leaves and soaking it in water. Designs were later carved on with a rat tooth. Bullroarers, pan pipes, flutes, masks, and other ritual and art objects were also made.

Kinakatem: Village, Hamlet, Household

In 1932 Mead recorded that 183 people resided in Kinakatem.[5] An additional 13 men from the village were away working, mostly in

Figure 4. Woman holding a baby, 1932. Photograph by M. Mead and R. Fortune.

Rabaul. These were among the first labor recruits to go away (informants in 1981, however, told me that some men were also taken by a priest to work in Marienberg on the main Sepik before 1932); they included married, betrothed, and single young men. The extent to which their absence affected village life is impossible to ascertain, but it certainly must have had some impact. It was probably not so much their absence that was noted but their return, for they surely came back to the village with new ideas, new goods, and new aspirations. Because men's subsistence role was not as significant as women's, their absence from this sphere was probably not critical, and because warfare and raiding had recently ceased, their defensive and offensive tasks were not necessarily required either. Their absence certainly affected marriage patterns: they were not present to defend their rights to use their sisters in brother-sister exchange marriages, and their female relatives were used by other men (especially their fathers and elder brothers) to acquire additional wives.

When discussing the village residents and the census, it is necessary to explore the possibility that perhaps others were absent from their homes. In *Letters from the Field* Mead (1977:135) wrote that "the *kiap* [patrol officer] has been here once and calaboosed half the male population over a stick fight. . . ." There is no mention of this event in her field notes and no indication which men were jailed or when. Elsewhere Mead notes that one-sixth of the men were missing, not half. Perhaps these men were from Kinakatem but had served their sentences and returned home, but the phrasing of this quotation suggests that the event took place during Mead's stay. It is possible, then, that some of the 13 included in the "away" category, presumably at work, were really in jail, but this too is unlikely. It is more probable that the "half" referred not to the village of Kinakatem but to the four river villages in general. As there are many references in the notes to a significant number of Biwat men being in jail, this is the mostly likely interpretation, and there is additional evidence to support it. Mead kept what she called a "Daily Events Diary" of Kinakatem from November 7 to December 8. From November 7 to November 15 it included a record of the exact activities of almost every member of 12 of the 20 households in Kinakatem, and it shows that all adult men of these households (plus a few from the remaining households) were present in the village at least during this week. Finally, given the relative ease with which census materials are recorded at even initial stages in fieldwork, it seems very unlikely that if "half" of the men of Kinakatem were in jail she would have failed to record it in her field notes. I think that this is an additional example of license and exaggeration in letters home but a more careful recording in field notes.

The population of Kinakatem then was 183 in residence and 13 away, presumably at work, for a total of 196. Although Mead estimated children's ages consistently, she did not do so for others, and it is not possible to extract a reliable age breakdown for the whole population. Only a rough approximation results by dividing the population into three categories: adult (married), betrothed, and unmarried. Betrothed males and females were almost always adolescent, but not all adolescents were betrothed: some were already married (and included in the adult category), whereas others had no definite marriage plans (and are therefore included with the children as unmarried). One woman included in the adult category was not married because she refused to marry. Nevertheless, these rough categories do reveal significant demographic trends, as table 1 illustrates.

Of the 13 men away at work, 6 were married, 1 was betrothed, and 2 were not married. Mead's notes do not specify the marital status of the remaining 4, but it is safe to assume that they were unmarried because if they had been married or betrothed, then the census of women would have revealed the names of their spouses or future mates. If these absentees are included, the result is the rough population distribution given in table 2.

The greater number of betrothed females in these tables can be explained by two factors. Five of the 10 were to marry the 5 young men listed as betrothed, and a sixth planned to marry a young local resident away at work. Thus the future brides of all of the men listed as betrothed were included in the betrothed category, and only 4

Table 1. Population Distribution (A)

	Male	Female	Total
Adult (married)	25	61	86
Away at work	13	0	13
Betrothed	5	10	15
Unmarried	44	38	82
Totals:	87	109	196

Table 2. Population Distribution (B)

	Male	Female	Total
Adult (married)	31	61	92
Betrothed	6	10	16
Unmarried	50	38	88
Totals:	87	109	196

females require further explanation. Two of these were promised to men from Akuran (both away), and the last 2 were betrothed to Kinakatem men who were already married and thus included in the tables as married men. Those betrothed to residents of other villages but who remained in the villages and those who were to marry men who already had wives account for the discrepancy of 4 females in table 2.

The most remarkable aspect of table 2, however, is the overall sex ratio. There were simply more women than men. This difference does not appear in the unmarried (children) category; here, in fact, males outnumber females (but see my later comment on the artificiality and possible skewing of these categories). If unmarried and betrothed people are combined, the difference is less: 56 males to 48 females. What is striking is the complete reversal of the sex ratio for married adults: 31 males to 61 females. If the betrothed and married categories were combined, the difference is even more pronounced: 37 males to 71 females. There are many possible explanations for this phenomenon. One might be differential mortality for adults. Perhaps because of differential child care or perhaps warfare, more women than men might have survived into adulthood. But such a factor was unlikely to affect men almost twice as much as women, and additional explanations for this sex difference must be sought.

Polygyny was certainly relevant. It was an ideal that men sought to attain, and table 3 shows that some of them were very successful.

Most men married at least once. Of the 4 in table 3 who had no wife, 2 were widowers who were unlikely to marry again unless to women no one else wanted, and only 2 adult men had never been married (one of these was lame).

The ideal of polygyny was complicated by the fact that marriages should be executed by brother-sister exchange. If Kinakatem men were acquiring wives from other places, for each one brought in a Kinakatem woman should have gone out. So the question arises, Where did these excess women come from? The answer involves several factors.

The first factor is a simple one: despite the ideal of exchange, if a man was able to steal, entice, or coerce a woman into marrying him without sending a return to her male kin, so much the better, especially if the victims were not Mundugumor. Indeed, Mead (1972:204) claimed that "they preyed on their miserable swamp-dwelling neighbors and carried off their women to swell the households of the leading men." Such was the case. Six of the adult married women were from bush villages, and of these 3 were married to the influential Mongova (who had a total of 8 wives), 2 to Alemi (who had 10 living wives), and the last to a third man. What is important is that no women were given in exchange for any of these wives.

A second and related factor has to do with the pattern of marriage with other Mundugumor villages—Biwat, Branda, and Akuran. Here the ideal of exchange was expected if not always fulfilled. Intermarriage was balanced between Kinakatem and Akuran, but there was a tendency for Kinakatem women betrothed or married to Akuran men who were away at work to remain at home rather than move to their husbands' village. Of the 10 Akuran women mar-

Table 3. Frequency of Polygyny

Number of Men	1	0	1	0	0	0	1	2	6	16	4
Number of Wives	10	9	8	7	6	5	4	3	2	1	0

ried or betrothed to Kinakatem men, all 10 lived in Kinakatem; but of the 10 Kinakatem women betrothed or married to Akuran men, 4 remained in Kinakatem rather than moving to Akuran. Three Biwat women married and resided in Kinakatem, but only one return had as yet been made. By the rules, 2 Kinakatem women should have eventually married and resided in Biwat. Thus, there were 6 women from Kinakatem who, according to the ideal, should have been elsewhere but were not.

The 6 bush women and 6 Kinakatem women who were or should have been married out but lived in account for 12 of the 34 excess women in Kinakatem, leaving an excess of 21. Some age skewing is undoubtedly at work here: surely some of the 50 males in the unmarried category were old enough to marry and be called adult (indeed, 6 of them were away at work), but because of their absence or the monopolization of wives by older men they were as yet unable to marry. According to an age criterion alone, there is no doubt that several young men in the unmarried category were old enough to wed, and had they been able to do so, not only would the sex ratio for married people alter but also the sex ratio for the unmarried would be more evenly balanced as well. Thus, my arbitrary classification of people as married, betrothed, and unmarried accounts for some of the discrepancy between the numbers of married males and females. An examination of the total population without regard to age substantiates this interpretation. There were 87 males and 109 females. If one subtracts the 12 excess women, it leaves a sex ratio of 87 men to 97 women, still somewhat skewed but not extraordinary, a difference that could probably be accounted for by differential mortality and other factors.

Although the figures are only approximate, later census data do not reveal similar age skewing: in 1969 there were 166 males and 168 females in Kinakatem, and in 1981 there were 133 males and 140 females. These data do reveal a drop in population, probably due to outmigration to cities, schools, and jobs and the movement of a few families to the Gavieng resettlement scheme near Angoram.

If by "village" (a term both Mead and Fortune use to describe Kinakatem) one means a nucleated settlement, then Kinakatem was not a village. The people lived in separate hamlets dispersed throughout the bush for several reasons. One was defense: the precise location of a hamlet was a secret, and occasionally secret paths were the only means of access. These paths helped the residents prevent surprise raids. Another reason was related to the hostility between individual residents, especially male relatives (brother-brother, father-son). Distance between residences decreased interpersonal interaction and thereby also decreased the potential for conflict. Mead seems to attribute the tensions between agnates to affective rather than structural causes, but she is never precisely clear and perhaps did not perceive the difference. In a letter to Boas Mead wrote the following of residential shifting caused by strife among kin:

. . . Reo [Fortune] followed shifting residence about and showed how it correlated with quarrels over women. A man gets involved with his own father and leaves, then his brothers, then more distant brothers, etc. He continually shifts his residence—if he is an aggressive person—or he drives all his near associates away.

Sometimes a hamlet was composed of a single household (large or small), but other hamlets included more than one. In either case, the household had a recognized male head and was the major residential unit. The actual composition of the household varied, but the ideal was clear: a man should have a number of wives, each with her own house. His compound would include a ramshackle hut for his unmarried sons and a more substantial house where he himself would receive meals from his various wives. Additional men—unassertive brothers, sons-in-law, and nephews—were attached to this ideal household. Of course, only a few men were able to attain this ideal; Mead estimated that only 1 in 25 came anywhere near this goal (1963:173–74). Table 3 reveals that most men had 1 or 2 wives. Recognizing that the ideal was not always possible, the Mundugumor stipulated that if 2 wives were to live in the same house, at the very least each had to have her own, separate hearth.

Of the 20 households recorded by Mead in Kinakatem in 1932, only 2 achieved this ideal (see table 3). The heads of these two households, Alemi and Mongova, were the village's two most important men. They were brothers-in-law, having exchanged sisters, and also intense political rivals. Their names appear again and again in these pages because their actions and the dynamics between them were central to almost every phase of village life.

The largest household was headed by Alemi, the *luluai*.[6] In all, he had had 13 wives, but only 9 were alive and living with him. His compound included 5 dwellings, and a sixth was under construction. In one house he lived alone. He summoned his wives, and they brought food to him there. The other houses provided shelter for his wives, children, and other relatives. Mead called these houses by the name of the particular wife in charge—thus, Mandjo's house, Malome's house, Orendena's house, and Kunma's house (see genealogy 1).

In Mandjo's dwelling, which must be considered something of a main house, lived 5 wives (3 of them childless), children of these wives, children of deceased wives, a married daughter with her child, and an absent son's wife. Orendena's house provided shelter primarily for children (foster and adopted) and a daughter-in-law. With Malome lived her offspring, a grandchild, and a future daughter-in-law. Kunma's tiny shelter housed only herself and her daughter by a previous marriage. Clearly Alemi had achieved a man's ideal for household and marriage.

Mongova was Alemi's closest rival in the achievement of this ideal. He had 8 living wives in 1932, and his extensive household numbered 27 people.

Most men, of course, never achieved this ideal. The fact that of the 18 remaining household heads, 8 had only one wife (see table 4) obscures the incidence of polygyny. Two of these 8 had previously had 2 wives, but 1 wife had died and left each with only 1 wife. Another man had been divorced by 1 of his 2 wives and was in the

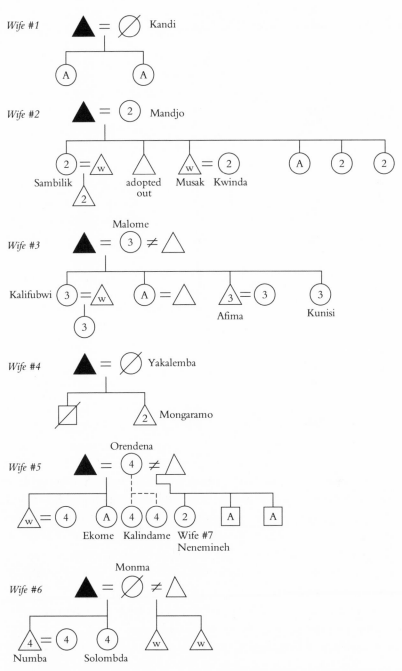

Genealogy 1. Alemi's wives and residence (*continued on next page*)

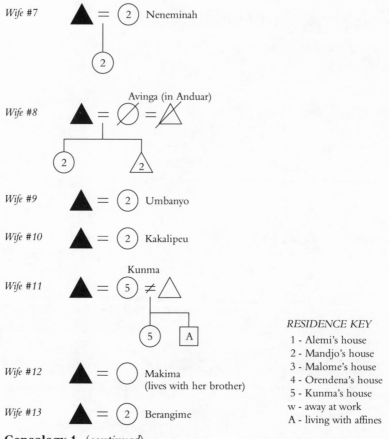

1 - Alemi's house
2 - Mandjo's house
3 - Malome's house
4 - Orendena's house
5 - Kunma's house
w - away at work
A - living with affines

Genealogy 1 (*continued*)

process of acquiring a second again. Only 5 of these 8 men had had only 1 wife. The man with 4 wives had previously had 6 but 2 had died. The man who had 3 wives had not lost any, but of the 6 men who had 2 wives each, 2 of them had formerly had 3 but again each lost a wife to death. Only one household head (residence no. 17) had never been married at all; the other 2 (both men in residence no. 20) were widowers who were cared for by a sister.

A comparison of tables 3 and 4 reveals some apparent discrepancies, but these can be easily resolved by noting that table 3 refers to marriages of all men whereas table 4 is concerned with residence

Table 4. Residence by Household

Household Number	Household Head	No. of Wives	No. of Children	No. of Wives' Children	No. of Children of Dead/Divorced Wives	No. of Adult Sons	No. of Adult Daughters	No. of Sons' Wives	No. of Daughters' Husbands	No. of Daughters' Children	No. of Sisters	No. of Mothers	No. of Adopted Children	Others	Total
1	Alemi	8	5	1	5	0	2	4	0	2	0	0	2		30
2	Mbunda	1	1	0	1	0	0	0	0	0	1	1	0		6
3	Mondamvu	1	1	0	0	0	0	0	0	0	0	0	0		3
4	Kalekumbun	1	2	0	0	0	0	0	0	0	0	0	0	(1)	5
5	Ndelong	2	1	1	3[a]	0	0	0	0	0	0	0	0		8
6	Kuainvoh	3	3	0	0	0	0	0	0	0	0	0	0		7
7	Omblean	1	2	0	0	0	0	0	0	0	0	0	0	(2)	9
8	Komeaka	1	1	2	1	0	0	0	0	0	0	0	0		6
9	Kiangenan	2	1	1	0	1	2	1	0	1	0	0	0		10
10	Ombani	4	1	5	0	0	0	1	0	0	0	0	0		12
11	Wheifon	2	2	0	0	0	0	0	0	0	0	0	0		5
12	Yeshimba	2	4	0	0	0	1	0	0	0	0	0	1	(3)	10
13	Ngangava	1	0	0	0	0	0	0	0	0	0	0	0	(4)	3
14	Mashamba	2	4	0	0	0	0	0	0	0	0	0	0		7
15	Mongova	8	9	1	3	0	3	0	0	1	0	0	1		27
16	Kwenandi	1	4	0	0	0	1	0	1	0	0	0	0		8
17	V'ren	1	0	0	0	0	0	0	0	0	0	0	0		1
18	Gavima	2	5	0	0	0	0	1	0	0	0	0	0		9
19	Nakwon	1	1	3	0	0	0	1	0	0	0	0	0		7
20	Vuvutpa/ Aulieh	0	4	0	0	0	0	0	0	0	1	0	0		7
															180

[a]one of these is an adult daughter

Others
1. 1 adolescent female
2. 1 wife's mother, her 3 sons, 1 lone male
3. 1 wife's sister
4. 1 wife's adopted child

and household heads. Table 4 indicates that no man had 10 wives, and yet one man—Alemi—is credited with 10 wives in table 3. Two of his wives did not reside with him: one had moved back to her home in Anduar, and the other lived with her brother (no divorces were noted). The second discrepancy relates to men who had 3 wives. Table 4 indicates that there was only one such man, but table 3 lists 2. The anomaly here was a man named Gavima, who did indeed have 3 wives, but only 2 were residing with him (hence he is described in table 4 as residing with only 2 wives). Table 4 shows 6 men with 2 wives (including Gavima), and one absentee also had 2 wives, yielding a total of 7 (the same as would be listed in table 3 if Gavima was categorized as having 2 wives instead of 3). Table 4 yields 10 men with only 1 wife—8 household heads plus a married son (residence no. 9) and a daughter's husband (residence no. 16). An eleventh was resident in residence no. 10, listed as a child of wife's former marriage (his betrothed wife is listed there as son's wife). Finally, 5 absentees had only 1 wife, and thus the total of men with 1 wife was 16, the same as in table 3. Of the men with no wife, 2 were the widowers of residence no. 20, 1 was the head of residence no. 17, and a fourth was a lame man who lived in residence no. 7.

Thus, household composition was variable, although almost all households had a single male head, his wives and children, and occasionally adhering relatives and other dependents (most typically future daughters-in-law). The size of the group was also quite varied, ranging from highs of 30 people (Alemi's house) and 27 people (Mongova's house) to a household of 1, a man who had never been married and lived alone. Actual composition is presented in table 4. The household count in this table yields a total of 180 people. The notes include mention of 3 other people as residents of the village, but it is impossible to verify their actual residential affiliation. One young woman, who was married to a man away at work, lived either with her parents or her husband's parents. A young betrothed man probably lived with his parents but was not listed as a household member. Finally, a boy (Kunma's 12-year-old son from her marriage previous to that with Alemi) most likely resided with his mother, but again the residential arrangement is not clear.

THE SOCIAL CONTEXT

Although the environment was rich, it was significantly lacking in shells and almost all stone. However, it did provide the resources that enabled the Mundugumor to trade. In fact, they did not manufacture many items they could have made (such as clay pots) because they had trade items (notably tobacco) and, just as important, held a central position as brokers in an elaborate trading network.[7]

Trade

In effect, the Mundugumor participated in two separate but articulated systems of trade. One was with bush peoples hinterlanders who lived in the swamps and grasslands away from the river. The other, with river peoples, was part of a network that stretched from the coastal and sea peoples up the main Sepik to the headwaters of the Yuat in the highlands and highland fringe areas.

With the bush villages the Mundugumor traded primarily areca nut, coconut, and tobacco for manufactured items such as pots, baskets, fans, and mosquito baskets (for protection from mosquitoes while sleeping). Mead's (1963:170–71) own description of the relationship between the Mundugumor and people of the Grass Country to the east is a vivid one:

For these miserable swamp people the Mundugumor preserve a contempt tinged with a sense of their usefulness as makers of pots and baskets. They said they were careful not to kill all of them, for then there would be no makers of pots left alive. They comment upon the advantage of having trade-connexions with two groups of mosquito-bag-makers: if one group becomes too depleted by head-hunting, they can always get mosquito-bags from the others. . . . [8]

The villages of Yaul, Dimiri, and Maravat in grassland specialized in potmaking, and most Kinakatem pots came from Dimiri (which occasionally acted as an ally in warfare as well). It was possible to affect a potter's work adversely by taking a piece of the clay, putting it in a section of swollen bamboo, and putting it in the fire. The bamboo exploded, and so would the pot when it was being fired or dried.

Trade for pottery was relatively friendly. Transactions took place between hereditary trade friends (usually inherited patrilineally). Pots were exchanged for tobacco, bananas, betel nut, yams, and coconuts. While making a large sago storage pot, the potter was provided with food and betel by the future owner.

Trade for other objects was conducted with other bush villages. On the eastern side, also in the Grass Country, was Bobaten, a village that provided the woven mosquito bags and fans (some of these bags were made in Bobaten, and others were acquired by Bobaten from other villages). A small mosquito basket was worth three large coils of tobacco. Large baskets for catching fish were also obtained from Bobaten (as well as from Yaul and Dimiri) in exchange for tobacco. Since people in these eastern grassland villages lived primarily in swamps and had little high ground for gardening, they were sometimes forced to purchase food from the Mundugumor. Although Maravat, Dimiri, Yaul, and Bobaten did not, some of the other grassland villages in return for tobacco prostituted women to the Mundugumor who visited them. The Mundugumor always paid for sexual services with tobacco and never reciprocated in kind if visitors from the Grass Country came to their villages. Intermarriages with these villages did sometimes occur.

If, however, the Mundugumor were fighting with Bobaten or its allies, they purchased their mosquito baskets from bush villages on the western side of the river (those villages left stranded when the Yuat changed its course), principally Nadvari and Mensuat. From these peoples they also acquired women's carrying baskets and small ditty bags. From Changriwa they obtained net bags and lime. Here, however, the predominant return was not tobacco but pots and shell rings, and thus the Mundugumor served as brokers in this context. Despite the existence of hereditary trade friends in these western villages, relations with them were often precarious, and child hostages were sometimes exchanged to ensure safe trading. Occasionally pots were traded to Maramba in return for paddles and lime.

Traditionally slitgongs were not traded, but they had begun to be used in exchange for European goods in 1932. The Mundugumor traded them to Grass Country villages and to Kamberamba, off the main Sepik. Formerly villagers from the main Sepik did not come up the Yuat to secure logs for canoe manufacture, but by 1932 they had begun to do so.

Trade with the various bush villages was conducted primarily on the basis of hereditary trade friendships. Although the trade relationships did not ensure continuously smooth and amicable relations, they did serve to channel the flow of goods between places through individuals. A man would have trade friends in several villages, and if exchanges were for any reason (such as fighting) precluded at one place, trade could continue somewhere else. Omblean, for example, had trade friends in Dimiri, Yaul, Bobaten, Nadvari, Maramba, and Changriwa. The first three he inherited directly from his father, the latter two from his wife's father. (It is not clear whether he maintained these latter two relationships in the name of his wife as her stand-in or whether he himself actually assumed the role.) Inheritance of these trade relationships is less than clear. It is uncertain whether there were various paths of inheritance or whether a person needed certain qualities, such as strength, to actualize a potential relationship.

The second trading system in which the Mundugumor participated was a more extensive one in which sea and river products were exchanged for mountain products. The system was almost exclusively a waterway exchange and was conducted separately from bush trading. The Mundugumor were an important conduit through which Yaul, Dimiri, and Maravat pottery entered this more expansive system. In this way they again played a middle role, and in the case of this second system their role as brokers was more important than with the tobacco trade.

From upriver villages, such as Asangamut and Sipisipi, they obtained stone adzes, bows and arrows, shell breast ornaments, bird of paradise plumes, and sago cutters. These upriver villagers almost certainly acquired these objects from other groups even closer to or actually in the Western Highlands. Some of each of these items the Mundugumor kept for their own use; the rest were traded to downriver villages, especially Anduar and Kundimo. Thus mountain products flowed downriver and were further traded to the main Sepik and perhaps all the way to the coast. To this downriver flow the Mundugumor added Grass Country pottery and the spears and paddles they made themselves. What went back upriver—that is, the items that were exchanged for these products—were shells and rings they obtained primarily from Kundimo and Anduar and traded in return for the mountain products, keeping some for themselves. Mead thought that many of these shells and rings, certainly those from large clams, probably originated on or near Wallis Island and were then traded for pigs to coastal peoples, who in turn sent them overland to the Sepik; these were especially likely to be cut up and used as nose ornaments or crescents.[9]

There seemingly were no hereditary trade partnerships in this second system, and only relations with Kundimo were consistently friendly. Mead noted one occasion during which attendance at a ceremonial was combined with trading by people from Anduar. For all trading with upriver villagers (especially Asangamut and Sipisipi) and Anduar downriver, child or half-caste hostage exchanges were required to ensure safe trading. (Fortune notes that child hostages were also required with the upriver village of Bun.) Mead notes that children and half-castes were used as hostages because they were less valuable if something went wrong and they were killed.[10]

Far more than material objects was traded along this route. From upriver villages the Mundugumor obtained significant charms and magic. (To pass on hunting magic to his son, a man had to ensure that both of them kept certain taboos during the learning period; because these were almost always broken, the magic had to be reimported by each generation.) From Anduar and downriver places they imported dances, ceremonials, and new masks and art styles. In this way they participated at least peripherally in the grand tradition of main Sepik art and ritual.

Politics and Leadership

Although neither Mead nor Fortune describes in detail the nature of political organization, both refer to it as a "big man" system. But achieved informal leadership, which is what I think they meant by that term, is manifested in various ways throughout Melanesia, and labeling a system this way describes it in only a very general sense. They were not aware of the diversity in these systems in 1932; glossing the Mundugumor as a big-man system is understandable because the major populations in the highlands, where achieved leadership assumes many forms, were yet to be contacted, and even classic descriptions of lowland leadership (e.g., Oliver 1955) had not been written.

It is possible to discern some characteristics of this big-man system and locate it at least generally among Melanesian systems. Alemi and Mongova were continual competitors and obvious rivals for the allegiance of others. Even in 1981, in discussing the past, an informant remarked on the rivalry between these two brothers-in-law. Clearly they were big men of some sort, but what was the nature of their power and how did they acquire it? An examination of contrasts drawn by two contemporary anthropologists, Godelier and Modjeska, can assist in teasing out critical elements of the system and thereby help us understand how the political process worked.[11]

Godelier (1982:31) makes a distinction in types of political leadership in Melanesia when he contrasts the big man with the great man. Godelier's big man is explicitly very much like the leader described by Sahlins (1963) in his classic model:

A big-man . . . is a man who possesses personal power acquired by his own merits, which is not inherited and cannot be passed on. These merits arise from the exercise of several talents: magical powers, oratorical gifts, courage in war, competence and effort in agricultural work, which have proved his superiority in these various contexts. (Godelier 1982:3–4)

. . . we discover a discerning man, a calculator, a great orator, who accumulates wives in order to have wealth and wealth to have wives, who is surrounded by dependents, who creates around him networks of obligations by paying for the bridewealth of young people too poor to marry. His name is known far and wide, because it is carried as far as his ceremonial participation in intertribal exchanges. More than war between tribes, it is exchange and competition in wealth between tribes which become the basis and privileged channel of establishing his renown. (Godelier 1982:31)

Aspects of this description fit the Mundugumor system well, such as the reliance on an individual's qualities and abilities, the manipulation of wealth, the accumulation of wives and the demonstration of skill in war and oratory, but two elements do not fit. First, there were no intertribal exchange networks comparable in scale and magnitude to those such as the Enga te or Hagen moka, found in the highlands; there were no elaborate cyclical pig festivals. Second, Godelier (1982:32) ties the generation of this big-man system to a particular kind of marriage structure:

. . . the big man appears to emerge in a situation where restricted exchange of women is not practiced as the dominant principle, where the generalized exchange of a woman for wealth is carried out and where the accumulation of wealth becomes a direct condition for the reproduction of kinship relationships.

The Mundugumor did not practice generalized exchange at marriage but rather preferred direct brother-sister exchange. Although this description of the big man fits the Mundugumor data in some ways, it does not in all.

But what of Godelier's image of what he calls the "great man"? He describes and contrasts the great-man system as one in which there exist restricted exchange of women and no large intertribal exchange ceremonies (1982:32). Furthermore, great men play specific and particular roles, such as warrior and shaman, and do not base their power on diffuse qualities and abilities; inherited status can also play a significant part in the generation of great men. Although the presence of direct and restricted exchange and the absence of elaborate ceremonial cycles would tend to place the Mundugumor in this system, there are no data to suggest that inherited status was at all relevant; skill in warfare, oratory, marriage brokering, and ritual rather than the performance of a specific role or the occupation of a specific status generated respect and therefore leadership. Thus, Mundugumor leaders fall somewhere between Godelier's big men and great men.

Modjeska's (1982) model incorporates a contrast between high-production societies and low-production ones. He compares the two in terms of political leadership; in the former, leadership is based first and foremost on eminence in ceremonial exchange systems, whereas in the latter it is based on eminence in elaborate ritual initiation cycles. Modjeska's data on the Duna place them in the middle of this continuum between "ritual and political-economic modes of domination" because leadership was based on several factors—no single one "constitute[d] an unequivocal cultural focus" (1982:86). Omblean's description of a leader (given to Mead in 1938) indicates that his power base was also a mixed one, similar to the Duna:

. . . he makes spirit houses, he plants many yams, he takes care of many pigs, he gives food to all people, he gives the best opinions on a fight. If people want to do something, they go [get advice] from him. If he's a big man from the [village], well, if they want to do something, they go ask him.

The sketch of a leader here includes ritual sponsorship (building spirit houses), industrious gardening and pig raising, generosity, knowledge, and sage advice. Alemi knew magic for yam growing that no one else knew, and all relied on him for the fertility of their gardens. Although there was clearly some overlap, particularly in the expectation of generosity, Omblean's description indicates that a good man and a leader were not necessarily the same. The attributes he used to describe a good man were "generous, hospitable, doesn't wait until people ask him for things, gives them [without being asked], doesn't quarrel or fight." In a parenthetical note Mead adds that one should "compare this judgement with the fact that when Mongova and Alemi [leaders who did not possess these characteristics] die, the whole place will mourn for them, but for Komeaka and Kalekumban [good men], only very near kin [will mourn]." [13]

Omblean described a rubbish man in this way: "His custom is not to do anything, really. He doesn't [say anything of significance]. He walks around like an adolescent. He just does his work. That's the custom of a good-for-nothing, he just does his work." The rubbish man, the ineffectual man, was one who just walked around and did not say anything of importance. He worked and had his gardens, but his opinions were not respected and his knowledge questionable.

Omblean's descriptions allow us to contrast the good man, the leader, and the rubbish man. What seems to have distinguished the leader was the force of his opinion and his oratorical skill as well as his generosity, initiative in subsistence and ceremonial sponsorship, and knowledge. Surely, although Omblean does not mention it explicitly, a prerequisite to leadership was skill in acquiring industrious wives and manipulating the marriage-exchange system, and the military prowess of leaders such as Alemi and Mongova is prominent in stories of raiding and warfare. It seems that, as for Modjeska's Duna, no single criterion was adequate to encompass all the prerequisites of becoming a leader, and again the Mundugumor fall somewhere between leaders characteristic of high-production societies and those of low-production societies.

Conflict and Warfare

Conflict was a common occurrence in Mundugumor society. Most disputes centered around arranging marriages and marriage itself; men competed for the rights to use a sister in marital exchanges as well as to receive her return as a wife. These sorts of disputes—by far the most common—are discussed in the next chapter in the context of kinship and marriage. Here it needs to be noted only that they were frequent, that they occurred between close kin and fellow villagers as well as outsiders, and that they often provoked physical violence.

Neither Mead nor Fortune provides any significant detail on the process of dispute settlement among members of the same village (other than the *kamain*-instituted peace described in chapter 4). One can only speculate that kinship norms dampened quarrels, that the relative richness and abundance of land inhibited disputes over material resources, and that the weak took shelter with the strong. In *Sex and Temperament* (1963) Mead stressed the individualistic nature of the Mundugumor and wondered that the society stayed together at all. But the cases provided here (and in chapter 4) provide ample evidence that the escalation of violence within one's own group was inhibited by a variety of factors, including kinship norms and values, fear of retaliation, and a system in which lesser men congregated around and supported more powerful men. The cases also illustrate that these inhibiting factors were not always successful.

Relations among members of the various Mundugumor villages were, ideally, amicable ones, but Fortune recorded a series of events illustrating that this norm was not necessarily always observed. This extended case is worth quoting at length because it reflects the nature of Mundugumor political relations as well as the treachery and stealth involved in disputes, the importance of reciprocating the killings of one's own people, the precariousness of alliances, and the significance of honor.[14]

. . . about 1920 the people of Biwat . . . adopted a [custom] of tying the
urethral skin of a male opossum . . . to the inside of the women's grass
skirts. . . .

A man of Akuran . . . who had seduced a Biwat woman, announced
scornfully that Biwat people hung grass skirts with urethral skins of male
opossums . . . up in their houses and ate their meals in the stench under
them. When the men of Biwat heard that their concerns were discussed
scornfully in the settlements downriver, they issued a challenge to the men
of . . . Akuran and Kinakatem to meet them on an appointed day in
Branda village which lay between their places. The challenge accepted,
Kinakatem and Akuran men arrived in Branda on the afternoon of the
due date. A go-between told them that the Biwat men proposed to use insulting language about their detractors. As a signal of the time and place
when this proposal would be carried out, they would see a grass skirt dis-
played at the head of a staff carried by a Biwat standard-bearer. If they
accepted the language . . . employed to detract from them, honor would
be satisfied, but if they failed to accept it, their blood would be on their
own heads. The Kinakatem and Akuran men remained in their canoes . . .
and the Biwat men stayed conversing with their Branda friends until night
fell.

Then the Biwat men, behind a leader carrying a grass skirt on a staff
. . . came, and their leader said, "you see this. Your wives are good and
ours not, do you say? You do not understand how to decorate your houses
with grass skirts. You lie with your wives only in the jungle, and not in
your houses, do you say? Your wives do not place their skirts within
houses." At this point, Tanguishengen of Kinakatem stood up and said,
"no. It is only your fashion that has been discussed. All places are laughing at it." His interruption drew a volley of spears. . . . The Biwat men,
having killed Tanguishengen, withdrew hastily and the Kinakatem and
Akuran men, after a short, futile pursuit of them, took the body and went
downriver to their homes.

The next day, the Kinakatem and Akuran men paddled upriver to Biwat
but found the place deserted except for one man whose mother had been
a woman of Kinakatem and who was protected . . . by his maternal relatives. . . . The invaders smashed property . . . but preserved the houses for
their own use and settled themselves in them. A man of Biwat permanently domiciled in Kinakatem was permitted by both sides to pass
between them, and brought amongst other requests one from the women
of Biwat to the women of Kinakatem for grass skirts.

. . . The Biwat people from their retreat in the jungle sent messengers
through to Andafugan asking for necessities. Then they sent word of an

expected arrival of an Andafugan party to the men of Akuran and Kinakatem and invited the latter to ambush the former and to return to their
homes. The backers of Akuran and Kinakatem debated the proposal and
decided to accept it with an aim of deluding Biwat into a belief that they
were satisfied with it. They ambushed the Andafugan party and killed and
carried six bodies which they cooked and ate in Kinakatem and Akuran.

It happened that in the Andafugan party there were some men of Dowaning and two of these were amongst the six killed. In the sequel the
Dowaning leaders considered a question whether their loss was a reason
for war between them and Kinakatem and Akuran. They decided that as
there was no . . . direct enmity between them to accept the loss.[15]

The Biwat people resumed the use of their houses and hopefully offered
the Akuran and Kinakatem men their help in acquiring a few bodies from
the nearest villages of the pottery manufacturers tribe to the east of them.
They offered a guide through their territory and into the territory of the
next people east. The offer was accepted, and Kakwaon, of the kinsmen of
Tanguishengen, was detailed to kill the Biwat guide before the party
reached the territory of the pot-makers. In this way, Kashwomda, a Biwat
leader, was dispatched and his body left for his villagers to recover.[16] The
Biwat people said that Kashwomda's death was fair return for that of Tanguishengen, but where was the return for the losses of Andafugan? The
Kinakatem men, recognizing this complaint, offered a guide through their
territory to ambush some manufacturers of pots to the east of them. The
offer was accepted and the leader of the Kinakatem men guided a party of
Biwat and Andafugan men through his territory to ambush a small party
of potters on their way to Akuran carrying pots. None escaped. The leader
of the Kinakatem men then went to Akuran and was told the news of the
deaths of the potters who had been expected to come that day.[17] He returned to Kinakatem, took a wife with him and the pair went to the village
from which the dead potters came to offer their condolences to the next of
kin and to divert suspicion that they were party to the action as best they
might do by not failing to put in an appearance. . . . It was said that the
Andafugan people were contemplating [losing] the Mundugumor language and using the language of the sleeping-bag makers which they
knew already, on account of the advantages that were taken of them in this
affair.

Mead's notes include only a passing reference to this protracted
quarrel. She added the following: "The war lasted a long time,
everyone was hungry, women had no grass skirts—only leaves, and

[the women] abused the men and demanded an end of the war." No further details, such as the mechanism by which the women pressured the men, are provided. She further noted that the end result was a "life for a life." It is interesting that the Biwat and their downriver neighbors, the Akuran and Kinakatem, settled their quarrel relatively amicably—only one man from each side died, and a goal of balance was achieved. Most of those killed in this dispute were not from the four river villages, and in fact some were not even Mundugumor at all. Here is some evidence that fights within the community were settled without resort to the more characteristic all-out violence that applied to outsiders. This case also clearly illustrates the ways in which trickery and stealth played roles in intervillage relations and raiding.

Relationships with non-Mundugumor villages were occasionally friendly. Trade ties clearly affected the nature of relations between villages, as did alliances against others. Fortune also noted that relations with the inland village of Changriwa were typically "friendly or neutral" (at least in 1932). A father and son from Kinakatem quarrelled, and the younger man escaped to Changriwa. His father was still angry and requested that the people in Changriwa murder his son, but they refused because they had no quarrels with Kinakatem. (Fortune does not provide additional evidence to support his interpretation that Changriwa's refusal was motivated by friendliness. It is certainly possible that it was an attempt to stay neutral and remain uninvolved in stormy Mundugumor affairs.)

Relations with some other villages, again at least in 1932, seem to have been typically hostile. The downriver people in Anduar were, in spite of the trade that went on, traditional enemies. Biwat people who wished to die would paddle to this village, knowing they would certainly be killed there. Fortune recorded three cases of such de facto suicide. In the first, two brothers quarrelled over the right to use their only sister in a marriage exchange. Their mother "reproved" the younger brother for trying to interfere with his elder brother's rights, and the younger brother committed suicide by paddling to Anduar. The second case concerned the same mother, who killed herself by following her younger son. The third case was a woman who was seduced by Alemi; her sister, one of Alemi's wives, shamed her for her actions, and she too paddled to Anduar.[18]

Hostages were sometimes exchanged or placed with enemies to ensure a peace between potentially hostile villages. Such hostages were typically children; half-castes were not trusted or valued and were usually unacceptable. Hostages were used with upriver villages and the downriver village of Anduar, but not with the downriver village of Kundimo. They were also used with the trading villages of Nadvari, Mensuat, and some other places where mosquito baskets were obtained, but none was used with the pottery makers of Yaul, Dimiri, and Maravat. Afima, who was a young boy when he worked for Mead and Fortune in 1932, had been a child hostage. He was sent to a Grass Country place, and his main complaints about his experience were that the place smelled, the water was not good, and the ground was too swampy to walk on. He was joined by another boy, and eventually the two of them escaped back to their own village. Apparently their escape did not damage relations with the hostage-holding village (with whom the Mundugumor wanted to ensure peace) for he noted no consequences. At least in his retelling, Afima did not indicate that he felt any fear, but that might be the bravado of a 12-year-old boy not willing to admit fear (in fact, he seemed more fearful of his father's reaction to the escape than of the enemy). Unfortunately, there are no further data on hostages; we cannot know if the practice successfully maintained peace or if hostages typically found their way home safely. It is possible that providing a hostage indicated a sincerity that was believed. It also seems likely that the identity of the hostage and his or her kin would be a factor: Afima was the son of Alemi, an influential leader, and causing him harm would probably have had more serious consequences than injuring the child of a less important man.

Mundugumor warfare entailed raids by stealth rather than open, confrontational battles. Men, women, and children were all appropriate victims. Although the goal was to kill as many of the enemy as possible, it was always important to reciprocate deaths and avenge the death of a member of one's own group. (Sorcery was a possible means of revenge as well as direct physical attack; see chapter 3). If a man was killed by an enemy, his relatives covered themselves with ashes and then went to reciprocate the death. When they were successful, they returned and washed off the ashes. The dead man's brother was obliged to provide a feast to all those who helped him avenge his brother's murder. The men who ate at this feast decorated the enemy's skull and presented it to the brother.

Fortune recorded an example of a revenge raid on Anduar. An Anduaran raiding party had killed some Mundugumor men (Fortune is not explicit as to how many) just after two Mundugumor committed suicide by deliberating intruding downstream into hostile territory. So men from all six Mundugumor villages and some allies from additional villages went to Anduar for revenge. Surprising their enemies in a dawn attack (signaled by the blowing of a conch), they killed all the men, women, and children in one hamlet, burned the houses, and destroyed all the property they found.

Another incident recorded by Fortune illustrates that political relations were not simple and that even within the village of Kinakatem there was not necessarily a united front against an enemy; it also indicates the rivalry between Alemi and Mongova. A man named Ndelong wanted to marry a woman, but she ran away to Anduar, and he was angry with the people there for taking her in. He heard that someone[19] had given the Anduar people an assurance of safe passage to come to Kinakatem to buy yams, so he got together with Alemi to plan an attack on their canoe.[20] Mongova opposed the plan because he thought there would not be enough people coming to make it worthwhile; he wanted to be nice to this particular group and entice more to come later. Fortune continued, "Alemi and Ndelong just ignored Mongova and went on with their plan. They did not apprise Mongova or let him in on the [attacking] party." They did enlist the aid of some of Mongova's brothers, one of whom inflicted the only wound. After the attack Mongova was furious and attacked Alemi and his allies. He threatened to leave

Kinakatem and let the people of Anduar take their revenge on Alemi (he apparently did not do so). This incident clearly illustrates the treachery and subterfuge of Mundugumor killing, the conflict between leaders, and the fact that plans were not always successful.

Neither Mead nor Fortune details the results of unsuccessful raids, nor do they comment on the possibility that inhabitants of other villages might raid the Mundugumor.[21] They did, however, record some details of the aftermath of a successful raid. First of all, the taboos on a man who had killed an enemy were minimal. He was not allowed to drink water or eat betel, but he could eat sago pudding and baked items. He did not seem to be viewed as polluting in any way; he could sleep with his wife, go into houses, act in a relatively normal fashion. Mead thought it "typical" of the Mundugumor that a successful warrior was not feared or seen as contaminated; by this I think she meant that killing was not seen as a disturbing act. A man who killed a member of his own group was not allowed to assume any homicidal decorations for such a kill, and in one note Mead claimed that he had to relinquish all such decorations for life.[22]

A successful raid was cause for celebration. Mead noted that feasting and dancing continued for several days and that such activity was believed to prevent an enemy attack.[23] A successful returning war party was met by sisters and father's sisters. In one note Mead recorded that these women removed their grass skirts and struck their brothers and brother's sons with them, but elsewhere Omblean told her that women whose relatives had been killed wore a special grass skirt made from the leaves of a betel palm; when the death was avenged, these women changed back to normal grass skirts. The women likely did not remove the skirts they were wearing; rather, the special skirt likely was used to strike returning avengers. Some women—presumably father's sisters—threw themselves into the river, and a few mother's brothers also fell into the water. (Fortune noted that this return greeting was also being used for young men returning from indentured labor.) Later, at the time of the ceremony for the shooting of the banana or soon thereafter, a brother's son reciprocated these services from his father's sister by giving her sago grubs.

When an enemy was killed, a ceremony was performed whose purpose seems to have been to banish spirits of those killed in war, but the details are sparse.[24] Enemy bodies were brought back for eating, and occasionally the ghosts would follow. These ghosts could not seriously harm humans, but they could frighten them, make them cringe, and make the hair on their arms stand up (a reaction comparable to seeing a snake). A wild banana tree was placed upright in a clearing, and it was believed that the banana stalk contained ghosts of the slain of both enemy and one's own people. A man (not the killer of an enemy spirit within) was chosen to shoot the banana with an arrow. The man who performed this act had to be one of several brothers, and he could never again smoke tobacco rolled in wild banana leaves but had to use what Mead called the inferior domestic ones. After the banana stalk had been thrown in the river, dry coconuts were painted and hung high up in a tree. These were shot with arrows, and the men shooting were later forbidden to eat any coconuts from the village (hence, these men were usually and conveniently from other villages).[25] A note in the margin indicates that shooting the coconut was done for play, but no indication is given as to the precise meaning of shooting the banana. Probably it involved a belief of setting free the ghost contained within, but where the spirits were released to or from is unknown.

Raids sometimes resulted in the capture of an enemy, although an occasional captive was purchased from another village.[26] Although it is possible that women and children captives were spared, more likely all who were captured were killed. Fortune provides data on the treatment and means of dispatching a captive. Grown men did not kill captives—that would be shameful. Children did the actual slaying (the act was not, however, according to Mead, considered a rite of passage); if the chosen child was not strong enough to do the job, he[27] would be helped by his mother's brother. The captive was tied to a coconut palm, and the people danced and sang

around the person, probably throughout the night. In the morning
he or she was offered food by a friend, and if no friend was present,
then the father of the child who was to do the deed (the man responsible for the capture or purchase) gave the food.[28] The food had
to be "good food," but just what that was is not specified. The captive was not physically tortured in any way but was spat upon and
verbally insulted. She or he was protected from physical abuse by
the father of the designated killer, who was concerned to see that
only his son shed the person's blood. After eating, the captive was
"made to look the other way," and the child killer speared her or
him in the back from behind. Other youngsters were then allowed
to spear the captive as well, but only the first assumed homicidal
decorations. (Note here a contradiction with Mead's data that homicidal decorations could not be worn for this act.) Then a *singsing*
ceremony was held around the slain enemy.

Cannibalism was practiced. One could eat enemies, and the
members of the four river villages (Biwat, Branda, Akuran, and
Kinakatem) had begun to eat the members of the two bush villages
(Dowaning and Andafugan). There are few details about the methods of cooking and eating a human body, but Mead did note that it
was first roasted and then cut up and boiled. There were special pots
for cooking human flesh, and care was taken that relatives and enemies were not cooked in the same pot, for if a person ate meat that
had been cooked in a pot used for a kinsperson, that person would
"go mad and die." Sometimes, presumably to be safe, human flesh
was simply cooked in a new pot (or, in another note, Mead wrote
just cooked in the fire and not boiled at all). The data on who ate
human flesh are contradictory. In one early note dated October 9,
Mead recorded that only men, not women, were cannibals. But
when Omblean talked of eating human flesh (a small bit only, so
small, in fact, that he claimed not to be able to taste it), he said that
everyone ate some of the meat, including little boys and girls. In
Bun both men and women ate enemies; the evidence seems to indicate that both male and female Mundugumor ate human flesh as
well, but of that we cannot be certain. Mead did make some notes

on the attitude people had in 1932 about cannibalism: "Boys of twenty have eaten human flesh, and they are all very merry about it. . . . [they think of cannibals as] men no good, in the sense of gay dogs, some guys. [They] don't eat man now for fear of the government; no horror expressed, just naughty glee."

The skulls of slain enemies, which were later presented by a mother's brothers to their sister's sons (see chapters 3 and 4), came in for special treatment. The killer first boiled the skull to loosen the skin and then removed as much flesh as he could. The skull was then hung on a tree where small black ants ate the traces of remaining flesh. When it was clean, the killer painted and decorated it and then hung it up in his own house or, if one was in existence at the time, a spirit house (see chapter 3). These skulls were either given to a sister's child while the killer was alive in exchange for a pig or were inherited by a sister's child after his death (see chapter 4).[29] The right to wear homicidal decorations was inherited with the skull.[30] This inheritance pattern did not pertain to skulls of captives slain by children. Whenever the acquisition of a new skull was celebrated, skulls of enemies slain in former battles were decorated anew and set out. These enemy skulls were stored in the rafters of houses, unlike the skulls of relatives, which were kept nearby, usually on the floor. If an enemy was killed but taking possession of the body, was not possible, people substituted the decorated skull of a pig.[31]

Although warfare, raiding, and cannibalism had ceased in 1932, the process of pacification had not been an easy one. In preparing to write her monograph on the Mundugumor, Mead (in 1973) wrote that

we found the Mundugumor in a state of cultural arrest: the earlier punitive expeditions of the German authorities had had no effect upon them, as they expected to die violent deaths, but the practice of the League of Nations Mandate authorities of imprisoning those who persisted in warfare and headhunting activities had broken their spirit. After the imprisonment of some of the leaders, who found a term in prison wondering who might have appropriated their wives thoroughly unpalatable, they

decided that there was to be no more fighting of any kind, and with this
decision, that all ceremonial activities were also to be discontinued. . . .

The way in which the Mundugumor ceased cannibalism, warfare,
and raiding and Mead's perceptions of this process bring us to an
examination of change in Mundugumor society.

THE HISTORICAL CONTEXT

No society exists in a temporal vacuum; all are shaped by events,
forces, and recollections from and of the past as well as perceptions
and expectations of the future. The same is true, of course, of anthropological conceptualizations of history and sociocultural
change—these too are shaped and molded by earlier theories as
well as the intellectual frameworks in which they evolve and against
which they react. Here I briefly sketch Mead's framework for describing and conceiving of change among the Mundugumor. Using
her visions and data as well as my own, I then attempt to outline the
nature of a Mundugumor past.

Mead's Conception of Mundugumor Change

Anthropologists generally conceptualize and organize their data in
terms of the paradigms prevalent in the period in which they work.
What is noteworthy about Mead, and what is apparent in her construction of change here, is that although she did assume a perspective of American cultural anthropology, her skills of observation
were such that she superceded the prevailing paradigm and included data, observations, and occasionally interpretations sometimes at odds with both the accepted theoretical model and her own
consciously stated framework as well.

Two aspects of Mead's depiction of history and change among the
Mundugumor require special attention in this context, both of
which illustrate her ability to perhaps unknowingly go beyond the

constraints of the prevailing theoretical model. The first of these has
to do with her tendency to see the precolonial society in a dynamic
rather than static way; this tendency both accords with and yet su-
percedes in significant ways the American cultural anthropological
paradigm about change. The second pertains to her picture of the
colonial and postcolonial society as one that had collapsed or just
stopped; although her model is generally one of loss, her perceptions and intuitions led her to acknowledge substantial accretions
and syncretic elements as well. What she failed to see, perhaps, is
that her perception of the collapse of Mundugumor society may
have been as much her informants' construction of past events as it
was a true rendering of "reality."

As noted at the beginning of this chapter, Keesing (1981:111–12)
depicts Mead's version of American cultural anthropology as assuming what he calls a "mosaic view"—that is, a tendency to see
each human culture as a unique creation, an experiment in possibility, almost unrelated to other societies in time and space. Each
was a separate tile, unconnected to surrounding tiles. Mead's presentation of the Mundugumor material in *Sex and Temperament*
might legitimately be labeled a "mosaic" view: the Mundugumor,
contrasted with the Arapesh and Tchambuli, were shown as one
example of human possibility, complete unto themselves and seemingly stable over time. However, her notes and a closer reading reveal that her perceptions about the Mundugumor were similar to
her perceptions about the Arapesh, a people she described as an
"importing" culture (Mead 1970): she recognized that the society
did not exist in isolation but was continually interacting with its
neighbors, and this interchange inevitably led to change within the
group as well. Although Mead often wrote as if societies were
unique creations that presented a natural laboratory of unrelated
instances, when she wrote about the Sepik she could not ignore the
various ways in which these societies interacted with and in turn
were influenced by groups around them. There is ample evidence
(see, for example, Tuzin 1976, Gewertz 1983) that the Sepik basin
in general had been seething with change for hundreds of years,

something Mead did not ignore. Despite the fact that she sometimes wrote wholly in a mosaic vein, her descriptions and analyses incorporated at least to some extent a more contemporary systems perspective.

American cultural anthropology in the 1930s exhibited not only a tendency to adopt the "mosaic" view, to deny change and analyze societies in some sort of perpetual ethnographic present, but also a profound interest in and recognition of change, at least insofar as groups adapted to changing environments and traits, customs, and ideas diffused from one group to another. Mead incorporated both these tendencies in that she sometimes wrote in a frozen ethnographic present, but she also clearly acknowledged shifts and changes. Her work in this way exemplifies these dual interests of American cultural anthropology.

Mead's actual perceptions and writings, however, reach further than the paradigm within which she worked allowed. That American paradigm tended to view change as having predominantly to do with adapting to the environment or as somehow being caused or initiated by some kind of external agent (e.g., the introduction of the horse, colonialism, or new traits being diffused from the society next door). Although Mead did incorporate this conception of the causes for change in her Mundugumor work, she went further. She saw change here as being only partly due to adaptations and importations and interactions with neighbors. A significant amount of change was brought about by an internal dynamic within the society itself, a dynamic with a momentum of its own, and this recognition put Mead far ahead of many of her anthropological contemporaries.

The major change that occurred before outside contact and was generated from within by structural elements of Mundugumor society was, in Mead's view, degeneration, a collapse of the kinship system as a result of ever-increasing complexities and impracticalities. She was convinced that because the social organization with its elaborate system of descendants of intermarrying pairs marrying four generations later (see chapter 4) was unworkable, there had previously been some other kind of system that had evolved—or perhaps devolved—into what she and Fortune observed in 1932. She thought that the kinship system contained within it evidence of an earlier time in which rules were followed and violence was less characteristic of the society (1963:228). The system, with its rules and requirements and additions (Mead believed that some kin notions had been imported from the nearby Banaro and that these served only to complicate an already complicated system; see chapter 4) had completely collapsed. In a letter she wrote that "the system has fallen completely to pieces," and she thought that fact explained why the Mundugumor had ideal rules in their heads that were rarely if ever carried out, rules that only made the people feel guilty and inadequate (see chapters 4 and 5 for a different interpretation of these data). From Mead's perspective the social organization had deteriorated to the point where it was no longer meaningful. Her main lines of evidence were twofold:(1) the system as it was supposed to work was unwieldy and, in essence, unworkable; (2) people did not even bother to try to follow their own rules. In essence Mead saw the past as one in which internal complexity increased to the point of complete disfunction. That she posited an internal dynamic within the culture that generated this change was remarkable for her time, but her theoretical view was still a simple one requiring integration between ideology and behavior, between rule and practice: she was not yet to the point of recognizing tension, contradiction, and dialectic as natural elements in sociocultural systems. Despite these theoretical blinders, she had the vision, perhaps peripheral, to recognize and wrestle with some of these significant issues.

Colonialism only caused further collapse. She wrote that the culture had "stopped like a clock," was paralyzed, arrested. She saw change predominantly as values that had been lost or customs that were no longer observed. She did note that some customs continued as before, but she seemed to frame her observations around the notion that there were few new ideas, that change had not in any way gone forward. Again, what is interesting about Mead's work is the extent to which her own analytical framework did not hinder her perceptions and observations, for although she wrote as if the culture had ceased, she proceeded to note the variety of ways in which it both continued and created anew. In part this can be explained by the concept of culture she operated with, one in which art, ritual, and ceremonial tended to take center stage, so that if the ceremonies ceased, the "culture" was gone. But it must also be conceded that Mead's ethnographic skills, as well as her powers of observation and perception, were exceptional and clearly superceded the theory she espoused.

A Sketch of Mundugumor History

Given what data are available, it is possible to sketch, at least in a cursory and admittedly Eurocentric way, the general outlines of the Mundugumor past and the major directions of change over at least the last two or three hundred years. Although Mead's published work (especially 1963) is presented in a timeless ethnographic present, the notes provide an eye-witness account of what the society was like in 1932 as well as some data on earlier life. We have further ethnographic reportage on change and continuity from Mead in 1971 and bits of information and impressions I gathered in 1981.

Mead and Fortune gathered few data on what the Mundugumor believed their origins to have been. In 1981 informants were interested in telling me more about where they came from. These stories tell of the founding of villages; the details of the establishment of the four river villages are not exactly clear, and informants differ as to particulars. All agree, however, that the river villages were founded before there was a river there, when only a small stream wound through the grassy land—a stream small enough to be crossed with a bamboo bridge. The founders, they say, came from the west, from what are now the inland villages but which seem to have been at that time dispersed hamlets and compounds near Andafugan. These ancestors established a village upriver first and then came to make Kinakatem. Informants also agreed that people they called "upriver Sepiks" from near Pagwi came later and settled across the river, again near what is now known as Andafugan and Dowaning.

Mead's perspective on the nature of change during this precolonial period focuses on one hypothesized event and one historical event. The hypothesized event was the degeneration of Mundugumor society caused by internal complexity. The historical event was the change in the course of the Yuat River, a change that literally brought the riverbanks to their doorsteps. Although Mead saw degeneration as the major element in precolonial change, she did allow for what might be called an efflorescence due to this environmental change. One cannot doubt that at least part of the hegemony they enjoyed was related to their possession of high, fertile, and relatively unswampy land along the river. In early publications Mead was unsure of the accuracy of informant statements that the river had changed its course, but in the draft of an introduction to the Mundugumor volume she verified the truth of the assertion by noting that aerial maps, not available until 1967, revealed the old riverbed clearly. What is somewhat puzzling about this dramatic event is the fact that the Mundugumor tell no tales of it. Informants in 1932, 1971, and again in 1981 simply state the change in the river course as a fact to be noted and do not attach much significance to it.

When asked about changes in the past, informants almost always began with stories of the arrival of Europeans, perhaps because the events were more recent or perhaps because the effects were more profound and extensive. Direct changes were imposed and indirect changes ramified throughout the region. Colonialism contributed to Mead's picture of the Mundugumor as a "broken culture" in 1932, and in fact this brokenness was one factor that led to the decision to leave after less than three months of fieldwork. As noted earlier, much of Mead's picture of the postcolonial Mundugumor was not specifically of change but of loss—this had ceased, that had been lost. Significant rituals, art manufacture, warfare, and cannibalism had ceased, and with these, Mead thought, the "living culture" as well had stopped.

In 1981 people were eager to regale me with stories of first contact. They told me that the people's initial reaction on hearing the sound of a motor was to hide in the distant bush, although a few intrepid souls did hide closer and peer out to see what was happening. They thought that these pale-skinned visitors were ghosts or spirits at first but soon realized their error when they passed out salt and metal tools (knives and axes in particular). Memories place a missionary named "Masta Bobby" as the first European visitor in the area, clearly in the first or second decade of this century. It was he who first contacted the people, gave them gifts, and took men away to work at the settlement of Marienberg on the main Sepik River. The first group of men to leave, a group of eight or ten, is remembered particularly because it met a brutal fate: only two returned because people reputedly from Moim and Agromara lied about returning them to their homes and, according to contemporary old men, killed them instead.

Although Mead's main framework for conceptualizing the impact of colonialism was that of cultural arrest and loss, she noted that there were additions as well, institutions that inculcated new ideas and new values and put an end to old ones. The first of these early in the colonial period was the practice of young men leaving the village to work, usually on coastal or island plantations. As noted earlier, the absence of several young men probably did not seriously affect the subsistence base of the society, but it did have at least two profound effects: new ideas, new aspirations, new customs were introduced by returning laborers, and marital disputes concerning their sisters and wives were common while they were away.

The advent of Christian missions caused profound changes. Although a mission station was not officially established in Biwat until 1956, Omblean described initial missionization to Mead while they were in Tambanum in 1938. He apparently reported changes that had taken place between 1932 and 1938, telling her that some people had converted to Catholicism, but some had not. If a person was unconscious, one of the two catechists would go and perform a baptism. He noted that both Mongova and Alemi had been baptized, but because they did not want to give up their wives, in reality they remained unconverted. Omblean's general impression seemed to be that the priests came, baptized, and taught, but that no one took them too seriously.

Mead's initial fieldwork with Fortune in 1932 was close in time to the period of initial contact and pacification by Europeans, and the data they collected provide a better glimpse into precontact society than any data later collected might have done; these data can also serve as a time marker. But Mead's visit to Kinakatem in 1932 was not her only visit there. In a draft introduction written in 1972, in a passage worth quoting because it reveals much about change, she described her decision to revisit the Mundugumor in 1971 this way:

> Furthermore, when I returned to the Sepik in 1967 . . . I heard quite a little of the Mundugumor, now spoken of as Biwats, members of the Biwat Council. Government officials spoke of them with approval, they were peaceful, hard-working, agriculturalists, so it was reported. The people of Tambanum [an Iatmul village of the Middle Sepik] used to make expeditions up the Biwat [Yuat] to trade for betel nut, and they too spoke of them as a people who presented no problems to strangers. They had been missionized before WWII by the Catholic Mission, and there was a mission station, church, school, and dispensary in Biwat. The spectacle of the Mundugumor having been transformed into cooperative agriculturalists, popular with a government which was interested in lack of trouble, intrigued me [see fig. 5], and I began to consider the possibility of returning to Mundugumor and taking a look at these conspicuously reformed and once very cheerful cannibals.

Mead arrived in Biwat on October 12, 1971, where she stayed at the Catholic mission station, making trips to Kinakatem, talking with informants, and working with school children until October 18. During these few days she accomplished a startling amount of work—everything from updating her 1932 census to visiting and talking to the upper-school students. Clearly, the Mundugumor had continued to change after Mead and Fortune's departure near Christmas of 1932—the mere fact that there was a school was a glaring change. But had the change been profound? Mead, although she could not avoid noting the changes that had taken place

Figure 5. Listening to political speeches, National Day, 1972, Biwat. Photograph by N. McDowell.

in almost 50 years, again conceptualized the Mundugumor as having stopped in place. This lengthy quote from her draft introduction to the proposed Mundugumor volume neatly summarizes both the changes and continuities that characterized Mundugumor society as well as Mead's conceptualization of them:

So, in October 1971, I did return to Mundugumor, and satisfied myself of what had happened and was happening [see fig. 6]. The culture had come to a full halt in the early 1930s and literally nothing had happened since, except a minor population explosion. The four villages once separated by shifting alliances, treachery and warfare, were now a continuous stream of settlement along the river. Swarms of children, bright-eyed eager children attended the Mission school, and returned later to their villages, or went away to do the most unskilled manual labor in European settlements. One boy had gone completely away to school, and had now repudiated his fiance, and announced he intended to marry a white girl and never return.

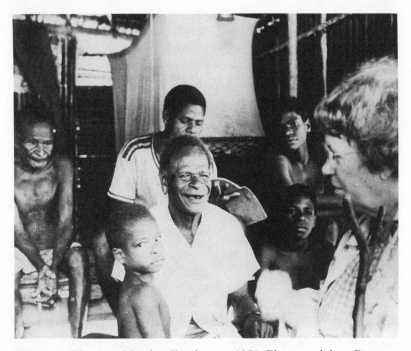

Figure 6. Margaret Mead in Kinakatem, 1971. Photograph by a Biwat teacher.

They were comfortably off; the betel palms still provide them with a sure source of livelihood, houses were better built than in 1932, and a few of them even showed some imagination and innovation. The old slitgongs, with their tongues cut out which the old *luluai* had mutilated in a rage, still lay where his house had been, and where his son lived. They were friendly, but not even enterprising enough to exploit my presence, by proposing expensive feasts or ceremonial exchanges as my other villages have done.[32] The culture had simply stopped like a clock; only the people were there.

Later she wrote that "the same sense of paralysis which was creeping through the culture forty years ago was there today."

She noted the "stop actions" (such as the mutilated slitgong still lying where it had lain almost 40 years earlier) and the losses carefully, but art, ritual, and ceremonial seemed to be central in her picture of what no longer existed. "They gave me, when I left, the last little old style carving left in the village.[33] A few men made rather shoddy things to sell in Angoram." Mead showed people a paper she had written (Mead 1934) that included photographs of earlier carvings and ceremonials, and it prompted her informants to say that they no longer had any of these things, including ceremonial carvings such as crocodile flutes. Everything, they said, was gone. They still performed a few *singsings*, but not with much interest or passion. Youngsters had not even seen many of the things Mead asked about. No longer were there ritual initiations and scarification, and even ear piercing had recently ended as well. There were no pigs in the villages: informants told Mead that the government had forbidden keeping pigs in the village, but she carefully noted that all the government required was that they be fenced in (the Mundugumor found it easier to do away with pigs than to fence them in). Mead continued:

It was reasonably clear from the general conversation, and later conversation with [specific individuals], that what one will get now from everyone is negative [there is nothing left from the ancestors, today's people don't know any more, you already recorded that before]. It would take a long time to get traces.

These words from informants in 1971 introduce an intriguing possibility concerning Mead's interpretation of Mundugumor change. It is possible that in seeing it to be predominantly loss and arrest, Mead was merely following her informants' perceptions of what had happened in their lives. It may be that the Mundugumor themselves see their history in this fashion and that Mead incorporated their ethnohistorical view into her own framework (I return to this possibility at the end of this chapter).

Much, then, had seemingly dropped out of Mundugumor culture. But much remained as before, and Mead noted several elements that had not changed. She noted that "rope inheritance seems to have survived intact" (see chapters 4 and 5) and that totemic associations continued (see chapters 3 and 4). Inquiries about a man's ancestor usually brought references to his mother's father, but land inheritance remained patrilineal. In a penetrating note she wrote that the

ethos seems unchanged, cheerfully disobedient and uncooperative. Endless joking, fight *garamuts* [beat slitgongs] and pretend to paraphrase talk, children and women always hitting at each other, children busy with little pieces of leaf, wood, etc., slap and threaten each other, and women threaten and slap at children. Men tell the children to leave and they don't. Women strong and unmodest. Roars of laughter. Little bit of sentimentality but very low in looking at old pictures. . . .

During Mead's visit she sat among a crowd that was comprised of both men and women; she did not note if women tended to sit around the edges, just that both men and women were present.[34] Women still wore their hair short and carried babies in baskets. People still used slitgongs to call relatives back to the village. Tobacco remained a major crop, along with betel, and there was no doubt that there was plenty to eat.

Despite Mead's conceptualization that change had not taken place or that it had been loss only, she did note significant additions. The existence of a population explosion and the school were major changes, as was the presence of the mission and people's adherence to Catholicism. Everyone wore Western clothing and had European artifacts such as saucepans (although native pots were still used as well). A cemetery replaced the traditional means of disposing of the dead (see chapter 3). Enterprising men owned three cows and were planning to clear a large pasture in the bush, and healthy chickens were common throughout the village. Three men owned outboard motors for their dugout canoes. House styles had changed somewhat, and houses were better constructed than before; there were also various small structures scattered around for specific purposes—carving, just catching a breeze, stripping tobacco. Mead thought that young men remaining on their father's land, as they did more in 1971, added a greater sense of unity (but whether it was unity of clan, agnatic group in general, hamlet, or village is not clear). The greater number of children was attributed by informants to better health care and people marrying at a younger age; many thought that they had too many children and that they entailed too much work.[35]

One of the most poignant events of Mead's return visit was her reunion with the earlier informant, Omblean. Afima, the young boy who had worked for Mead and Fortune in 1932 and had visited them in Tambunam in 1938, had been killed in 1971 while working as a native police officer,[36] but Omblean was alive. He had had, Mead thought, a stroke and could not talk but seemed to recognize her and understand much of what went on around him. Many thought that Omblean might magically be cured by Mead's return visit.[37] Omblean's wife served Mead a lunch of boiled chicken and sago in her house (she had tried to get rice but no one in the village seemed to have any).

Mead's notes from 1971 detail many significant changes, and my visit in 1981 revealed even more. It is impossible to discern whether the pace of change increased between 1971 and 1981 or whether Mead did not note changes as thoroughly as she might have in 1971; I suspect both are true. What I saw in 1981 was an area of significant development and change. The Catholic mission has grown, and today most people claim adherence to the Catholic faith. Attendance at Sunday morning services is high: of the two I attended in 1981, I estimated that more than 200 took part in one (for which the priest was absent) and more than 400 in the other (when the priest was present). Vespers, although not well attended, is held daily. The church is beautifully decorated inside with traditional paintings by local artists. The resident priest thinks that it is time for the people to stop thinking of themselves as a mission or outpost and begin to conceive of their community as a congregation or parish.

Changes unimagined in 1932 were unremarkable in 1981. The provincial minister of education was from Branda, and several youngsters (including at least one of Alemi's grandchildren) were not just in high school but were attending the University of Papua

New Guinea in Port Moresby. Enterprising people formed cooperative associations; one bought a vehicle to use on the road between
Angoram and Wewak while others sought loans from international
agencies to buy a cargo ship[38] to ply the waters of the Yuat and
Sepik. There was a small herd of cattle. Biwat had a village "club,"
which sold alcoholic beverages (see fig. 7). Most children went to
school; certainly those of elementary school age went to the school
(which went up as high as Standard 6) in Biwat. Village stores sold
a variety of goods, and contemporary entrepreneurs chartered airplanes to sell their betel nuts and tobacco in Mount Hagen in the
Western Highlands Province.

That fact—chartering airplanes to sell betel and tobacco to
people in the Highlands—can serve as a paradigm for what has
happened to the Mundugumor in the last 50 years because it neatly
encapsulates both change and continuity (see also figs. 8 and 9).

Figure 7. The village club, where alcoholic beverages are sold, 1981.
Photograph by N. McDowell.

The people are indeed chartering airplanes and driving cars and sending their children to university, but they still rely on the traditional commodities of betel nut and tobacco. For subsistence, the same is true—sago processed in the traditional way, fish acquired by women with their nets, and slash-and-burn gardens predominantly of yams, taro, and bananas, although supplemented by purchased foods such as rice and tinned fish, remain the staples eaten daily. Sago, which one man referred to as "the rice of our ancestors," is still of central significance in the diet.

Much had not changed in 1981. Old slitgongs still lay around the village (see fig. 2), perhaps just where they had been left and where Mead saw them again in 1971, and men pointed out to me the head of a slitgong that had been made with stone tools while we sat near a house under which were stored piles of old war shields. The style of dugout canoe seems not to have changed at all. There was at least one case of infanticide in recent years, and men still aspired to many wives. Sister exchange was the ideal form of marriage, despite the fact that people believed it was not achieved nearly as often as it had been in the past. Brideprice was becoming more common, and out-marriage in general was no longer an aberrant phenomenon; young men and women who went to high school and on to jobs in towns frequently married people from other areas of the country.

The population explosion Mead mentioned in 1971 continued, and in 1981 demographic pressures were beginning to be apparent. People up and down the Yuat[39] (including the Catholic priest whose parish includes the four river villages) recognized that the population pressure in Biwat, Branda, Akuran, and Kinakatem was a problem.[40] The preliminary national census figures for the area in 1981 only tell part of the story: there were 412 people in Biwat (197 males, 215 females), 201 in Branda (97 males, 104 females), 258 in Akuran (134 males, 124 females), and 273 in Kinakatem (133 males, 140 females). An additional 63 people were associated with the Biwat mission station (32 males, 31 females).[41] In 1932 Kinakatem had 196 people; less than 50 years later, it had 273, a rather substantial increase.

The increases in population are even more staggering than these figures indicate because a significant number of people from these villages do not live permanently in them any more, and it is unlikely that all away were included in the census. Many youngsters went off to school and got jobs in towns (as taxi drivers, schoolteachers, mechanics, bank tellers, soldiers, foresters, and police officers and took various other civil service jobs); they return to visit but do not rely upon the land for their subsistence. Father Michael Fiedel (personal communication), the Catholic priest in Biwat, thought that if all absentees returned, there would be absolutely no way to support the population with the land available. In fact, the indications are that those who remain in the villages rely upon those who leave for cash and commodities. I did not have ample time to acquire reliable or quantitative data on the topic of remittances, but they are no doubt significant. Several adults proudly told me of what their wage-laboring children provided for them (including relatively expensive items such as outboard motors). One means of relieving the land pressure is for people to leave and send remittances back, and this the Mundugumor seem to be doing.

The people who remain in the villages, however, unlike those who leave and enter into completely new lifestyles in towns and cities, seem to combine both old and new in their economic dealings. They rely upon relatively traditional means of subsistence but add new crops and new markets to the old items to obtain cash. Tobacco and betel remain essential items, both for intracommunity consumption and extracommunity sale, but now they sell their products in Angoram, Wewak, Madang, and Mount Hagen (and possibly other places in the highlands as well). They use planes and cars and motor-powered canoes to market both old and new products. Traditional crops make their way into the market sales, especially betel nut, tobacco, and sago but also yams, sweet potatoes, and bananas; some people occasionally sell fish or pork as well. And of course there are new cash crops: copra, rubber, peanuts, pineapple, and coffee. In addition to pigs, there are now also cattle to raise and sell. Crocodiles, however, whose skin might have been sold to traders for a significant cash income, have become less common on the river, and although they do still inhabit swamps and *barets* inland, they are not a significant source of cash.[42]

There are changes and continuities in trading as well. Once a week people from Yaul, Dimiri, or Maravat come to the mission station in Biwat to sell their wares, particularly to the teachers and mission workers who have no access to land. What is especially interesting is that pottery continues to be made in these villages and that not only outsiders but also Mundugumor continue to purchase and use it. Although Western-style pots and pans have a place in every household, traditional pottery, purchased from the "Grass" peoples, is still used. Other trading networks, however, such as the exchange of mountain products for sea products with upriver and downriver groups, ceased many years ago. Trade for mosquito baskets, of course, ended with the introduction of mosquito nets purchased with cash. Only trade for pottery still continues (and even that, of course, on a much reduced scale).

My impression of the economy of the four river villages is profoundly colored by my previous work in upriver Bun. Father Fiedel, who visits Bun regularly, also noted that radical differences exist between Mundugumor villages and upriver villages in general. The upriver villages are a different world—there is less education,[43] less development, less sophistication, less money. I was continually impressed during my visit to Kinakatem by the small signs of what I considered to be relative affluence. I unexpectedly visited a house and was served tea and biscuits (Mead had been given chicken for lunch in 1971)—I cannot imagine that happening upriver at that time. Guests, of course, were treated hospitably and served refreshing foods, especially green coconut milk, but I doubt that they would have been given store-bought food if not expected (indeed, until 1980 or 1981 there was no store in Bun). Although most houses are still built with traditional materials and in basically traditional styles (but with innovations),[44] indications of money were everywhere: clothes lines, discarded tin cans, bicycles (fig. 8), a baby stroller (fig. 9), canvas, metal and plastic buckets (fig. 10), innumer-

Figure 8. Continuity in change: path lined with old coconuts and traversed by bicycle, 1981. Photograph by N. McDowell.

able outboard motors, newer clothes, and a whole host of material possessions contrasted significantly with the state of upriver groups. Parents seemed to have no difficulty finding money for school fees, and many young people attended high school in Wewak.

My perspective, looking from my experiences from upriver peoples, was not the same as that of the Mundugumor themselves. They had little but disdain for upriver peoples. The people in Biwat, Branda, Akuran, and Kinakatem looked at their villages from the perspective of urban dwellers or at least small town inhabitants. I thought them affluent because I compared them with Bun and other upriver groups; they thought themselves extremely poor because they compared themselves with highly developed urban areas or, on occasion, with highly developed rural areas such as the coffee belt in the highlands at its peak of affluence. They perceived themselves

Figure 9. Continuity in change: house constructed from traditional materials with a baby stroller parked in the doorway, 1981. Photograph by N. McDowell.

to be victims of government neglect, lack of development, and poverty. Almost all noted that a few individuals were somehow able to generate significant and profitable businesses, but on the whole most were not. They also wanted far more business in Angoram, the district headquarters and nearest town. I must mention, however, that my informants were all adults who predominantly remained in their villages.[45] I did not get a chance to talk with many who had significant business interests that kept them away from the village for periods of time because most were away; the kaunsilman from Kinakatem, for example, was in Madang at the time. My sample of informants might be skewed, but even if it is, it is significant that almost all men with whom I talked complained that they had not developed sufficiently. Many described their villages as being "corner places," out of the mainstream of national economic develop-

Figure 10. Washing clothes, 1981. Photograph by N. McDowell.

ment. They blamed the government and its representatives, including their elected officials, for this state of affairs, and some remembered Australian colonialism with fondness. This attitude may, of course, have been merely a front for my benefit, but I think not entirely. There especially seemed to be bitterness that campaign promises, which people had believed, were not kept.

The perception that the people here were comparing themselves to urbanized and developed areas rather than their own neighbors helped me understand what I at first thought was an anomaly. When I arrived and people asked me why I had come, I reminded them of the visit of Mead and Fortune almost 50 years ago and told them that Mead had written part of a book about them. But much time had passed and much had changed, and now if I too was going to write something about them I had to know what life was like to-day—after all, cannibalism and warfare had ended, they had political independence and some education, a variety of important

changes had taken place. I asked what had changed and was repeatedly surprised by the usually vehement assertion that in fact
nothing had changed in the past 50 years. "We still sit down as our
ancestors did—nothing has changed," I heard over and over again,
the same refrain Mead had heard 1971. One man said that they just
put trousers on old customs—nothing underneath had changed,
only the surface. And yet I saw obvious changes all around me—
schools and burgeoning literacy, a well-attended Catholic church,
material goods, and obviously new ideas and customs. My informants were not using their ancestors as the baseline of comparison
but the highly developed cities and towns of Papua New Guinea.
Especially in terms of subsistence and the reliance on fish and sago,
they were more like their ancestors than their own children who
lived in Wewak, Rabaul, or Port Moresby. Men still wove fish traps,
women still fished in *barets* with handmade nets, people still processed sago taken from the inland swamps. They did physical labor
and produced their own food directly; they did not participate totally
in a cash economy and get wages to spend in a store on their daily
bread. Store-bought foods had, I suspect, become necessary supplements but no one could get by in the village without access to traditional resources; only at the school and on the mission stations
were there any full-time salaried positions.

In sum, the people perceived more continuities than changes in
their lives because their point of reference was not their ancestors
and the past but their children and the towns (and perhaps the future). There are, of course, elements of both change and continuity
throughout their lives, and they are aware of both, but it is the comparison with the more developed areas of the nation and the appearance of more continuity than change that concerns them. Perhaps another factor is relevant here, though, as well: Mead may
have echoed earlier Mundugumor informants when she asserted
that things had collapsed, that the culture had "stopped like a
clock," that nothing new had been introduced. Perhaps Mundugumor perceptions of time, change, and history are relevant here as
well as their tendency to compare their lives with the lives of urban

dwellers. If we examine their comments since Mead's 1932 visit up through my 1981 visit, their vision is a consistent one. They themselves continue to assert that their culture has not changed or at least that it has not changed enough or in the right directions. It may be that as long as the subsistence base remains the same, as long as day-to-day living requires fishing and gardening and sago processing, as long as their time is spent predominantly as their ancestors spent it, people here will continue to assert that little has changed. Perhaps that is how they have always seen things, and one can only wonder what kinds of changes would be required for them to shift to another perspective.

RELIGION |3|

The Mundugumor had already ceased much ritual activity by 1932. There were to be, for example, no more initiation rites until Mead and Fortune commissioned one to be performed, and that one was abbreviated and partial. Despite the changes that the Mundugumor had recently undergone, the notes contain a wealth of data on traditional religion and offer a rich resource for comparative analysis. In this chapter I divide this broad subject into six general topics: (1) water and bush spirits, (2) souls, death, and ghosts (3) sorcery, (4) magic, ritual, and belief, (5) initiation, and (6) myth and folktale.

WATER AND BUSH SPIRITS

The Mundugumor pantheon was not a complex one. It was composed mainly of two kinds of spirits: those of the bush *(maindjimi)* and those of the water *(saki)*. Mead often lumps these two kinds of entities together under the pidgin term *masalai*, making it sometimes impossible to differentiate adequately between the two. Further confusion stems from the Mundugumor practice of representing some of these spirits, particularly the bush spirits, in material or mask form, and it is occasionally difficult to discern whether a note refers to a mask or to a spirit. Finally, people often possessed the names of these spirits, and the relationship between the person and the spirit is problematic as well. The potential confusion of spirit, mask, and person is never addressed by Mead or Fortune; we cannot know whether there were complex interrelationships among these entities in Mundugumor thought. The possibility certainly exists, however, that mask, spirit, and person were intimately connected.

Both kinds of spirits lived in defined territories associated with particular kin groups (see chapters 4 and 5). A spirit could take the form of a human being, but it had never been human. People encountered bush spirits primarily as cassowaries and water spirits primarily as crocodiles (occasionally these spirits took the form of other animals such as wild pigs), but they were none of these animals. If a cassowary or crocodile behaved in a peculiar way—if, for example, a cassowary failed to run away when a person approached it—then this was a sign that it was a spirit in animal form and not a real animal. If a person saw such a spiritual manifestation while in his or her own territory, he or she addressed the creature as grandfather or brother and said something such as, "Lo, it is I your relative who walks about." A person entering her or his own territory did not address the spirits present unless some unusual event occurred, such as a rare or unusual bird cry.

These spirits lived in groups composed of husband, wife or wives, and children. All of them had specific names, and these names were bestowed upon members of the group associated with the territory. The ghosts of the dead lived with the spirits as well. The kin groups were agnatically based: land was associated with patrilineal groups and was inherited patrilineally (a woman was allowed to name her own children after her patrilineal spirits). A different kind of association, however, held for the material representations of some of these spirits. *Peleva*, snakelike carvings associated with the water spirits (but not with any particular named spirit), were inherited patrilineally, but Mead claimed that the masks of bush spirits were handed down along the "ropes" (see chapters 4 and 5)—that is, a woman took the carving and bestowed it on her son. A man would first acquire it from his mother and later hand it on to his daughter. Women brought these items as well as flutes to their marriages. The spirits themselves, however, were associated with the patrilineal group and territory, and although neither Mead nor Fortune makes anything of that fact, it does indicate a significance of patrilineal connection and personal identity that cannot be ignored. (See chapter 5.)

Human beings, often but not necessarily patrilineal kinspeople of the spirits, made offerings primarily to placate their potential anger. Although spirits occasionally helped their human kin find game, especially pigs, angry spirits prevented them from finding game. Offerings were especially important when people were cutting down a tree in the spirit's territory in order to make a canoe or slitgong. When a slitgong was being made, for example, the carver provided an offering of betel, tobacco, and shells to the human kin of the spirit, who then made a speech and hung the offering up near the tree that had been selected. (The goods eventually were returned to the original donor.) A similar offering was made when a tree was cut for a canoe. An additional action was required for canoe making: when the canoe was ready to be pulled out from the forest, men struck it with leaves of oil palm and breadfruit charmed with ginger, thereby ridding it of any bush spirit who might be within it.

Such precautions were necessary because spirits were potentially harmful to humans. They frequently caused the deaths of infants, and parents often warned their children of the danger (despite the warnings, children were not afraid of spirits and said that these were of no concern). Folklore had it that when angry the spirits caused storms and heavy rains, and they could also cause yam vines to wither if they visited a garden. Spirits were known to have killed one old man and caused a large sore on the leg of another, which eventually led to his death. If a man slept in the bush, a spirit might come and, unbeknown to him, burn his skin with lime, causing sores.

Although bush and water spirits were not particularly offended by menstruating women unless some especially sensitive process such as slitgong making was underway, they were easily offended by sexual activity. These spirits became angry if anyone, man or woman, who had recently had sexual intercourse came near. One woman had been blinded by a water spirit for this reason; in 1932 she was pregnant and because of her blindness had to be led out of the house by the hand even to urinate. In 1981 informants told me that it was still forbidden to work in the bush immediately after sexual intercourse because spirits were offended by the smell and caused a person considerable harm. Although I could not discern the extent to which this taboo was observed in actual behavior, the people clearly believed that the spirits continued to be dangerous.

Women were sometimes accosted and tricked by spirits in the bush who assumed the human form of their husbands and copulated with them, and death in labor and childbirth was usually attributed to this cause. In 1938 Mead recorded a text from Omblean describing a woman who had had sexual intercourse with a spirit and her husband and gave birth to twins, one the offspring of the human father and one of the spirit father; mother and both children died. Sometimes the spirit took this form of revenge if a couple copulated near his or her home, and Omblean attributed these three deaths to this cause. Women were not the only ones to be tricked sexually by these spirits; men were sometimes the victims too. The brother of a man living in Kinakatem in 1932 had sexual intercourse with his wife under a banyan tree in which lived a powerful spirit and his family. The spirit-wife came and assumed the form of the human wife and had sex with the man while he was processing sago. He then went home and died.

Mead also recorded a magical act performed in order to cause death in childbirth, an act that informants told her had formerly been done by humans but now was done only by spirits. The spirit stretched a thin piece of bark along a path where the victim would step on it. Then the spirit tied it in a tight knot and placed it in the mud nest of a particular kind of insect. This procedure caused a difficult delivery and eventual death to the woman. Why a spirit would do this is not specified, and Mead also questioned why informants told her that people no longer did this; she wondered, "Is this 'done by a *masalai*' a blind, an alibi, a change in practice, or what?"

These spirits often punished a trespasser on the land or the enemies of their human kin. Unlike their physical representations, they were said not to be able to leave their territories, but anyone who entered therein, especially an enemy, was in danger. A man could instruct his spirits to harm or not to harm particular people. For example, two men made a yam garden on land that belonged to their mother's patrilineal group. The proper patrilineal owner was angry, and they quarrelled. The two left, saying that their yams could rot. The angry man later relented, and they returned, but the man died and the yams would not grow. Blame was laid on kinsmen of the angry man for having called upon the spirits and ghosts of the land. If a man did not leave specific instructions with the spirits, they might harm anyone who entered. If a person became ill after having gone to another's bush, the other would assume that his or her ancestors were to blame. The spirits, possibly assisted by the associated ghosts living there, purloined the soul of the sick man, and the soul's absence was discovered during the process of seer dreaming.[1]

Sometimes people took a more active role in encouraging these spirits to cause harm. In addition to talking to them there were two specific methods of inducing the spirits to act. The first was to hang bamboo spears in the banyan trees where bush spirits lived and instruct them to kill a specific person or certain people. The bush spirit then either turned into a wild pig to accomplish the task or it directly attacked the victim, removed his or her heart, and sewed the chest back up; the victim then returned to the village to die. A man need not invoke only the spirits of his own group in this way. He could call the spirits of others to act in order to avoid being suspected or discovered; if anyone later found the spears, they would tend to blame the owners for the victim's demise. The notes provide two examples of calling upon the bush spirits in order to get revenge. A man from Branda was killed by sorcery by known members of another village. In revenge the people "took the spears to the spirit." The second example is more specific. A man was angry with Safun because Safun had seduced his unmarried sister. The angry man called upon the spirits by "taking the spears" to the bush. Safun and a companion went hunting in this bush and encountered a pig. Their dog attacked the pig, but it behaved suspiciously and demonstrated no fear. Safun's companion was cautious and retreated, but Safun stayed and attacked the pig. His spear merely glanced off the animal, which then attacked and killed him. His death was interpreted as caused by the spirit who had been invoked by the brother of the woman he had seduced.

Water spirits also were sometimes invoked to cause harm. A man made a small bow and arrow or pronged fishing spear and threw it away near the water of a prime fishing place, a known home of a water spirit. If later a woman who had been having an illicit affair or a man who had been performing harmful magic went to this place, the spirit attacked. The notes do not specify the means used by the spirit.

The second main method of forcing the spirits to act against other people involved placing the victim's "dirt" near the home of any spirit, a kind of spiritual sorcery. This was a dangerous act because if the spirit's associated human ward had instructed it to attack enemies or people who had no right to be on the land, it would harm the person placing the dirt. Mead's notes include an illustrative example. A group of boys playing in the bush saw a man copulating with his wife, and they laughed at them. Later, one of the boys became very sick. He fainted when people chewed betel near him and wanted all betel chewers to go away. Divination by dream revealed that part of a pepper catkin was the dirt at work. A search of spirit homes was conducted, and finally the searchers uncovered a coconut shell containing part of a catkin with a spear through it. The man who had been laughed at was blamed, and he temporarily left the village.

Spirit attacks were not necessarily fatal. If the spirit stole the soul, there were two methods of retrieving it and thus restoring the victim to health. People sometimes used dreams to divine the cause of an illness and determine whether a spirit was to blame. If they discovered that a particular spirit had caused an illness, the human kinsperson was approached. He[2] was given shell rings, which were then taken with a meal of cooked bananas to the spirit's abode. As he hung up the rings, he said, " 'Don't make this man sick anymore, send back his soul. They have given me rings. Now if you make him sick more, they will be angry with me. Bring back this man's soul. I'll keep some of the rings, and some I will share with you.' " Then the man waited for a sign—the appearance of a butterfly or a bird but also possibly a cassowary or a snake or another living thing— that the spirit had heard and accepted the offering. When the spirit had released the soul, a seer could see many ghosts coming into the village in a procession, carrying the soul. The man himself kept the rings until the sick person either died or recovered (and probably afterwards as well). Of course, if a man did not want the victim to recover, he only pretended to ask the spirit to return the soul and secretly told the spirit to continue to make him ill.

Even if all steps were done properly, sometimes the treatment was inexplicably ineffective. In the case concerning the argument over gardening rights, the offerings simply did not work. The case of the woman who was blinded for copulating near a spirit's home is even more revealing. She was ill and in danger of dying when a man divined the cause of her illness in a dream. He dreamed that she was sitting down fishing and saw a fish leap up and away. She chased it, but it kept leaping up and away (odd behavior for a fish). Finally she caught it, brought it home, and ate it—then she became ill because in the dream the fish was a spirit. In this way the dream identified the cause of her illness. Several people went to the bush and offered rings and cooked bananas to the spirit. The spirit sent back her soul but kept her eyesight, and she remained blind.

The second method for retrieving stolen souls seems to have been used more often but not exclusively for souls captured by water spirits. Only an old woman could perform it. She tied an old grass skirt on an old basket and offered sago to the basket, which she ate herself. Then she put tobacco, betel, and a knife in her personal carrying basket and put all these in the old basket. She said, "'I have filled up these things. You [the old basket] go. Ask the spirits for the soul back. If they are strong, fight them with this knife.'" She then entered her sleeping basket. The spirit of the old basket left, eating betel nut and carrying the old woman's basket, followed by the old woman's spirit or soul. They journeyed to the spirit world, where they retrieved the spirit of the ill person. While these spirits were away, other people in the house could not walk, talk, copulate, or make any noise. If the old woman saw success in her dream, the ill person would sneeze, a sign that his or her soul had returned. Only old women could use this method (Mead listed the names of five) because young women would be sexually attacked by the water spirits.

Mead's notes include brief mention of two other ways of fighting spirit-induced illness but give no details. The first is this: "Illness from a [spirit] is combatted with a wooden figure called *ngaungau*, a shield and a spear are set in his hand, and a ceremony performed." Second, she mentioned in a listing of various kinds of magic that one man (and the only one in Kinakatem) had a "curative [ceremonial] for [spirit] illness." If a man dreamed that he was going to be the victim of a spirit, he could take action to prevent it. He took some earth from the footprint of a preadolescent girl, the base of a coconut, a particular (but unspecified) kind of fruit, mixed all of these ingredients in sago pudding, and then ate the mixture. This procedure protected him from attack.

These spirits obviously played a role in Mundugumor life, but there are few myths and tales involving their activities. One tale concerned a spirit who tried a beard on a pregnant woman. "It looked awful so he tried it on a man. It looked good so he left it there. If only he had tried it on a pretty young girl, women would have beards now, and men wouldn't be bothered." Mead asserted that the Mundugumor did not have an elaborate body of myth; she recorded some myths from Omblean in 1938, but neither she nor Fortune recorded a significant body of myths during their original trip in 1932. However, it may be significant that the only long and relatively elaborate myth Mead recorded concerned one of these spirits—Bilishoi, the offspring of a spirit and a man—and it was this same myth that informants wanted me to hear and record when I visited Kinakatem in 1981.

SOULS, DEATH, AND GHOSTS

Bush and water spirits were not the only spiritual entities in the Mundugumor conception of the world. Human beings also had an incorporeal aspect to them, most easily represented as a soul. Although no one knew when the soul of a human being animated the body, all people had souls (and some other creatures such as pigs did also). The state and location of the soul were major factors in conceptions of illness, and curing often involved restoring a lost or damaged soul. The free soul of an unconscious person was somewhat feared, and people tended to congregate in the village, especially at night, if one was abroad (usually they had no fear whatsoever of being in the bush at night).

Mead's notes do not specify what happened to this soul at death, but it is likely that it became the ghost *(shigon)*. The evidence for this assertion is only indirect. Mead used the terms almost interchangeably in the notes. Among the upriver Bun the spirit or soul *(mwi)* becomes the ghost *(shigeun)*. There were no beliefs in reincarnation; the spirits did not recycle back through the living world.

The process of dealing with death and the resulting ghost was a long one. When a person died, he or she was first physically prepared. The body was anointed with an oily tree sap; the jaw was fastened shut but the eyes were left open. The body was decorated with rings and put on a scaffold outside. The person's food, yams, coconuts, tobacco, betel, net bags, bow and arrows, spears, and skulls of slain enemies were placed near the body. The crosspiece on which the body rested was covered with the unworked strands of a grass skirt.

A slitgong call announced the death, and relatives gathered, their faces, backs, chests, and arms covered with white clay as a symbol of their mourning. If the deceased was a man, his wife or wives sat near him, sometimes holding his hand. Other relatives who were especially fond of him also took his hands and occasionally talked to him. The deceased's tobacco, betel, and coconuts were distributed among the mourners. The heir also told the man's father's sisters to "'go on, climb the trees [of the deceased] which you helped to plant, and help yourselves.'" Close relatives shaved their heads, and in the case of the death of a big man almost everyone in the village shaved his or her head. Women had a special costume for mourning that consisted of short strings in their noses and ears and a modified skirt, shorter in front than the usual one and made of strings rather than grass. If the person had been ill for a long time, he or she was put in a coffin on the same day; otherwise, the body was kept until the next day on the scaffolding.

After the body had been removed from the scaffold, the area of ground surrounding the structure was swept with a stiff piece of sago palm spathe. The person's net bag was carried far away, either to the river or into the bush. The scaffold and broom were thrown away, and the ghost followed. At this point the ghost left the house but not the village and its surrounding area. Then the net bag was returned to the village. If a deceased man had joked with his mother's brother or, more likely, his sister's son or daughter during his lifetime, then the bag went to this relative along with his bow and arrows, spears, and skulls of slain enemies. If there had been no such joking, these items were given to a sister's son or sister's daughter. Skulls of slain enemies were especially important and were always inherited by a sister's children, never one's own children (see chapter 4). If inherited by a sister's daughter, she usually gave them to her son. Food was set out for the ghosts, sometimes eaten by an old woman of the household, sometimes thrown away because others (especially the sister's children) feared to eat it. Neither Mead nor Fortune hint at why an old woman might eat this food without fear. There are many possibilities, but the most likely one is that the elderly were less likely to cause the recently dead to be jealous and angry at their continuing existence and therefore were less likely to be harmed.

The body was then measured for a coffin made from an old canoe or the hollowed trunk of a sago palm. Sometimes baskets served as coffins for children. The rings were removed before the body was placed inside, and the coffin was fastened over with a covering and placed in the center of the house. A hole was bored through the body to allow the body fluids to escape, and it hung over a gap in the floor. Beneath the floor, under the hole, hung a palm bark sheath to catch the fluids lest they touch the ground. These fluids eventually dried up and were thrown away in the river for fear that a pig or dog might eat them (presumably this action would have caused harm, probably to the pig or dog). The encoffined body remained in the house until it was completely decomposed.[3] If the deceased was a man, his wife stayed with his corpse in the house and kept a big fire going. If the fire was adequate, the smell of the body might not invade nearby houses. This was the prescribed way of dealing with a corpse, but Mead noted in *Sex and Temperament* (1963:172–73) that it was not always observed. She wrote that

> the children held their noses and fled before the stench of their father's decaying flesh, and the widows were only too likely to have already chosen new husbands, so many a man was bundled unceremoniously into the earth on the plea that the survivors were not strong enough to undertake the long mourning.

After the body had been placed in the coffin, a bundle of the totemic leaves of both the mother's group and the father's group was fastened to a banana stalk and placed on the ground near the ladder to the house. The ghost, which had earlier been led from the house when the scaffold was taken down, came and entered into the leaves. The deceased man's sister's son then carried the leaves up onto the roof of the house and left them—and the spirit—there.

The widow observed a number of taboos. She was not allowed to cook and could eat only dried food, which she warmed in a small fire. (This taboo also applied to widowers and parents.) She could not wash or walk around and was allowed to leave the house only to urinate or defecate.

Events in the death of a woman are not as clear as for a man. If her relatives were influential or more numerous, they took the body and saw to the mourning rituals, but if they were not, her husband and his family did. On the death of his wife a man paid all her brothers, presumably with a feast, and sometimes all his other brothers-in-law as well. It is likely that these feasts were all reciprocated and that men trying to increase their power would vie for the opportunity to initiate a feasting series. Thus, a woman's husband and male kin (fathers and brothers) might compete for the right to see to her burial.

It usually took the body a month to decompose fully. The widow then washed the skull in water without ceremony. The arm bones were scraped, and when the scrapings were eaten with lime they became a form of war magic that gave a man superior strength and cunning. The deceased's son, full brothers, mother's brothers, and sister's sons could not, however, eat the bones, or their own breastbones would crumble and "they will go mad and run away in the bush." The notes do not indicate whether Mead or Fortune witnessed this mortuary cannibalism or whether they only reported informants' statements. (Because the notes are general and do not include reference to any specific individuals, it is likely that they did not observe any death rituals during their short stay.)

Subsequent events reveal the significance of the skull. If it was the skull of an adult, it was taken by the dead's sister's son; if the skull of a child, it was taken by the mother's brother. He made holes in the jaw bones and upper jaw and fastened the two together and applied the first coat of paint. At this point the skull was elaborately decorated with modeled clay, paint, hair, and shell rings. The mourners themselves might decorate the skull, and if this happened no payments were involved. If, however, a man had rings to invest and wanted to get food in return, or if he was just ambitious to initiate exchange transactions, he would take the skull and decorate it himself and then return it to the family. They were then obliged to give him a feast of cooked food. Later, they had to give him a large feast in repayment for the rings that decorated the skull. When this prestation was ready, they removed the rings and buried the skull. Until this feast, they were obligated to care for the skull and guard it from harm. Widows often carried the skulls of their dead husbands around with them, and even when they were remarried (sometimes to a brother of the former husband), the skull went along. (At this stage a man's ghost sometimes caused anxiety for the new husband because it followed its wife around and could cause potential harm.) The skull was not stored in the rafters of the house but was kept close at hand. (Enemy skulls were often stored overhead in the rafters.)

Anyone could decorate the skull, but if a special relationship called *kamain* was in the process of being made (see chapter 4) and the child of one of the two *kamain* died, the other was obligated to be the decorator. This service was reciprocated at the next death in the decorator's line. Feasts were held as well.

In the final feast, before the removal of the rings and burial of the skull, the dead person's sister's children had a special role to play. The skull was put on a chair or stool, and food and betel were set out before it. The sister's children, particularly her sons, ate the food and chewed the betel. There was then a ceremony in which the sister's sons escorted the ghost out of the village and turned the ladder of the house in so that the ghost would never return. It was sometimes several years before this final feast was made and the ghost banished forever.

If a death occurred but the body was not recovered (if, for example, a person had been killed by enemies), a pot was filled with water, cordyline leaves, and totemic leaves, and these were boiled. Then the pot was placed on the ground amid ashes and left overnight. In the morning the dead person's footprints were visible in the ashes because the ghost had come to bathe in the water. It was believed that the ghost went back and forth between its home and wherever its skull was.

Drowning, frequently a cause of death especially among children, caused special problems. The body polluted the river water, and women then had to carry water from sources more distant than the convenient river. Mead included a specific case of the drowning of a child in which the general taboo lasted for three months, while close kin of the dead child observed the taboo even longer. Close relatives released the other villagers from the taboo by presenting rings, but to whom the rings were given in general is not clear. In this specific case rings and a cup of water were given to Alemi, the *luluai*, but whether this action reflected his political importance or a particular kin relation is not clear. Mead did note that when a relative of Alemi's drowned soon after, he presented rings to the man who had originally given him rings in order to release the second taboo.

Finding the bodies was also problematic. In at least one case, in which a man was in the water for four days before passersby smelled him, the body was buried immediately on discovery because of the stench, and ceremonial actions were abandoned. (Surely it was easier to ignore the burial rituals for an unimportant person such as a woman or child or ineffectual man; perhaps their ghosts were feared less as well. Mead's presentation of burial in *Sex and Temperament*, noted earlier, suggests that almost any excuse to abandon mourning rituals could be cited.) The downriver peoples sometimes found the body and decorated the skull with the expectation that return feasts would be elaborate, an action that did not please the Mundugumor.

Once permanently released and sent from the village, ghosts lived on their own kin's territory in the bush with their associated bush and water spirits, and they assisted these entities in their activities. Unlike bush and water spirits, however, the ghosts of dead people were not capable of transforming themselves into material representations such as pigs or cassowaries. The attitude toward these ghosts was one not of fear but of mild respect. There was a taboo on calling the name of a ghost while in the bush, and violation of this rule caused poor hunting or fishing.

Ghosts were invoked if their living descendants cursed in their names. If a woman went fishing on her husband's territory without asking her husband's sister to accompany her, the latter might curse the woman in the name of these patrilineal ghosts. A father cursed his children if they abandoned him, although Mead noted that no one remembered anyone doing so. Ghosts could be invoked by other than their patrilineal descendants too, for they "listened to the talk" of their mother's brother, father's sister, and sister's children as well.

In 1981 informants told me that funeral customs continued substantially as they always had. No one mentioned the old custom of allowing the body to decompose in the house, and I did not think to ask whether they remembered it. Nowadays, bodies are buried in a local cemetery. What does continue, they asserted, were the signs of mourning such as not shaving or not cutting the hair and the exchanging and feasting among the deceased's kin. Skulls are not decorated and are not kept separately but are buried with the rest of the body.

SORCERY

If one defines sorcery as the conscious carrying out of actions that will invoke elements of the supernatural to hurt others, then the means people used to induce a spirit to cause harm, such as hanging up the spears, were a kind of sorcery, and in her notes Mead refers to these activities as such. But the Mundugumor had at their disposal other techniques for causing illness and death that also fall under the general rubric of sorcery. In most cases they did not perform the actions themselves but hired people from other villages. Most sorcery involved operations on the victim's "dirt" (food, partially smoked tobacco, feces, woven armbands, clothing, or semen). Only occasionally could a sorcerer operate without dirt. They attributed to sorcery almost all deaths except those of the very elderly or those caused by obvious accidents and possibly those in warfare, including the malevolent actions of the spirits described earlier.

Fortune's notes reveal that river villages did perform sorcery on members of other river villages, but there are only a few clear cases of a sorcerer harming someone from his or her own village.[4] Fortune suggests a simple reason for this: in order for the sorcery to be effective and for the sorcerer to remain safe, the activities had to remain secret. Keeping such a secret within a community would have been an exceptionally difficult thing to do, and word could easily have leaked to the intended victim or her or his relatives. If someone did try to perform sorcery on a member of the local group, only two or three people could know about it.

At least three main methods were used (besides the spirit types described earlier), each loosely associated with a geographical or cultural group. There was a belief that bush peoples (on both sides of the river) performed one kind of sorcery, downriver peoples a second kind, and upriver ones yet a third. Which direction a person took the dirt he or she wanted acted upon seemed to depend on language: there tended to be more sorcery transactions with the Dowaning and Andafugan because their shared language facilitated the transactions. Mead also noted that people who could speak "Ramu languages" tended to hire sorcerers from there. Although the ability to speak the language may have determined to which place a person went to hire a sorcerer, familiarity with the language likely reflected close ties of some sort with individuals in another location, and these close ties, rather than linguistic fluency, likely led one to hire the sorcerer.

The limited evidence available indicates that when the Mundugumor themselves performed sorcery, they used the method of the bush peoples. The sorcerer dug up a wild taro root, put dirt in it, buried it, and built a large fire of hardwood over it. When the victim's death was desired, people gathered and pretended to be relatives, weeping in mourning. Then the dirt was placed in the open with tongs and cut into pieces. A person who was the victim of this kind of sorcery (and perhaps other kinds as well) would feel feverish, and relatives poured water over the victim to cool the skin.

The Mundugumor believed that a different method was used by the peoples in villages downriver from them, one that involved the use of water. The sorcerer took the victim's dirt and fastened it to a piece of wild sugar cane before throwing both into the water, or the sorcerer cut off the head of a crocodile and put the dirt in its mouth, sewed the mouth shut with flying fox bone, wrapped it in coconut fronds, and threw it away in the water. The victim would then drown, be eaten by a crocodile, or be lost in the bush.

The third method, used by their upriver neighbors, did not require the use of dirt because a sorcerer here had special abilities. The sorcerer scraped some mildew off a particular tree with his arrows and then spent the afternoon and evening in his sleeping basket. His spirit, however, left the basket and encountered his intended victim. The sorcerer's spirit cut open the unfortunate person, took out his or her heart, and then sewed him or her back up again. When the victim returned to the village, he or she died. The Mundugumor claimed that villages upriver from Bun practiced this form of sorcery. (People in Bun in 1973 also claimed this to be true. In fact, most deaths in Bun were then still attributed to this form of sorcery.) Upriver villagers claimed that they could not be harmed by this technique if others practiced it.[5] One of Mead's informants also said that he had heard of a cure for this sorcery that involved eating a "special mash made with a young girl's footprint and sago."

In 1932 Mead recorded from Omblean information about another kind of sorcery, but where it was believed to have been practiced is unclear. The sorcerer took the dirt, put it in food, and gave it to a snake to eat. The victim was then unable to talk, his or her mouth was full of spittle, and she or he died. Omblean knew of victims from both Biwat and Branda. Mead also made one short note on "crocodile magic," which seems to have been practiced by the river Mundugumor. The sorcerer constructed a model crocodile,[6] then put food in its mouth and a potion in its eyes, and talked to it. Then the model would tell other, real crocodiles to go eat the victim. Mead thought that this technique might have been imported from Anduar. Finally, there is one brief reference to sorcery in "frog form," in which the hands and legs of the victim swell, but no other information is available.

There were many cases of sorcery or suspected sorcery, and a few examples can provide ample illustration of its basic nature. In one case Mbunda, a Kinakatem man, had heard that his trade friend's eight-year-old daughter in Andafugan had drowned and had been found hidden under a ladder in a *baret*. He journeyed there only to discover that the rumor was untrue but that his trade friend was very ill. He lit a cigar and as he puffed the smoke his friend fainted, proof that the dirt involved in the sorcery was a piece of tobacco. (Note that what causes the sick person to faint is one way of discerning the specific kind of dirt involved in a sorcery incident.) He returned to Kinakatem after having arranged to meet a delegation of men from Andafugan the next day in Dowaning. They were going to give rings to those whom they suspected of sorcery (the reasons for their suspicion of this particular place are not given). When they arrived, the people of Dowaning refused to accept the rings. Their refusal signified that they were either not guilty or not willing to reverse the actions of the sorcery and ensure the victim's recovery.

A second case involved the death of a Kinakatem child. The child's father suspected and accused a man in the village, and the accused temporarily fled to another village. However, later a prominent man from another place reported that yet a third village had done the dirty work after having been feasted by some members of his own village. They had given a feast and said, "'Drown a child of Mundugumor,'" and shortly afterwards the child died. No action was taken, but those close to the parents of the dead child refused to go near either place and even refused to eat a pig that one man had received from there.

One case from Fortune's notes illustrates not only the process of sorcery but also the enmity between a husband and wife and the rivalry between Alemi and Mongova. These two influential men were brothers-in-law, having exchanged sisters. Ndavukuwei was Mongova's wife but Alemi's sister. She fed Mongova a piece of smoked pork and saved a small piece of it for Alemi so that he could have sorcery performed with it. Alemi gave it to Kwenandi, a distant relative of Mongova, for forwarding on to sorcerers in Dowaning, but because Kwenandi did not know who the intended victim was, he held on to it for awhile. He tried to discover who was in danger because he did not want a friend or relative to be the victim. Mead says that he tried "the omens" and "sure enough, the simbax bird flew in front of his face close to his eyes" so that he knew a relative was threatened. He performed further (unspecified) divination techniques and discovered that it was Mongova who was in danger. Kwenandi returned the piece of dirt to Mongova rather than Alemi and told him that one of his wives was responsible but would not reveal which wife. Mongova reputedly removed all of his wives from their houses and made them stay on the ground with no food, only water, for five days. During this time he repeatedly beat them as well, trying to discover the identity of the betraying wife. Every day they went to Kwenandi to beg him to reveal her name, but he refused. Mongova forced his wives to offer Kwenandi their own shell rings in order to get the name, but Kwenandi refused the rings as well. On the fifth day Kwenandi felt sorry for the women who were being starved and beaten and finally revealed to Mongova that it was Ndavukuwei who took his dirt. She fled to the protection of her brother, Alemi, until after colonial pacification, when she returned to her husband Mongova.[7]

A complex case followed the death of a man named Kombevom. Mongova accused a woman named Yopou of sending Kombevom's dirt to sorcerers, and the resulting conflicts were prolonged. Eventually it was recognized by most that Yopou had been innocent of the charge, and Kombevom's relatives sought the truth about his death. Fortune detailed a means by which one could discern the guilty party in this case. Kombevom's brother Minduli put the victim's finger in a hollow oil palm plank and as the finger rotted, the guilty person sickened. People apparently knew that Minduli suspected Mongova, the original accuser of Yopou. After Minduli placed Kombevom's finger in the plank, Mongova's brother-in-law

Yaunga became sick, and when Minduli cut the oil palm containing the finger, Yaunga died, proof that he had been the guilty party. People assumed that since Yaunga was not in good health before this affair and could barely get about on his own Mongova himself had personally carried the dirt to the sorcerers; he accused Yopou of the act to deflect suspicion from himself and to get revenge on her for her refusal to send him a daughter to marry.

The identity of a sorcerer could be discovered in other ways. If a person was unconscious, it was a sign that his or her spirit was wandering around, a cause for great fear. Someone close to the victim— a wife or household head, for example—called out to the wandering spirit a series of questions answered by a set code of whistles. The spirit thus revealed the community in which the dirt was being burned. A dreamer-diviner could discern who was causing the harm, but if that person was kin, the dreamer might not reveal the identity for a year or more, when the anger had faded, in order to protect the relative. In the case of Kombevom's death Minduli tried an alternate means of discovery before Yaunga died. He took shell rings around to other villages in an attempt to solicit or perhaps purchase information. The people of Akuran and Biwat both protested ignorance and innocence and were believed because Kombevom had brothers in both places (the assumption here was that the secret could not have been kept from his brothers and that they would have revealed the truth). Dowaning's denial of guilt was also believed because Yopou's children lived there, and they would have been eager to reveal any information that absolved their mother. Other communities escorted the investigating party through their bush, thereby demonstrating that there were no places where personal leavings could have been burned recently. Only the village of Branda refused; because of this and their attempts to blame almost any other village, it was decided that they were really the guilty ones.

One case recorded by Fortune indicates that a means existed by which a person could prove his or her innocence of the charge of sorcery, but the note is only suggestive. Mashamba accused Kombokata of sorcery in the deaths of two men, and they fought. Kombokata ate the bone scrapings of both of the victims and said, "'You see perspiration come out on me?'" It seems plausible to suppose that a lack of perspiration indicated a lack of guilt in the sorcery deaths of those to whom the bones belonged.

Who were the likely victims of sorcery? Neither Mead nor Fortune is explicit on this point, but clearly anyone who caused another to be angry or jealous could be a victim. Boys and young men were cautioned not to play around with others' wives because such actions could lead to the husbands' anger and revenge via sorcery. Political rivals, anyone with a grudge, or wives who wanted to be rid of their husbands could hire a sorcerer. And these were the people who were likely to be accused of sorcery—those with grudges, recalcitrant and malcontent wives. Or, as when Mongova accused the innocent Yopou, the accusation could be directed at someone a person wanted to be rid of or get revenge on.

If the sorcerer was identified before the victim's death, it was possible to get the malevolent action reversed and save the victim's life. An initial payment was sent to the sorcerer or his community; the sorcerer might then throw the dirt away in water, thus restoring health to the victim. When the ill person recovered, a final payment was made to those responsible. Of course, frequently the sorcerer was stubborn and would not revoke the action.

The task of identifying the purveyor of dirt, the originator of the malevolence, became one of discovering the road to revenge after the victim's death. The identification of the guilty party was not random, as Fortune argues in one of his notes:

The suspected seller of dirt was always chosen from a group [which was] very inferior in strength—hence the seller of dirt was ostensibly "given up" by his or her group, who always said at the time that it was a horrid "crime" and the "criminal ought to be killed." Hence there is also a saying that a person killed in a feud over women or other property must be revenged, whereas a person killed as a seller of dirt must not be revenged. He or she has killed and therefore deserves killing and when killed all is "square." In practice, however, the saying by the suspect's own group that the suspect deserves killing and may be taken without resistance is a "saving of face" merely by a group surprised by a vastly superior fighting force and looking to their own skins. In practice, moreover, the group of the killed suspect subscribes to the idea that a seller of "dirt" was [not] to be revenged, but they do not believe that the suspect who was killed was guilty—that is, they do not take the killing party's word for it and accordingly they look for a chance for revenge later.

For river villagers personal leavings were not always a necessary intermediary in causing harm to others. Three men knew of a spell that was put on trees and creepers, and any person who came into contact with these would go blind. Another man had a spell to cause dysentery. There was also a method for taking revenge on a woman who spurned a man's advances; if he was angry, he would utter a spell and spit into the fire used to heat the dye for her grass skirts and thereby ruin the dye. The inhabitants of one hamlet also owned an interesting ceremonial object of some sort named Kukaleame (Mead called it a fetish but gave no further information about its nature). They dressed this object in a new grass skirt and tied bands around its belly and waist, and then its spirit roamed around and breathed into people's mouths. This caused an epidemic of colds and respiratory diseases. The house it was in collapsed, and it was never recovered, despite ardent searching.

Although contemporary residents of Kinakatem have converted to Catholicism, many believe that sorcery did kill and still can kill. Some deaths by sorcery were identified to me, and the kind of sorcery in which the practitioner leaves the body and murders by stealthy actions (such as theft of the heart) is still attributed to the people upriver.

MAGIC, RITUAL, AND BELIEF

The Mundugumor also had ways to ensure good fortune. Although it is unlikely that Mead and Fortune recorded more than a fraction of these activities and beliefs, the variety of their data on spells, charms, taboos, magic, and rituals clearly indicate that the Mundugumor had a rich ceremonial life. Some of these practices, such as those associated with spirits, have already been described, and because of the relatively large amount of data available on initiation rites, these are presented subsequently in a separate section. Here I present material on a variety of topics, all of which have to do with ensuring one's own good fortune by supernatural means.[8] Neither Mead nor Fortune provided any framework in which to understand these relatively miscellaneous pieces of information; most were recorded as separate notes and not related to one another.

Subsistence

Hunting charms and spells were often purchased with rings from groups upriver; because parents usually failed to see that their children kept the taboos necessary for inheriting them, they were continually being repurchased. (Mead seemed to believe that this failure demonstrated a lack of concern on the part of parents for their children.) Pig-killing charms were bought from the Sipisipi and other groups near the mountains. One man would organize an expedition and go in the company of several others. He became the sole owner of the charm, but the others helped him learn and remember it. Later, he distributed to them parts of pigs killed with the charm. The owner of the charm could not eat any pig he killed using it; in fact, men could never eat their own kills, or they would never kill again. Households kept two pots for cooking—one for meat provided by the household head, which he could not eat and the other for meat given to them by others, which he could eat. Also, a hunter was not supposed to eat a pig killed with a charm he possessed, whether he or someone else killed the pig. The skulls of all wild pigs hunted with or without magic had to be kept, for if they were discarded and covered with dirt, the hunter would not be able to kill more pigs.

Fortune recorded several bits of magic that enhanced hunting success. One spell was received by a man from two female spirits while he was asleep; they put ginger in his hand, and he awoke with leaves in his hand, now in possession of a charm for finding casso- wary eggs. Another spell affected a particular kind of bird. The hunter called upon the river mist to cover over the bird's eyes so that it could be shot easily. A man chewed and spat ginger with another spell to make a trap for catching pigeons. Hunting fortune could also be effected through the medium of one's hunting dog. The hunter cooked grubs, put ginger inside them, and then placed the grubs inside a shell. He recited a spell and spat on his chest and armpits; then he said the spell again and spat on his hunting dog on the chest, under the front legs, and on the feet. He recited the spell again and then spat on the grubs before feeding them to his dog. The dog was not allowed to eat anything else the entire day. This magical act was performed in the afternoon, and the hunter could not go out the next day (or he or his dog would be killed by a wild pig), but he would kill a pig on the following day. The special form of ginger planted for this purpose came from the mountains and was supposed to work best with large pigs with tusks.

According to Fortune, one man had magic for shooting pigs from a platform by the light of the moon. Informants said that this magic came from the upriver village of Bun.[9] The man who first used it, however, said that it did not work, and the pigs ran away. If the hunter met someone as he was going off to wait on the platform, that person was required to give him some betel nuts and say, "'You go first, I'll come later.'" (Thus the hunter would arrive before the pig.) The nonhunter would wait quietly for awhile and then return home. (Hunters were apparently not supposed to encounter others on the path; if they did, sometimes they hid.)

If a hunter did everything properly and waited but no pig ap- peared, it was an omen that, according to Fortune's notes, a ghost was about in the forest and someone was going to die or had died. When someone died, no hunters from the village of the deceased were successful (although other people from other villages could be). When a man planned to hunt pig, he was not supposed to cop- ulate with his wife. If he was hunting pigeons or searching for cassowary eggs, however, no sex taboo applied. Also, some food taboos were associated with hunting.

Mead noted that charms for dogs used in cassowary hunting were also acquired with rings from upriver groups, but some charmed plants for cassowary egg hunting were obtained from the Grass Country. Spells with special herbs were used in hunting cuscus, and a charm as well as special plants were used to catch bandicoots. Not all men possessed hunting charms, and some of those who did discovered that they did not work. Magic was also used to enhance fishing. One charm involved the male owner of the spell spitting over bodies of water before women fished, and the other involved spitting on the barricades made to trap fish in *barets*.[10]

If these spells required the use of a special or magical plant, the plant was grown as inconspicuously as possible. If someone noticed it and asked about its use, the owner lied about its purpose, not wanting to share with others the knowledge of the spell or access to special magical plants.

Long yam gardens were a focus for ritual concern, but neither Mead nor Fortune acquired much data on the special ritual requirements for growing and caring for them. I base my assertion of their importance on the significance they had in Bun and the importance they had according to informants in 1981. People told me that a man should not have sexual intercourse and then go to a long yam garden to work, nor could he go (even in 1981) if his wife was menstruating. Informants were not certain that these taboos were consistently followed, but they did maintain that they *should* be. These concerns are not exclusively associated with ideas of sexual pollution; for example, a man could not wash with soap and go to the long yam garden because the long yams dislike the smell of the soap, as they dislike the smell associated with sex. According to informants in 1981, birds and bandicoots also were sensitive to smells, and a man had to be careful about sex and soap when hunting them as well.

Only one man in Kinakatem—Alemi—knew yam magic (as did only one old man in Akuran), and therefore he performed it for everyone. He could not eat any of the yams he had charmed (or he would die), and he was required to purchase yams from distant places. No one in Biwat or Branda knew this magic; they merely planted their yams with ritual ginger and then put rings on a plate with herbs and water and scattered the water over the yams, saying, "'By and by you will drink this water and your bad qualities will vanish.'" Alemi was also capable of discerning the cause of a poor yam crop. He stood at the edge of the garden and "saw" the cause— the ghost of a menstruating woman or perhaps a water or bush spirit. Various methods were used to cure an ailing yam garden.

Material Manufacture

Some minor observances were associated with house building. Builders always left a house with a small section of roof unthatched until it was almost completely finished because the Mundugumor believed that a fully thatched house might run away. On the day that the house was totally finished it was tied down with rattan and left unoccupied for one night. Three feasts were associated with house building: one for bringing in and setting the posts into the ground, one for erecting the ridge pole and the side poles, and one for placing the thatch. Finally, when the new hearth was constructed and the first fire made within it, a bunch of grass with yellow flowers was held in the smoke, and then the smoke was wafted upwards with it. The grass was then placed in the rafters and never removed, thus ensuring that smoke from the fireplace would always rise upward and out of the house.

A ceremony was held for the launching of a war canoe. (The context in which such a canoe was used, however, is not clearly specified, nor does either ethnographer address the problem of a recently watered people having war canoes.) The canoe was painted; a special "super-prow" was constructed with a palm frame and painted palm spathe and decorated. This elaborate prow was removable and kept after the ceremony to be used in other launches and possibly other ceremonies. The ceremony itself was performed by a mother's brother and sister's son who, according to Mead, stood in no special relationship to the canoe owner; furthermore, they were not paid for this service.[11] The elder relative scraped some bone dust from one of his dead brothers into the husk of a dried coconut and then hung the coconut from a palm over the river. He instructed his brother's spirit to dodge the arrows that the younger relative would shoot. The group that actually performs the ceremony is divided into two parts: those who paddle the canoe (the sister's sons) and shoot at the over-hanging coconut with arrows, and those on shore (the mother's brothers) who are armed with mash made from coconuts and ba-nanas, which they hurl at those in the canoe and "call out to the Crocodile Mother."[12] The party in the canoe tries to shoot an arrow into the coconut over the river, a ritual called "trying the canoe."

The manufacture of a slitgong was circumscribed with ritual and taboo. An offering was made to the spirit that inhabited the bush from which the log was taken. The man who began the manufacture could not drink water or green coconut milk, eat big fish, or have sexual intercourse until the tongue of the slitgong was carved out. While this initial carving was being done in the bush, women and children were allowed to go near the work, but a pregnant women or a man whose wife was pregnant was not permitted because if she or he stepped on the shavings of the slitgong the instrument would be "no good." After a small feast given by the owner, men pulled the partially completed slitgong into the village or hamlet, where it now had to be hidden by a fence from the sight of women and children. In the final stages men seared the inside with special torches. Cane stalks were used to test the sound, and if the test was successful, pieces of this cane were thrown outside the village in every direction so that the sound too would travel far and wide.

Pregnancy, Birth, and Childhood

A variety of beliefs and ritual activities surrounded conception, ges-tation, birth, and childhood. The Mundugumor believed that con-ception was caused by frequent, multiple acts of intercourse. If a couple had sexual intercourse frequently—two or three times every day—the woman became pregnant quickly, in about two months. If they copulated less frequently, it would take longer. If a woman became pregnant when she and her husband had not been having sexual intercourse frequently, then her husband knew that someone else had been copulating with her and would be angry with her and try to kill the child when it was born.

Pregnancy was recognized by changes in the woman's breasts and demeanor: she was lazy and tended to sleep late when pregnant. Once pregnancy was recognized, further sexual intercourse was forbidden, or twins might result. If a woman seemed to be pregnant for a long time and her belly came down over her thighs, people predicted twins. Disapproval of violation of the intercourse taboo was strong, and women who had twins were likened to pigs. (Although anomalies, twins were not necessarily killed; see chapter 4.)

The child was formed by blood collecting in the woman's stomach. Copulation served to stimulate the skin so that the blood would collect; semen was the irritant or stimulant, but it did not unite with the blood to form the child. The chest formed first, the arms and legs then extended out simultaneously, and the head came last. No one was certain when the soul came into being. Children were sometimes named before they were born, thus making it impossible to match names appropriate for one sex with children of that sex. If a man was very young when his wife conceived, people believed that he would be worn out by the frequent copulation and grow thin and pale. It was also believed that if a fetus was quiet and the parents thin and unhappy, the child would be a boy, but if the fetus was active and the parents plump and healthy, it would be a girl.

In addition to the taboo on sexual intercourse during pregnancy, the parents were subject to other restrictions. The prospective mother could not eat cuscus because it hid well and thus the child would not emerge quickly. Nor could she eat cassowary, because one might then step on the child, or pig and bandicoot, because they too could kill the child, or large fish, because they would make the child sickly and its skin pale. The father could not fasten anything with rattan; he could not plant house posts or any kind of stake. All the father's restrictions served to facilitate a quick and easy delivery; if he failed to observe them, the child would stick tightly in the womb.

When the time for delivery arrived, a portion inside the house was sectioned off with mats. The husband was not allowed to be present, nor could he work, walk around, or use an axe or knife for fear that such activities would kill the child. Women who had not themselves borne children also were not present because if they witnessed childbirth they would become afraid of bearing children themselves. The woman was cared for by the newborn's father's sister—that is, her husband's sister.

At birth other women handled the child; the mother need not. Both head and foot presentations were recognized. Stillbirths were the result of breaking the pregnancy taboos, and a woman's death in childbirth was caused by her intercourse with a spirit disguised as her husband. A child born with the cord around its neck was destined to be bad-tempered, a craftsman and artist if a boy and good at netting and plaiting if a girl. Children born with their hands free and no cord wrapped around them were destined to be gay, friendly, good-natured, and inept at making anything. The cord and afterbirth were wrapped in palm bark and discarded. People remembered the circumstances of birth and expected these talents to develop.

The day after the birth, the husband went to the forest, cut rattan, and pretended to pull it down from a tree. Then he got a vine and brought it home. The mother took this vine, put it on the newborn's back, broke it into pieces, and hung it in the rafters. When the wind blew, it rustled and made the child sleep.

More taboos were in effect after the birth of the child. Both mother and father were forbidden to eat fish, pig, cuscus, sago grubs, and coconuts. If one of the parents ate part of a pig, the next day the devil or spirit of the pig would return to murder the child. When the child's skin turned dark, all these taboos except on fish and pig ended. Fish and pigs were forbidden until the child was strong, and these two restrictions had to be lifted in a special way. A special charm had to be said over fish freshly caught by the father; only four men in Kinakatem knew this charm, and one of them had taught it to his wife. Then and only then were the taboos ended. A man who was a slitgong maker had to observe all these taboos even longer, until the child laughed and ate regular food.

There was a postpartum sex taboo, which lasted about five or six months. A couple could then have sexual intercourse but only infrequently so as not to cause pregnancy immediately. If a woman became pregnant again too soon, the living child would suffer from the ensuing bad milk. Its back and bones would become weak, and it would defecate the bad milk instead of retaining it.

The father's sister of the newborn played a significant role in the birth process and was repaid with a feast (see chapter 4). These women were usually not actual fathers' sisters but classificatory ones. The father was in charge of this feast "to wash the hands of the father's sister" and told her that "'if you had not been here, the child would have died.'" The feast consisted of pork and other food and was reciprocated with shell rings. These sisters of the new father not only cared for the new baby and mother but also cooked. The mother remained inside for only three or four days but did not resume cooking for her husband until she felt fully well and strong.

The father's sister had another significant role in relation to a new child. Certain foods including the child's totemic emblems were taboo to a child, and she was the one who first gave these foods ritually to the child by passing them under her armpit. If the children were very young, the taboo was lifted by merely touching the food to their lips, but if they were old enough, they ate what was given. If a man was lazy, he would have his real sister perform these actions and, thus, owe little in return. However, others made them important feasting occasions. A man presented a distant sister with a very large quantity of meat, including pig, cuscus, and sago grubs, for which she returned rings.

An additional exchange took place on the birth of a first child.

The wife's family provided pots, carvings, and net bags while the husband's family presented a feast in return.

First-achievement offerings were given when a child performed particular subsistence activities for the first time. A girl gave to her father's sister her first fish and the first batch of sago she processed, and the father's sister reciprocated with a small feast. A boy gave to his mother's brother the first pig, cassowary, and marsupials he killed. Parents were strictly forbidden to eat this meat. The kill was usually given to a classificatory mother's brother because a mother's real brother was felt to be "too much in the family." One assumes that the same is true for father's sister.

Mead perhaps had been impressed with the Iatmul ceremony of *naven*, or at least Bateson's description of it (see Bateson 1936), and in 1938, when she was in Tambunam and her informants, Omblean and Afima, visited her, she asked Omblean if the Mundugumor had such a custom in which parents' siblings celebrate the achievements of siblings' children.[13] Omblean replied that if he did something significant such as killing an enemy, his father's sister might "do something." Or if he killed a pig, she might celebrate. He said that it was not a major event; she did not really construct an elaborate ritual affair around it but just asked that her good brother's son be brought to her, then danced and held him tightly, and told him how good he was, what an effective warrior or hunter he was.

The offerings of first achievement to the mother's brother developed into an important reciprocal relationship between mother's brother and sister's son, which was more elaborate than between father's sister and brother's daughter (see chapter 4). Men and boys presented pigs to their mother's brothers even after their first kills, and these were reciprocated with what Mead called crocodile-yam feasts. A man built a model crocodile frame, filled it with yams, and gave it to his sister's son. A large triangular palm spathe painting, which resembled Sepik spirit house facades (see Mead 1934:236 and 1970: plate 3 for photographs) was made to adorn the yam gift. Some of these exchanges were relatively small and simple affairs and involved perhaps only one pig, but others became large and elaborate. In one case whole villages were active in helping the principals exchange; the people of Akuran had sent seven pigs to Branda and were waiting for the return feast. It is likely that ambitious men used the occasion for display and exchange transactions while the unambitious were content with modest affairs.

The ear-piercing ceremony was also accompanied by feasting. Here the father's sister played a central role, especially for young girls. The feast was not necessarily a large one—one pig sufficed for several children whose ears were pierced at the same time (and often only one child's ears were done). Fathers usually performed the actual piercing, especially if they were to make a ceremonial occasion of the event. Mead's notes also include a reference to nose piercing, but no details—other than the fact that a feast was given that included father's sister—are given. That ear piercing was not a central focus of ritual concern and that, indeed, it was not always even a ceremonial event is evident in a text recorded from Afima in Tambunam in 1938, in which he describes the piercing of his own ears. There was, for him, no ritual occasion—he just wanted to do it. One of his father's wives simply used a flying fox bone to do the piercing; no pigs were killed, no ceremonies held.

The ritual reciprocities between mother's brother and sister's son and between father's sister and brother's daughter were important elements in intergenerational exchange, but this system is best examined after marriage rules have been discussed. Thus, further elaboration on these ritual reciprocities is postponed until chapter 4.

Totemism

The intricacies of Mundugumor totemism are never clear in the notes. We do know that an association between particular species and social groups[14] was recognized. Each group had a totemic animal and a totemic plant. There were eight such groups, and more totems were being imported through intermarriage with people who recognized others; for example, one man obtained through his wife from Dowaning *vanma* (sun). Three of the eight animal totems were pigs; five were some kind of bird.

The particular totemic plant associated with a group was taboo to its members for firewood and house building (a violation caused skin disease), but most people did not strictly observe the taboo. Three of the bird totems were theoretically taboo for life, and members of the associated groups were never allowed to eat them. The other taboos were all lifted for a child when his or her father's sister presented it with the taboo-releasing feast.

Each animal and plant could be symbolized by a unique set of strokes on the slitgong. If someone wished to summon a person who had gone to the bush, he or she would beat the signal for the person's father's and mother's totemic groups. If ambiguity remained, other calls, such as his or her spouse's totem, were added to specify which individual was intended.

Leaves from a person's totemic plant were worn if he or she was angry or wished to elicit sympathy from others. Totemic leaves were made into *tangets*, which were used in dispute settlement as well as in death ceremonies. These totemic associations played a part in the construction of personal identity, but we do not have enough data to specify further just how totemic association and identity were intertwined.

Dreaming and Divining

A few comments remain to be added on dreaming and divining. It has already been noted that one could discern the cause of an illness, discover the identity of a sorcerer, or be warned of impending sorcery in a dream, that some people had the ability to see the cause of a poor yam garden, and that souls could be recaptured in dreams. But dreams could also foretell the future. If someone dreamed of a future spirit attack, precautions could prevent it. If a man had gone pig hunting with a sago lure and his wife dreamed that she saw someone—especially one of his ancestors—give him betel, then she knew he would kill a pig. Similarly, if a man dreamed of being given betel, he considered it a good omen for his next hunt. A dream of a flood meant that the river would rise; of a corpse, that someone would die; of a birth, that a wife was pregnant or someone would soon give birth; of a house on fire, that there would be a fire. A dream of police fighting with everyone meant that white people would come. But some dreams were not as straightforward as these. If a man dreamed of killing a pig or cuscus, it meant that his hunt would *not* be successful. A form of dream divination was associated with giving rings to a spirit; the man would take the branch on which he had hung the rings to bed with him, and presumably these would induce portent-telling dreams. Certain men and women, including both Alemi and Mongova, were known to be particularly adept at dreaming and divining through dreams (these must have been the people Mead referred to as "seers"); others were not.

Miscellaneous Beliefs

Mead and Fortune recorded a few other miscellaneous activities. Several men knew a spell that would quiet a crying child. There was also a kind of love magic. If a man was desirous of an unmarried girl (it is not clear whether this technique worked on married women), he would spit in the water where she fished. Later, she would become lazy and think only of him or of joining him in the bush. Her parents knew that there was trouble if their daughter became lazy and "dreamy" about fishing. It was believed that all but arranged-marriage courtships involved the use of love magic.

Only two additional omens were recorded, and Mead described their use as "slight." If a flying fox flew around a house in the afternoon or if a pigeon cried out during the night, it meant that someone would die.

Various taboos have already been described in the context in which they are relevant. Here it is necessary to mention only two additional ones. First, bird bones or tuber skins could not be thrown on the ground where a pig might eat them. If a domestic pig ate bird bones, it would go wild permanently. Further, women who fed the pigs were not allowed to eat birds. If a domestic pig was to eat tuber skins, it would go immediately to the gardens and break into them to eat the crops. Second, men were afraid to accept food from a menstruating woman. Whether or not this is best described as a taboo is difficult to tell from Mead's note, which I leave for the reader to interpret:

Menstruation is a matter for privacy and hiding. Women will comment to their husbands on girls whose black breasts show that they are menstruating. Men are afraid to receive food from menstruating women, but women only tell their husbands and don't even do that if they think they won't be discovered.

When I was talking about the old days with informants in 1981, another taboo came up: many people said that formerly people had handled the problem of where and how to defecate quite differently than they did today. I had heard similar stories from people in Bun but found it remarkable that neither Mead nor Fortune noticed and indeed that Mead was able to note that attitudes toward excretion were "pretty casual." Comments about these bodily functions, Mead said, were freely made in mixed company. "All men just urinate over the bank into the river. The custom was to defecate on a leaf and throw it away into the river." What informants told me in 1981 was that there had previously been a strong taboo on seeing people of the opposite sex defecate, so strong in fact that special houses *(haus pekpek)* were built, one for men and one for women. Only within these latrines could one defecate; if one was far away, it was all right to dig a hole, but it had to be covered up carefully so that someone of the opposite sex never saw it. My male informants stressed that women were never allowed near their latrines: if a woman was caught, she would summarily be dispatched.[15] A story was told of a man who told a woman about men's defecation; the man was killed, and his head was put through the legs of young boys at initiation. Men remembered names of women who were killed for this infraction. Strange men were dangerous because fecal matter was ideal material for the sorcerer's spell. Men were careful to hide their feces and use the special houses.

In telling this story informants laughed at some of the silliness of it (including the idea that all men had to defecate before going on a raid—they didn't want to have to worry about it later and get shot!), but they also emphasized that there were very serious taboos associated with the house and defecation. What is remarkable is that nowhere in Mead's or Fortune's notes is there mention of this as a recently abandoned custom. They have data on other sensitive issues, but nothing on this. There are, I think, only two possible explanations for this gap. The first is that when Mead and Fortune arrived the topic was still so sensitive that they did not get data on it during the short time they were there. And yet it is difficult to understand, then, how Mead could write that attitudes toward excretion were "pretty casual." If people were still so sensitive and the taboos so strong that they did not want to talk about defecation habits, I doubt that Mead could have so written. I think that the second explanation is the more likely one: that in a sense the story of the *haus pekpek* is really a myth, firmly believed, but a myth nevertheless. As such, it reveals something about the Mundugumor—their values, how they saw the relationship between male and female, how they feared the danger posed by others, perhaps how they saw body boundaries (see Douglas 1966), and certainly their sense of humor.

INITIATION

Despite the short length of fieldwork, the notes contain a wealth of data on initiation rituals. The reason Mead focused so heavily on initiation is impossible to determine, but it may have something to do with what she conceived to be the core elements of culture; initiation was somehow more central, more revealing, more fundamental than some other behaviors. Also, this kind of ritual activity could be viewed almost on demand rather than waiting for an appropriate occasion (unlike, for example, a funeral ritual). And, of course, the fact that this is the form of ritual activity on which Mead and Fortune decided to focus first may be accidental.

Although the Mundugumor had various kinds of initiation rites, all of these shared certain general characteristics. An individual, usually an influential man, sponsored each occasion to allow initiates, especially his sons, to view ritual objects for the first time and to induct them into the cult surrounding the specific object or category of object (details of the ceremony varied according to which ritual object was the focus). The mother's brother played a significant role in all of these. For each initiation a separate ritual house was constructed. Youths and women were not allowed near during construction, and noise-making instruments were forbidden. A propitiary meal was made to an especially powerful spirit and eaten by the sponsor or the spirit's ward. The spirit was asked to ensure that no one be killed or injured by accident during construction. These houses were not permanent structures but temporary places for specific ritual activities that had no use once the initiation was complete. Hunting magic, usually including ginger, was placed in bowls and left when the structure was in use.

Various food taboos were imposed on initiates. Mead insightfully noted that these taboos were significant as "markers" or "punctuation" for the beginning and ending of events or states and that they served to separate "the ceremonially or supernaturally tinged event from everyday secular life. . . ." There are no systematic data concerning which foods were taboo for which initiations. In one note Mead observes that initiates (presumably during their seclusion) could eat no soups, only dry, cooked meat; this pattern is comparable to the special meal of sago pudding that ended the seclusion period as well as the similar restrictions on mourners. Initiates were subject to a variety of food taboos; these were later lifted in special ceremonies.

In content, emphasis, purpose, and organization Mundugumor initiation rituals differed from those in many other parts of Melanesia. First, as noted earlier, there was no permanent men's or spirit house. When an initiation ceremony was held, a special structure was constructed to house the paraphernalia and activities for that one particular occasion. At other times ritual objects were stored in dwellings.

Second, an individual sponsored each initiation separately from others; a social group of some kind, such as a clan or community, never sponsored the ceremony although many people participated in it. Thus, initiations were held at the whim of the more powerful men. If no man wanted to sponsor a ceremony in which initiates viewed, for example, the crocodile flute, then all young boys could grow to adulthood without having seen this ritual object and having been initiated into its mysteries.

Third, there was no single initiatory system or cycle but several apparently unrelated rituals. There seemed to be no unifying cosmology, and initiates were taught little esoterica. Initiation meant undergoing the ritual requirements that allowed one to see special objects, and because there were many of these objects, there were many initiation rituals. Possibly a more coherent ideology or cosmology existed that unified these different rituals into one coherent system, but Mead and Fortune did not record it or learn of its existence in their short field period.

Fourth, Mead asserted that enduring the ritual did not really change a person's status in a major way: the initiate acquired the right only to view particular ritual objects. A person could have gone through two or three initiations and, despite physical and social maturity or even advanced age, be chased away like a child from a fourth if unwilling to endure the hazing and rigors associated with the actual initiation. Mead did not think that acquiring the right to view a sacred object marked a significant change of status. However, in 1981 informants remembered that going through initiation made a boy a man and ready for fighting and warfare. One man likened it to school—one goes in a young boy but comes out a man.

Fifth, and perhaps most striking of all, is the role of women in these rituals. Whereas in most places in Melanesia initiation was

girls included!

for men only, here girls were included and initiated along with the boys. A young woman could join the men and be initiated herself if she was willing to undergo the taboos associated with the rite. Some association was made between scarification and strength in fighting, and because women did not participate in warfare, they were not subject to scarification. Females who chose to see the objects were not subject to any ordeal, but the onus was on them to observe the food taboos. Most girls and young women based their decisions to be or not to be initiated on whether or not they were willing to forego these foods. Often one sister would be initiated and a second refrain so that the latter could eat the foods her sister could not. (There was no observance of the first menstruation; it was a private matter only.)

Finally, there was almost no real secrecy involved in these rituals, and Mead likened them to a pantomime because actors performed as if there were secrets when there were none. Women knew all about the preparations and performances; men knew that the women knew. Mead thought that the pretense of secrecy was a remnant of a previous time when secrets really were kept from women. Symbols from this earlier time were retained, such as smearing a plate with mud and saying that the crocodile had eaten from it when everyone knew very well that it had not. Mead does not attempt to reconcile her notion that what she saw contained remnants of some former "true" initiation with the fact that girls were initiated; that is, she does not consider the possibility that girls were not traditionally initiated but were included only as a consequence of more recent disruptions. In her autobiography (1974:204) she ambiguously remarks that females "had already been admitted to initiation"; did she later think that perhaps women's admission to initiation was a result of colonial disruption? Her observation—and she did at least observe girls undergoing the ritual to release them from food taboos imposed by initiation—may have been of a relatively new behavior. In 1981 no one spontaneously mentioned to me that girls or women were initiated or allowed to see *tambaran* objects in a ritual context,

and when I asked, some informants said that women were completely excluded (others were unsure).[16] The initiation of girls, then,
may have been a historical anomaly observed in 1932.

All these generalizations, of course, must be regarded with a
small degree of skepticism. Mead and Fortune saw only an abbreviated version of one of the initiation ceremonies, and Mead herself
(1963:181–82) believed that initiation rituals had undergone profound changes as a result of the various precolonial shifts in social
organization; she thought that Mundugumor initiations had formerly been more like other Melanesian ones. Furthermore, the ethnographers witnessed an *ashin* (crocodile) initiation performed specifically for them, and most of the data on initiation refer to this
particular performance. Commissioning a ritual to be performed
raises methodological issues, the most obvious of which is the extent
to which a possibly unnatural performance may deviate from what
otherwise might have been done. But it cannot be assumed, either,
that a seemingly artificial performance is necessarily false or wrong;
such an assertion presupposes that there is only one correct way to
perform a ritual. We know, of course, that ritual performances show
a wide range of variation, and perhaps no two are ever exactly alike
anyway. Informants in 1981 assured me that this particular performance was the last initiation ever performed by the people of
Kinakatem.

I divide the remainder of the discussion of initiation into two
broad topics: the *ashin* (crocodile) initiation witnessed by Mead and
Fortune, and other kinds of initiation rituals, including the ceremony for releasing all initiates from the food taboos.

The Ashin, or Crocodile, Initiation

The *ashin* initiation had as its symbolic centerpiece the crocodile.
The flute itself was called *ashin* (which I translate as "crocodile"),
and the initiation involved a large model of this then-common
beast. Neither Mead nor Fortune speculated on just what the croc-

odile's symbolic significance might be, but that it was central is clear throughout their data.

There were three essential items in the crocodile initiation: the flute, water drums, and a large rattan model crocodile. The drums and model were said to be crocodile mothers, and the drum provided the voice for the model; the flute represented the child (always male), but because these elaborate flutes were rarely capable of being played, smaller plain flutes provided the voice for the flute-child. (See also Mead 1934:237–38.) New flutes had to be borne by their mother spirits, and in Mead's description of the ceremony for a new flute and initiation to that flute this birth process pantomime is apparent.

The water drums were not elaborate. They were shaped like the common hourglass drums but lacked a membrane for striking. They were played by a person who held one end and "thumped down on the water," resulting in a "hollow, plumping, zooming" sound, rather like "a monster beating the water with its tail." The drum made another sound as well: the player held on to a piece of rattan attached to the handle of the drum but flung the drum into the water with a splash. Mead likened this sound to a "heavy animal diving."

The model of the crocodile was large enough for initiates to enter, although for the performance witnessed by Mead and Fortune only a smaller model was made (see Mead 1934:243 for a photograph of this model). During construction of a model, two plain flutes were played daily, and food was offered to both the model and the flute before the craftsman ate it. If food was not given to the model, it was believed that the work would not go smoothly, that the craftsman would be clumsy and take a long time. Mead astutely noted in parenthesis that "this is a good personification of the carpenter's attitude if he is not well fed." If the sponsor provided many pigs, then a large model was made, but if there were few pigs, then only a small one (about three feet high) was constructed. Heavy rattan was used to make the main structure of the model and a lighter rattan for tying on the shell made of palm spathe. On the day that the palm spathes were collected, a pig was cooked and a piece given to each worker as he returned to the work house. A bowl of water containing hunting magic was placed in the middle of the room, and each man washed his hands in the bowl on return as well, presumably thus ensuring good hunting. The palm spathes were sewed on the model and painted; eyes were carved on, teeth attached, and decorations added. The model's head had to face the bush, or it was believed that an innocent, uninitiated person might pass by and be seen by it, an act that would cause the person to have serious nightmares and perhaps eventually die.

The model crocodile played a major role in the initiation of the young men. It emerged from the men's work house; if it was large enough, adult men crept along inside it to move it, but if it was smaller they carried it by the outer edges. The model had to be moved backwards, tail first, or it would "eat the whole village." The model frightened the young boys and chased them into the river, where they were scarified (probably by classificatory mothers' brothers) with crocodile teeth. The model was then taken back to the house. Initiates were fed a large meal before they slept. The next morning they were covered with mud and matted hair and carried down to the river to the music of flutes and the sound of water drums. The model appeared again, and young boys were forced to crawl through it on their hands and knees with their real mother's brothers;[17] classificatory mother's brothers remained outside the structure and pushed the initiates through, being sure that the crocodile's teeth cut them. (It is important to note here that real mother's brothers were supportive but that classificatory mothers' brothers were the agents of scarification.) Water drums continued to sound, ostensibly to drown out the cries of the young boys. The initiates passed all the way through the model in this way, until the tail was lifted and they were freed. They lay outside the model in a single row "as if dead." The model returned to the house, making tracks as it went, and the men informed the women that the crocodile had devoured the boys. A large stone was bounced on the floor to simulate the crocodile's vomiting the youths out, and then a large fire was made to revive the returned youth.[18] The boys cried out for their mothers.[19] After the initiation the model was destroyed to prevent the initiates from having nightmares during their adult lives.

The flute was the centerpiece of the *ashin* initiation ritual. Mundugumor ritual flutes were elaborate objects, which, according to Mead (1934:237–38), had been "developed and decorated" to such an extent that they were more like idols than flutes and were virtually unplayable. "The whole surface . . . is encrusted with shells, and in the top is set a small carved figure with an enormous head and diminutive body upon which a great number of valuable shells have been arranged." (See Mead 1934:240 and 1970:plate 8 for photographs of one such flute.)

Ashin flutes were given specific names, but unlike bush spirit images these names did not correspond to any particular spirit. In fact, the notes include almost no references to spiritual or cosmological concerns regarding the flutes. A spirit did inhabit the flute or at least was associated with it, but beyond that few data are available. Crocodile flutes were sometimes used in the process of making a *kamain* (see chapter 4) as well as in this initiation. They also accompanied women at marriage, and sometimes women would attempt to steal an *ashin* flute or another flute when they eloped. Flutes were kept in domestic dwellings, carefully wrapped in mats. Mead wrote (1934:237–38) that the flute was unwrapped and "fed" by initiates.

A special new flute was constructed and given to Mead and Fortune (the construction of a new flute was not, however, necessarily a part of the ritual). Making such an elaborate flute was a complex process. A craftsman, who had to be fed throughout the entire period of manufacture, made the head. A man could make an *ashin* flute and decorate it secretly, but such an action was likened to stealing because the owner had to validate his possession of the flute by feasting the community. More typically a group got together for the final decorating. In the case of the *ashin* flute constructed for Mead and Fortune, Mongova was the sponsor, and he arranged for workers to convene and be fed a pig and other foods. He provided many of the decorations, but other men did so as well without comment or apparent accounting. Food was offered to the carved wooden head, then to the hole in the flute, and then again to the head before workers were allowed to eat. Hunting herbs were hung from the center of the flute, and it was believed that the flute's spirit would assist hunting. Apart from the period when the flute is fed, Mead's description of this decorating procedure is one of merriment and easy joking with others present. There was no solemnity; everyone had fun.

Sacred flutes were frequently broken in anger or because people wanted to use part of their decorations, so spare parts for new flutes were easily available. It may be surprising that such seemingly sacred objects, subject to elaborate ceremonial, could be broken in anger, but Mead noted cases in which these flutes were destroyed in exactly this way. Slitgong drums were also subject to destruction during fits of anger or rage. I think that Mead would argue that material possessions really were not all that important and could always be replaced, and hence a rather casual attitude toward their destruction was not unusual, as it might have been elsewhere. Many of the decorations on the flutes were also used for other purposes; rings were worn on arms or in the nose, women often wore long strings of shells, the woven bands were put on lime spatulas and cowries on lime gourds, and cassowary feathers were used in head-dresses or as fly whisks.

Some leeway was allowed in the adornment of the basic flute, but Mead did not indicate under what circumstances additional decorations would be added or what significance they might have; given the rather casual attitude toward these supposedly sacred objects, people might add whatever they had on hand that they thought would look attractive, things that might have little or no ritual significance.[20]

Following is Mead's description of the actual sequence of events as she observed them in 1932. I reproduce this long text here because it is an excellent description of the atmosphere of the ceremony, its informality and casual character. I have, however, deleted many details as well as the sections that describe the construction of the flute, which was decorated on Monday November 21. On Tuesday the 22d and Wednesday the 23d palm spathes were painted, and Mongova, the ostensible sponsor of the initiation, sought out and acquired two pigs[21] with rings contributed by a variety of people (he had a third pig ready). Work on the model crocodile frame occurred on the 23d and 24th.

Mongova returned with the first pig [on the 24th] and made an offering of food to the crocodile model and went around it with a firebrand (if this were omitted, sickness would result). Offerings to the model were phrased in terms of [not having] sickness or nightmares, and also . . . to make the work of the carpenter go swiftly and well. . . .

On the 25th, they painted the palm spathe on the model, and Mongova returned for the other pig. There was very little commotion or special work. . . .

[On the 26th] a sense of the nearness of the feast begins to be felt. They finished the model except for [decoration]. A water drum . . . which had never been completely carved was brought and laid beside the model— both of these are crocodile mothers. The flute was taken back from our house to the working house. . . . [22] However, when the [youths] went in they were chased away with good humoured roars. . . . While the other preparations were going on, Yeshimba was painting up an old [ritual object]. . . . He was working behind a barrier and a boy from Akuran peeked over to see what he was doing. The next day he had to prepare a meal of the forbidden foods . . . and come and eat half of it after it was offered to [this sacred object]; his mother's brother ate the other half.[23]

When the water drum and flute were assembled, food was offered to each, and to the model a spoonful was offered and then eaten by the offerer. Meanwhile Wheifon and Yeshimba went out and got the trees for the yam hopper. . . . [Alemi's allies from the Grass Country] are here helping him build a house and also a party of Anduar youths arrive prematurely for the dance. In the evening the hopper is moved to Yeshimba's, and dancing by [undecorated] men begins. Grass men and Numba sing an Aitape *singsing* which Mondamvu brought back . . . and [Mondamvu] protests vigorously and rudely, and they all slink away and beat slitgongs in Alemi's half of the village. . . . But it is a rule here that during . . . a *singsing* there must not be the slightest dysphoria; just a hint of disagreement is sufficient to accomplish this result. The Anduar youths erected a pole, piled all their baskets around it and sang in a separate group. Our [Kinakatem] youths and a few girls sang around the yam hopper. Rain came down about eleven o'clock and dispersed them.

Early . . . the 27th, the yam hopper was filled. People unostentatiously produced a dozen or so yams [elsewhere Mead recorded an average of 8 to 10 yams] and they filled up the hopper, end to end, rattan being tied around in bands as the hopper was filled higher and higher. They were piled about with little regard to donors; Mongova was not there to note each contribution, and a general feeling of spontaneous and unconsidering general contribution was in the air. Mondamvu tried out the new water drum and decided it didn't make enough noise. . . . After practicing with this for some time, he declared it poor, and someone was sent to get a better one. . . . In the ceremony both were used. . . . At noon a small house (with a rounded top) about three feet high was built of oil palm leaves right on the brink of the river and sheltered from view by the high bank. (Note that during the informal playing of the water drum, women and children of all ages strolled by and looked over the edge at the performance. From the time the little house was built, however, the players assumed an air of great secrecy and importance.) A piece of strong wild sugar cane was secured in the mud bank back of the little hut . . . and the water drums were concealed in the hut—to fool the women—and fastened by their rattan cords to the cane so that a sudden rising of the river could not carry them away. Up the side of the bank a straight trail was cut, ending in a small V-shaped ditch about a foot over the upper surface. This was to be the track of the crocodile mother, about which there was much mysterious whispering, but everybody strolled by and over it all afternoon. During the afternoon, some more fine touches were put to the crocodile model. . . . A Biwat boy and Yeshimba and some of the girls painted . . . coconuts red and painted patterns on the tips of . . . long yams. . . . The painted coconuts were tied on the outside of the yam hopper (note that I call it a hopper for convenience, but it converged to a point at the top rather than at the bottom). The coconuts had slight designs painted on them too. This was all done very casually. Some many-handed yams . . . were also hung up. A group of women made more . . . streamers. . . .

At sunset came the first real ceremony. The two plain flutes were taken out, and the players went down to the water's edge by the little house and played them. This shows the women that the bones of the child, i.e. the new flute, are getting stronger now. They think it is the new flute playing—crying. The water drums were simultaneously plumped about in the water. Mongova came up solemnly with a plate of sago pudding and pig. The new flute was brought out and stood up at the end of the track. Then

Mongova called "nuff, nuff, nuff," as one would call a pig or fowls to food, and the two drums were dragged up the riverbank, along the made track, by the rattan attachments, and made to pause at the end of the track where the plate of food had been laid down. Some argument as to who could eat the food . . . took place. Spoonfuls [were] offered to each drum and to the mouth and flute hole of the new flute. Then he [the one who ate the food] hurriedly ate the rest while the flutes played, and everybody enjoined him to hurry up and finish. The drums and flute were taken into the work house, the drums being dragged animistically along the ground. The plate was sent down to the water's edge and smeared with mud to show the women where the crocodile had eaten. The small flutes which had played all this time were put away with the new flute. (General impression left by this ceremony was a pantomime which everyone enjoyed and for which the transparent excuse that they were tricking the women gave a dignified raison d'être.)

Dancing began soon after; the Grass men [danced] at Alemi's; the big men of this place danced with spears in front of Wheifon's house . . . and all the youths and girls [danced] around the hopper.[24] The big men danced with spears, in pairs, which changed with position at fixed points in the dance. The girls and women danced around them in a line, with arms entwined. The young boys danced with hourglass drums in a circle around the hopper, the small girls in a circle outside them holding hands (sometimes all with hands on hips). One small girl of seven was set in the line by her father. . . .

The next morning very little was done. People were making . . . streamers, getting out their headdresses, fixing up feathers, etc. (Note a [party] from Mensuat of about fifteen, six of whom were women, arrived the night before. . . . Some of them danced with the big men here. A large party from Dimiri and Yaul also arrived after dusk, danced all around the house and in front of it, and went to sleep in Akuran about nine o'clock. Most of these did not come back again. They danced with spears, shields, tightened bows, etc.)

The morning of Monday the 28th, they fenced in a small rest house overlooking the river in which to put the initiates. The painted yams were stuck in the ground in a circle around the base of the hopper. The flutes played from the work house, and the water drums, which had been taken back to the river quickly early in the morning, were played by the youths. The normal procedure would then have been to dance first and initiate at dusk, but because we wanted to photograph, this order was reversed. Mongova set up a banana tree with a big bunch of bananas just beyond, in the end of the crocodile track, and set up two long yams on either side. (The *ashin* is supposed to attack these when it comes out of the water, and they are later eaten by the new owner of the *ashin* and his household.) A particularly graceful . . . streamer was set in the top of the banana tree. The two plain flute players went down into the water. The flutes started to play and the water drums to sound. People produced baby crocodile heads from all angles and began playfully cutting at each other, feinting, scratching, dashing about, laughing merrily the while. Two dried palm fronds were laid over the crocodile track. Under this the people to be cut were to go. The flute, head and stem separated, was brought down and carried down the bank. Wheifon rushed down under the fronds, being cut as he went. Yeshimba was also down the bank, and the men who carried the flute. There was a cry that there were no youths [to cut], all had run away to the bush, shouts and threats and admonitions. Finally Mondamvu mustered about ten, two of whom . . . had seen the *ashin* and had not yet been cut. He lined them up; they put ornaments and shells in their mouths . . . and shouting, puffing, rushed in a line to go down in the water. There was a wild scramble down the bank with everyone cutting indiscriminately. As no one had paid a pig for their son, there was no special cutting. The *ashin* stem was held between their legs in the water. They then dashed up the bank [see fig. 11], holding the stem and rushed up and down the village with it shouting the new name of the *ashin*. This should have been done the night before when it was carried into the house after the feeding ceremony, but they had not shouted loud enough for all the women to hear. A bowl of food was passed down the bank and returned empty, smeared with mud. Then men rushing up the track cut down the yams and the banana tree, hacked the stalk to bits, and the yams and bananas were brought to us (the new owners); the flute was carried solemnly to us, and the . . . streamer which had been stuck in the banana stalk was fastened above our house ladder. Then the *ashin* was taken away again and taken to a small fenced hut. Here the novices were gathered and betel leaves put in their mouths. Otherwise the taboos did not begin until the morrow. The plain flutes were also taken into the little house and played from there at intervals during the afternoon and night.

(Note, in relation to this part of the ceremony, that the youths are not coerced as long as they are small, but they are believed to become cowards and remain small and womanlike until they dare the initiation. . . . Mandjo [one of Alemi's wives] appeared at the end of the scuffle and pretended to be angry over having the boys cut. A group of women and girls who had seen the *ashin* gathered on the bank at some distance and

Figure 11. Initiation, 1932. Photograph by M. Mead and R. Fortune.

watched the proceedings. But while the show was being organized, they
scurried along the back of the village behind the houses. If older people
were not cut also there would often be no show likely. The cuts are mostly
mere scratches which heal by the next day [another possibility is mentioned later; see also fig. 12]. The whole atmosphere is merry and
scuffling.)

Everyone then retired to decorate themselves, the men in one group and
the women in two. . . . It was notable how few people touched each other;
each man put on his own decorations. Endless numbers of . . . streamers
had been prepared. The women each carried these and had them fastened
about their necks, to their skirts, etc. Everything carried was also decorated with them. The men presented a great variety of costume. . . .
Orendena, a big woman,[25] carried a fish net. They advanced in a great
mass, women first dancing backward waving the . . . streamers, then the
men, led by Yeshimba with spear and shield. Fake attacks between two
parties were staged, and they surged up and down the place, attacks in
which children and women had to scuttle. Drums were played throughout

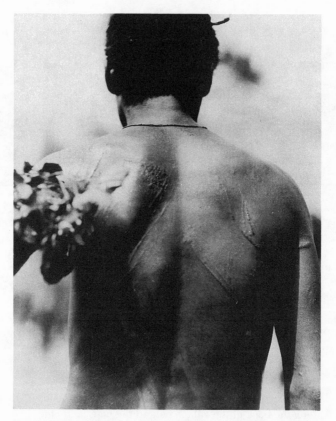

Figure 12. Initiation scars, 1932. Photograph by M. Mead and R. Fortune.

this, the flutes sounded from the fenced house in the intervals when the singing stopped. . . . After about an hour of this, the Grass people arrived, less bravely attired and making principal use of ferns. A part of this crowd surged out to meet them. They then settled down into four big dancing groups, not divided as to age nor strictly according to place. People were fed informally during the night. . . . They danced straight ahead until morning. Only a few strong young women with young children carried them, as the dance is very active for carrying a child. The little children went to sleep on leaves and pieces of oil palm, not in their mothers' arms. The dancing went on without a pause all night, but people from Akuran and some Grass people had melted away by dawn.

At dawn it stopped. Quietly, the yams were taken down from the hopper, and each place was summoned and given some. They went away, each carrying a yam, still merry and amiable. . . . Very few children cried. There was no irritation, no quarrelsomeness. Mongova made a slight speech with eyes twinkling about the youths who had run away and demanded what kind of warriors they would make in a time of fighting, said they were women and would only do to wash sago. No one minded. The group melted away to sleep happily. . . .

The whole emphasis was on having a good time, dancing, decorating, enjoyment. No deadly earnestness, no talk of hardship or hard work or great generosity in the matter of pigs, just a jolly time. [There is no specific reciprocity], although other places will invite them in due course. . . . everywhere the point is dancing and then sending your guests home with favors in their hands.

There are several things to note about this text because it describes a special performance, one significantly influenced by the presence of ethnographers in the village. It is possible, for example, that the merry tone might have been inappropriate in traditional context, although I suspect that the atmosphere Mead described is probably a typical one. But this performance did combine two rituals that were not necessarily always united—the initiation of youth into the *ashin tambaran* and the production of a new crocodile flute. There was no need for a new flute to be made for the initiates to view; an old one would have been sufficient under ordinary circumstances.

It is also important to note that this performance was a somewhat abbreviated version of the initiation (to what extent these rituals usually deviate from the ideal or "complete" form is impossible to determine). A large model crocodile, through which the initiates went while being cut with crocodile teeth, was not made, and it is possible that the relatively minor cuts observed by Mead would have been more serious had the cutting continued as the novices went through the model and the ritual performed in its entirety. In 1981 several informants stressed to me the severity of this hazing. An old Kinakatem man underscored the acquisition of strength as a reason for undergoing initiation, but he associated that acquisition with the spilling of quantities of blood—black blood that a boy was born with and that was acquired from the mother, blood that debilitated a man. A boy's mother's brother, particularly a classificatory one, performed the scarification task, and the more blood that was shed, the stronger the boy became in fighting enemies. Boys cried a lot during this process; special grass skirts were made to clean up the blood, according to men in 1981. Although accounts of the trials of the past may be exaggerated here, it is also likely that Mead thought boys were not seriously harmed because in the contrived version that she saw they were not. The ritual hazing may have been curtailed significantly in the abbreviated version. Informants in 1981 were probably right that blood was shed and that the boys were scarred seriously, but I do not know whether the notion of "mother's blood" is a new or an old one. Public health officials, for example, sometimes talk about using family planning to conserve women's "blood," so the ideas here concerning blood may not be old ones.

Other ritual activities, such as the crocodile's vomiting up of initiates as described in Mead's general notes, were also not performed in this shortened version. Probably the most significant deviation was the failure to include a seclusion period (this was also missing from Mead's general description but was included in Fortune's notes). In 1938 Mead recorded a text from Afima in which he described his own initiation into the *ashin tambaran*, and a significant part of this event involved remaining in a seclusion enclosure for a period of one month, subject to taboos. The structure itself was a small house that Afima likened to a pig house, and food was provided by the initiates' parents. Also important were rites that marked the end of seclusion, activities that significantly involved mothers' brothers again. Initiates proceeded to the village and put yams in the houses of their "mother's brothers' wives." They then returned to the seclusion house and with their mothers' brothers ate a meal of sago and meat. In the afternoon they left the enclosure and returned to their parents' homes, thus ending the seclusion.

Informants in 1981 said that the seclusion house was full of carvings and food and that a boy's mother's brother watched out for him. They claimed that initiates slept on a shelf over an open fire, just like pork being smoked (and like corpses were traditionally allowed to desiccate). When the boys emerged from seclusion, they were measured with woven bands, and people exclaimed about how big they were. Women, often even their own mothers, did not recognize the boys and got very excited over them. They came out of seclusion and danced and sang and washed. (It was, again according to informants in 1981, necessary to wash three times before having sex; if a young man did not do so, the woman would be killed and he himself endangered.)

Finally, although Mongova was the official sponsor and was clearly in charge of orchestrating this ritual, the actual sponsorship was divided with Mead and Fortune; as a result, it was an out-of-the-ordinary affair, and the kinship relationships among the participants were not the ideal ones. The mother's brother–sister's son relationship, for example, which was an important one in this ritual, was not especially apparent. It was the classificatory mother's brother who was obliged to cut his sister's son and received pig in return.[26] If such a man had no appropriate ritual object of his own, he was required to borrow one from a brother or sister and then share the pork he received with them.

Other Initiations

The *ashin* initiation was only one of several (although informants in 1981 clearly remembered it better than any other). Seeing any kind of ritual object for the first time necessitated a ritual introduction. Very few data are available on these other initiations, but it seems that the *yakat* initiation was as significant as the *ashin*. (In 1981 Alemi's son Vai remembered that the *yakat* initiation had been an especially vicious and painful one; he claimed that viscera often fell out of the wounds!) Like *ashins*, *yakats* were named but corresponded to no particular spirit. These single-hole flutes were decorated differently from the *ashins*. The faces on the flutes were built up with paint, and they were decorated with shells, a fringe of hu-

man hair, and a headdress of cassowary feathers. The *yakat* flute
also had two pig tusks as well and was often decorated with flowers.

If the *ashin* initiation was one of crocodiles, then the *yakat* was
one of pigs. Not only were the flutes distinctively decorated with pig
tusks, but also the cutting of the initiates was ideally done with pig
teeth.[27] No references exist to any specific association with pig spirits or pig mothers, however. The initiates' foreheads, arms, legs, and
backs were cut, and occasionally flaming fronds were inflicted on
the boys. In 1938 Omblean described his *yakat* initiation at the age
of about nine as a painful affair. He presented the real mothers'
brothers' role as extremely supportive. This relative went with him
and held his arm while he walked through two lines of men while
the flutes were playing. They approached a platform and went underneath while the men who did the scarifying were on top. In this
initial encounter they cut him only a small bit on his forehead, but
Omblean cried anyway while his mother's brother led him away to
the other side of the platform. There he stood with his mother's
brother holding him firmly when a relative Omblean described as
his mother's brother's son-in-law came to cut him seriously. The initiate put his arms around his mother's brother's neck and was held
there on the back of his elder relative. Here the serious scarification
was done—legs, arms, and back, and Omblean claimed that he
really cried out with the pain. After the scarification initiates lay on
the ground until late afternoon, when they went back to the *haus
tambaran*, where they stayed for two more days. Then there was
more scarification. After that, Omblean said, they remained in seclusion in the bush for about a month. The procedure for ending
seclusion was very much like that for ending seclusion during the
ashin initiation. The initiate and his mother's brother processed
sago and then bathed. They then put clay on their skins, got wild
yams, and threw them at the house of the mother's brother's wife
before returning to the seclusion enclosure and eating there after
offering food to the flute. Mead specifically asked Omblean if he
had been decorated for his return, and his answer was no.

Few details of the *maindjimi* (bush spirit) initiation are available.

Maindjimi flutes resembled *yakat* flutes except that they lacked the pig tusk decoration and had two holes. Those with short bamboo stems were female. The *maindjimis* and *pelevas* (representations of water spirits) were associated in one initiation ceremony in which fire was used in the ordeal, and men danced with the *pelevas* between their legs. (A *peleva* could also be associated with a *saki*—another water spirit representation in flute form, like the *maindjimi* but with more paint buildup on it, possibly also the focus of an initiation—and a *yakat* but never with an *ashin* or *baika*.) The *maindjimi* representation did correspond to a particular, named bush spirit, and it was also significantly involved in transactions between kin (see chapter 4). Although *maindjimi* as physical objects were sometimes flutes, in one place in her notes Mead recorded that they were made "as their ancestors had made them, made of pieces of wood and worn as masks." [28] In the same passage Mead also indicated that *yakats* could be masks as well (and to add to the confusion she also noted that a large woven mask was also a *yakat*). *Nggau*, which "went with *maindjimis*," were carved like human beings, but no other data are available concerning their use or context. Finally, the large *baika* object imported from Anduar also had an initiation associated with it (discussed briefly later).

Seeing a ritual object in any initiation imposed food taboos on the initiates that were later lifted in special ceremonies. Data are available on the taboo-releasing feast for breadfruit seeds which Mead observed in November 1932. In this case the initiation object was *baika* (a woven mask). Mongova had purchased the method of constructing this mask and the rights to do so from Anduar, and he presented it to his brother-in-law and rival, Alemi. After ritually seeing the object, all initiates were forbidden to eat breadfruit seeds (as well as numerous other items). A peculiar aspect of this object was that all the taboos imposed on seeing it the first time could be lifted only in the presence of the mask itself. When the group was initiated, two young boys from Anduar went to see the sacred object, thinking that it was an *ashin*. They assumed that since the *ashin* cult was present throughout the area, they could undergo the releasing ceremonies at home or somewhere closer to their village. But because it was the *baika*, they had to return to Kinakatem for the taboo-releasing feast, and they did so. Just how long the taboo lasted is unclear, but the initiates were anxious to be released because a new harvest was at hand. All the initiates who saw the *baika* when it was shown by Alemi participated in the feast—seven males and seven females from Kinakatem and the two young boys from Anduar. Some people believed that at least one child had already broken the taboos and developed boils as a result.

The day before the feast to lift the taboos, the initiates roasted breadfruit and removed the seeds. On this day (or perhaps the morning of the next, the feasting day) the actual taboo was lifted. This ceremony was required to release the initiates from all meat taboos as well as the breadfruit one. (Taboos on grubs, coconuts, and fish were "released on the spot," while those on cassowary, bandicoot, and eels were lifted later.) To release the initiate from the taboo, a piece of the food is touched to each joint and then discarded. In the breadfruit seed–releasing ceremony, for example, all the initiates did this with a piece of unripe breadfruit in order to "keep their joints from malfunctioning."

On the day of the feast the ritual objects were set up in a relatively secluded house. Inside, a triple scaffold, similar to the one used to hold the dead, was constructed and to it was attached an elaborately decorated *ashin* flute. The *baika*, itself highly decorated, was set out on an elaborate water drum with a decorated net bag hanging behind it. Also behind it an old woman's rain cape and net bag hung from a forked stick. In Mead's text is an ambiguous pronoun reference that is especially frustrating. Her sentence reads, "Behind it [the mask], on a forked stick, was an old woman's rain cape and a net bag which represented its wife." I assume that "its" refers to the mask, and thus the rain cape and net bag would represent the mask's wife, but "its" could also refer strictly to the net bag, which would then be the symbolic wife of the rain cape. Later in the text Mead wrote that "Omblean sat in a line with the big mask and

Mongaramo in a line with its 'wife' as symbolized by the net bag," a sentence that does nothing to clarify unless the net bag alone acts as a symbolic wife to the mask.

In any case the rain cape and net bag were across from the flute and faced the door of the house, while the flute faced the right side of the house, where the novices sat on a long high bench. While all these arrangements were being made and things put in place, Mead noted that "there was a certain amount of respect shown, but little real awe." Yams were cooked and coconuts scraped and mashed up with some of the breadfruit seeds. One plate of this food was put under the mask.

For the ceremony itself the fathers of the initiates sat to the left of the door, along with a few other male observers. Again, I present a text from Mead's own notes in order to preserve the texture of her observation and to communicate the atmosphere of the ceremony.

Kalekumban officiated. Taking a cupful of food, he held it to the lips of the *ashin* and said . . . "breadfruit seeds they eat" but which means "they saw you before, now they wish to eat breadfruit seeds."[29] The name of the novice was called. All the girls' cups were handed out first to a girl who came to the door to get them. There weren't enough cups, and they were told to bring theirs back when they had eaten. Alemi was presented with a large plate as owner of the *ashin* and maker of the former ceremony. The food for the mask was presented to Ndelong, who verbally bade Omblean [an initiate] to eat it. He sat beneath the idol with his back to the group and ate. . . . Alemi handed his big plate of food out to his wife and ate from another. Food was passed about to all the fathers. One initiate was neglected and not remembered until Kalekumban had left, so Mongaramo [an initiate] picked up the cup and shoved it to the *tambaran* without saying anything.

When the initiates have seen the *tambaran*, they perform the following ceremony: (1) they wash their hands in water in which herbs for hunting have been put; they wash their eyes also, and later they will be able to find meat; (2) they heat immature bananas, immature coconuts, in the fire and press these scorching hot to their . . . major joints; (3) the mother's brother hands them betel nut on a ring which they keep and return when daughter's child is initiated (see chapters 4 and 5); (4) the mother's brother hands them tobacco on a ring. In this last show, there were no mothers' brothers, so fathers arranged to give rings to each child in pairs, and so get the ring back at once.

The last paragraph in this text is a puzzling one. It seems to be about an initiation ceremony rather than a ritual to release initiates from taboos. The paragraph is set off from other parts of Mead's text with the title "Meaning of the Ceremony," but which ceremony is meant is not clear. The paragraph included in a typed, one-and-one-half page note specifically labeled the "Taboo Releasing Feast" and does contain the reference to touching the insides of joints with forbidden food, so I include it here but note that some of these observations probably apply in a broader context.

MYTH AND FOLKTALE

The Mundugumor did not possess an elaborate body of mythology. According to Mead, Fortune was to record myths in 1932, but men preferred to recount stories of former wars and battles, and when Mead began to organize the material in 1973, she discovered that there were few myths. Omblean had told her some in 1938, but these few were the entire corpus. Mead specifically asked Omblean at that time about particular tales and recorded that there was no "swan maiden" story, no myth of when women did not know how to give birth, no tale of a girl who did not menstruate, no story or explanation of menstruation. She noted that "toothed vagina" appeared not as a myth but "just folklore."

Omblean, assisted by Afima, did tell Mead a few tales in 1938. One humorous story, which Mead labeled "The Story of the Dogs and Rats," was about a time when women married dogs, men married rats, and neither sex knew of the existence of the other. Then one day a man happened on the place where women defecated, discovered women, and learned from the scratches on the women's backs that they copulated with dogs. One woman complained that the dogs were always screwing and scratching them, and the man felt pity for them. When he suggested that the two of them copulate, the woman said fine and then turned around, "dog fashion," but the man corrected her and taught her the better way, which she liked so much that she wanted to marry him. They talked things over and decided that men and women should marry each other, so the men killed the dogs and the women chased the rats away so that humans could marry humans.

Another story, which Mead called "The Woman Without a Vulva," was about a woman whose genitals "weren't open." A man discovered this, inserted a sharp shell in the skin of a large tree that the woman had already climbed, and told her to rush down. When she did, the shell broke open her vulva, and she cried. The man eased her pain with warm banana leaves before they had sexual intercourse. In "The Story of Fire" human beings sent a dog out with two rings to buy fire and excrement; the dog returned and gave the fire to people and was stuck with the excrement.

Omblean also told Mead two relatively elaborate myths in 1938, myths that were still held to recount sacred truths in 1981. Their staying power reveals something about their significance, and the continuities as well as the differences between 1938 and 1981 are interesting.

The Story of Bilishoi

The story of Bilishoi was collected first by Fortune in 1932, but he did so as a linguistic text, and his notes are fragmented and do not provide adequate translation. For that reason I present only Mead's version, recorded in pidgin, in its entirety. Fortune's is substantially the same but includes incidents that Mead's version does not, two of which are in my 1981 version (I include a summary of these two incidents in their proper place in the text in brackets).[30] What follows, then, is the version Mead recorded from Omblean in 1938.

Mongaramo went to fence in a watering place in order to hunt a pig which always went there. He went and slept there. He thought it was a pig, but it

was really a female spirit [*maindjimi*]. This Fonbalime[31] was the child of a
spirit, and this watering place was where they all drank. They looked like
pigs, and Mongaramo thought they were pigs. So he set up the trap and
waited for a pig. While he was waiting, Fonbalime went down to get water
and saw Mongaramo. When she saw him, she said, "Who is this, guarding
the water? This is our drinking place." Mongaramo said, "I thought pigs
came here. I was waiting for a pig." "You didn't see our footprints?" she
asked. He replied, "I only saw the prints of a pig; I didn't see human footprints." She said, "Still, our prints." Then she said to him, "You come
outside." He came out, and she started thinking and said, "I think I'll
marry you." Then she said, "Let us go up into the house."

Fonbalime's father had been in the bush. He came back and saw Mongaramo and asked, "Fonbalime, where did you get this man?" "I just got
him in the bush." "What bush did you get him in?" She said, "The place
where you and I drink water." "He just appeared where we drink water?"
the father asked. She replied, "He came to hunt for us; he thought we
were pigs." Then she told her father, "He's mine now, my husband." Her
father asked, "You want to marry this man?" and she replied, "Yes, that's
what I want."

The two were married and slept together two days. Then Mongaramo's
father began to search for him. He searched all night but didn't find him,
then the next day he waited. He waited until dark, but Mongaramo didn't
show up, so he searched for him by canoe. He searched and came up to
. . . a bush spirit's place. He went and asked [Fonbalime's father]. [After
hearing the reply] he asked, "Eh, my child is already married?" "Yes, my
daughter married your son." Mongaramo's father said, "I thought he was
lost in the bush, and I was searching for him."

Mongaramo's father said, "I want to take the two of them back to my
place." [Her father] said, "No, they can stay with me." His father said,
"No, they go back with me." The two argued, both were strong, but Mongaramo's father got them. He took them back to his place.

The version of this tale that I recorded in 1981 does not include
anything up to this point but begins with the two married in the
village, as does Fortune's. It continues with the following incident.
Fonbalime went fishing with the human women and caught fish,
but she never came back to the village with them; instead, she said
that she was looking for firewood. She ate all the fish she caught
and gave only bones to Mongaramo, who apparently did not know

any better. Finally, he asked a friend what he ate and discovered the truth—that his wife was a spirit who fed him bones with no flesh. He followed her one day, confirmed her behavior, and reported to his friends. He followed her again and shot her in the shoulder, but she escaped and went wild in the bush. She was always insulting Mongaramo by telling their son that his father never planted any bananas, which he often cried for, but she did go to the gardens to get bananas, and Mongaramo tricked her by digging a big hole near the bananas. When she came, he shot her and threw her in the hole. In anger she sent all the pigs away and told them to hide on nights with a good, bright moon; she also told pigs to reciprocate to humans the pain they received from people, and now pigs attack people as a result. The narrative picks up with Bilishoi, their child, growing up in the village.

They went back to Mongaramo's place and stayed there. Fonbalime got pregnant and gave birth to Bilishoi, a boy. Bilishoi remained there because he wanted to do so. He stayed until he was about eight years old.

One day he said to all of the young children in his place, "Let's go up a betel palm; we want to chew betel." They all went to the base of a betel palm, then one child said, "Alright, I'll go up first." Bilishoi said, "No, I'll go up first. All of you follow me. Let's go all the way to the top of the palm." So they all followed him up. They all went up one palm. They came close to him, then he kicked them, and they all fell down. He stamped on them with his feet, and they all fell down and died.

He went and told their parents. "All of your children—we went up a betel palm, and they all fell down and died. I alone held the palm tightly and came down; they didn't." The parents went to get their children. They cried as they carried them to the house; they put them in the house until the mourning was over, then they made a hole under their houses and buried them. When the burial was over, they were angry with Mongaramo, Bilishoi's father. "Why did your son, Bilishoi, take our children and go up that betel? Now all the children fell from the palm and died. You must compensate us. You are Bilishoi's father. You give us compensation." Mongaramo gathered rings, put them on a stick, and gave them to the parents. After giving them the rings, things just went on as before.

A little later Bilishoi persuaded some young boys to go bathing. He found a piece of oil palm in the water. He stepped on this piece of oil palm in the sand. He took it and said to all the boys, "Let's go. We've finished bathing. You go to your houses, I'll go to mine."

He went and told his father, Mongaramo—"Sharpen a spear for me from this piece of oil palm. When it is sharp, make a woven band and decorate it with some feathers." His father did it and gave it to him. He went down and speared a banana plant, and the spear went through it and came out the other side. He took it out and started to think, "I'll go down to the water, take some young boys, and when we've finished bathing, I'll try one of them."

He went down, put his spear in the sand, and called all the young boys in the village. "All you young boys come, let's go bathe." The boys heard his words, and they all went. "You come up and lie on the log." They went up and lay on the log. "Now you can't watch me. Close your eyes. I'm going to play on your skin. I'd like to scratch your skin with my finger." They listened to him and lay down. He got his spear and speared all of them. He skewered them all on one spear. They all died. He took out the spear and left; he went away and put the spear in his house.

Then he went and told the parents. He said, "Your children—we all went to bathe, and they died on the beach." The parents replied, "They weren't sick; we think you killed them." Bilishoi was adamant: "They just died." The parents were already convinced. They were angry with his father again. Mongaramo got out all of the rest of his rings from his basket to pay compensation for the children. He gave the rings to the parents. Then he was angry with Bilishoi. "Why did you kill the boys? I don't have any more rings now—if you kill more, I can't pay. You can't remain here."

So Bilishoi cried. He cried for his home. He finished crying, went up some betel palm, picked it and put it in his bag, went and got some pepper catkin, put it in his net bag. His father said to him, "Let's go cut wild sago in the bush." He listened to his father, and the two of them went. The two went and Mongaramo scraped sago. Bilishoi said, "Father, I'm going first to cut some sago." The father said, "Go ahead." So he went and cut only one. He then talked with the bone of a flying fox. Bilishoi was always taking out sago thorns from his legs with the bone of the flying fox which he kept in his hair. He opened the bark of the sago palm. He said to the bone: "You cut the sago. You are just like me, a man. You can cut sago." The pounder fired up, and his father came and heard it.

The flying fox bone cut the sago. Bilishoi already went home. His father [not knowing he was gone], asked him, "Bilishoi, where are you?" "I am cutting the sago," the flying fox bone replied in the native language.

Bilishoi came back to the village and said to his two sisters, "You two come." They came and sat down, and he came and sat next to one. He said, "I'm going to kill a pig and pierce your ears." They said, "Why didn't father come?" "No, father is angry with me; he insulted me. I can't stay. Today I will pierce your ears." The two said, "Father will come; he'll invite everyone [to the associated feast], and he can pierce our ears."

Bilishoi was adamant. "I can't stay to see you two. I'll go travel around many places." The sisters gave in and said, "You go kill the pig." He got his spear and went and shot a pig. The pig died, and he carried it back, cooked it, cut it, and when it was cut up, he took a piece, the liver, and put in it one [sister's] mouth first. Then he got the flying fox bone and pierced the ears of one sister, and when he was done, he yelled to all the villagers. . . . When he finished, he said to the two, "You two wait for the sore [to heal], then eat the pig." Then he got up and shook hands with them [to say good-bye].

The two sisters cried for their brother. "Brother, where are you going? Wherever you go, tell the two of us, and we'll go with you." He replied, "I can't stay put; I must wander. To many places. You two stay. Father will come, and you can stay."

The two sisters cried. Bilishoi got up, cut some bamboo, and put his spear in it. He cut another bamboo, put fire in it, and left. The two sisters cried after him. He chased them back, "You two go back home." He ran off. The road was full of swordgrass. The two sisters followed him, calling his name. He responded from a long way off—"You two go back." For the two of them, the grass was too much. They were afraid. They cried and cried. They said, "We can't go home. We will stay here." One of them said, "You can stay on the ground. I will go up a tree." One became black ant, the kind that stays on the ground, and the other went up a tree—she remained up the tree. The two turned into ants completely. The second was white. . . .

Bilishoi went and came upon two women. They were dyeing grass skirts. They were cutting sago shoots [for making grass skirts]. He shot a goura pigeon with this spear of his. The pigeon fell with the spear in it in the women's sago. They took it, removed the spear, and put both aside. They covered them with palm bark. Bilishoi went and asked if they had seen the pigeon. "I shot it. It fell with the spear still in it." They said, "No we didn't see it." Bilishoi said, "It fell down right here. You two are stubborn. I will kill you both." The two got the pigeon and returned his spear, and Bilishoi took them. "I see. Alright, the pigeon is yours."

He got his spear. The two women were afraid of him. "Your ways are no

good; you're going to kill us. We heard—you are no good." "What do you
mean, I'm no good?" "You kill people." The two lay down. Bilishoi said, "I
want to have sex with you." "Eh, just don't kill us." "No, no, you two just
lie down. I won't shoot you." The two lay down. "You can't look at me."
He got his spear and shot them both at the same time. They died. He cut
their heads off, put them in his net bag, and carried them to the next
village.

An incident recorded in Fortune's version and by me in 1981 (this
particular rendition is from my notes) goes like this: He came upon
an old woman and her grandchild. He asked them why their skin
was such a mess, so full of cuts and sores; they told him that little
red parrots attacked them every day at 4 p.m. He felt sorry for them
and killed all of the birds; he used the feathers to decorate his spear
and left the birds for the women to eat.

He carried the heads to a village; he came up and saw the men building a
haus tambaran. They were making it with little logs, and he said, "Your
logs aren't big enough. Don't bother with these. Get real posts." He said,
"I'll go up. You give me a log." They gave him the log; he didn't hold it
well—he only pretended and threw it down. He dropped it on a man
standing below and said, "You fellows can't run away. Hold the post. Hold
it tightly. Bring it back." He tricked them. They heeded his words and
went closer. But again he really didn't hold the post well—he let it fall and
killed all of the men standing below.

Some witnesses were aroused and said, "Let's go get our spears. This
custom of his—killing people!" Some had stayed far away, and these men
went and got their spears from their houses. They said, "Let's go kill Bilishoi. We can't let him go on, or he'll kill all of us. Now let's really kill
him." They then got spears and went to shoot him. Bilishoi was up on the
peak of the *haus tambaran.* The spears didn't get him. He used his elbow
to flick them aside. One man lived across the river, a rubbish man who
had a sore on his ass. He yelled, "You guys come and get me." They yelled
back, "You're no good. You have a sore on your ass. You stay!" "No, I want
to try to shoot him with my spear." His friend[32] said, "Never mind, you
fellows stay, he's my friend, I'll go get him." He got his paddle and went in
his canoe to fetch him.

They came back and went ashore. He put his spear in a piece of bamboo, like the people of the Sepik do, and shot his first one—and it just missed Bilishoi's head. His friend said, "You fellows look at this rubbish man, my friend, today he's going to war on Bilishoi." The second time he shot, he really got him (in the left temple). He fell down and died. They recovered him, cooked him in boiling water, and when he was cooked, they cut him. They ate, but their mouths were full of nothing but liquid. His meat was too soft, so they threw it away.

They threw away part of his head (forehead), the part like a coconut shell; this part went and came up in a water hole near Dimiri. One woman went to get water there and saw this part of a skull of a man in the hole. She ran away. She went and told people in the village [Dimiri]: "A part of a man's head is in the hole." So they didn't go get water out of this hole. They slept and dreamed. The devil [spirit, soul] of Bilishoi said [in the dream], "You want to get my head and kill a chicken. Put them well in a hole. Go fetch me."

In the morning they got up, and this man who dreamed said to all the men of the village, "We all must go kill a chicken. Get the head of this man." They all asked, "What man?" He said, "Bilishoi." "Ah, let's go get him." Then they all went to get him. He went and brought him back and put him in the *haus tambaran*. Night came again, and everyone slept. All right this man dreamed again. Bilishoi said, "You fellows must cut a hardwood tree, carve arms and legs, carve it just like a man, make a belly too; all right, you can put a head on it too. You can put my head on it." They put the head on—first they put it drooping down. Then all the men of the village died. Bilishoi said then, "Put my head so that I look up into the clouds." They arranged him in this way, and then the place was all right. They didn't die more. Then Mundugumor, Andafugan, they all went and paid. They paid Dimiri. He didn't belong to a family there—he didn't belong to Dimiri, they went and got him back. He remains in Andafugan. . . .

Now he's there. We give him pig livers. If he talks, talks [to someone] in a dream, we send livers. All the four Mundugumor villages do; Dimiri doesn't send any. The men who take care of him eat [the pig livers]. The rope of . . . Fonbalime's father, looks after him.[33] The mission [Catholic] thinks—you [Bilishoi] have no passage for defecating, why do you talk of eating? If I dream of some meat, I send my father's line, of Kinakatem, to give pig livers. . . . Now he's there, the mission says hide him, but he says "You fellows want to test me; I think the people are good," and the people are afraid. Bilishoi's bones are in one place behind Kamberamba. Some send livers there, but we don't—it's too far. That's where they killed him, where his bones are. If you want to make a man die, alright get these bones, some splinters from the bones, and put them in food and the man [who eats it] will die. That's why they are afraid still. Now us, we don't buy these scrapings; we don't want to buy the bone splinters and finish everyone in the village. We're afraid; we don't want to destroy the village.

When I was in Kinakatem in 1981, I was sitting with a group listening to stories and talking, and a young man approached and announced that he had things to tell me about Satan and Satan's activities. The name of this satan was Bilishoi, he said. The young man told me that he and others had heard the missions' stories of Satan and had figured out that Satan and Bilishoi were really the same thing. His face was very animated as he explained the association to me, obviously pleased with the intellectual play and achievement. Throughout the telling of the tale, other men helped recite the story, clarified points, added episodes, and interrupted to correct others. Despite the satanic association and statements that this Bilishoi was evil, they clearly admired Bilishoi's exploits and were impressed and humored by his trickery. The narrative was frequently interrupted, not just by someone adding or correcting but also by general laughter.

There were some differences between Mead's 1938 version and my 1981 one. The data are too incomplete to suggest any substantial conclusions about the meaning of the variations, but it is interesting to note some changes and speculate on possible meanings. The 1981 version of this myth begins without any prelude—Mongaramo and Fonbalime are already married, there is no story of him finding her footprints, his father searching for him, and so forth. But in the version Fortune recorded in 1932, the same was true: the story begins with the fish bone incident and its ramifications, so not much can be made of this difference.

However, the 1981 version does differ from both Mead's 1938 version and Fortune's 1932 one in a startling way: the sisters are lost entirely. There is not even a mention that Bilishoi might have sisters. There is no ear-piercing incident, and no one seems to mourn Bilishoi's departure from the village. In the early version the brother-sister tie is portrayed as one of deep affect, but it has vanished from the later version. To suggest that this change reflects a diminution of the strength and importance of the brother-sister tie over recent years is simplistic Durkheimian speculation but far more likely to be true than the reverse.

Perhaps the lessening of the brother-sister tie is related to the increasing prominence of the role of affines. My 1981 version highlights the significance of in-laws in an elaborate episode not even suggested earlier. Bilishoi marries a woman from a place where people make war on frogs and celebrate these kills. He told his brothers-in-law that they were silly to kill frogs and not people, and he sent them out after human prey. He did not, however, share his good spear with them but let them go ahead with their very inferior spears, which were inadequate for killing people, and he shamed them with his success and his human trophies. One of them spied on him and discovered the secret about his spear. They used rat teeth to saw through the spear, but only partially, so that when he went to use it again, it broke after he had only killed one or two people. He was sad and cried, as if his parents had died. He set about to make a new spear from an oil palm. The palm fell on the men who had lined up to catch it and killed them all except his true wife's brother (who only lost his ear), for whom he felt pity. (My informant remarked here about the importance of brothers-in-law.) He made two spears, one for himself and one for his affine. (When the women found the dead men the next day, they discovered that Bilishoi had desecrated them by putting a stick in each man's anus. Then they knew Bilishoi's true identity.) This added episode is a clear and unequivocal statement of the importance of the tie between a man and his wife's brother.

Finally, Bilishoi's nature seems more ambiguous in my version—he is not wholly evil but able to demonstrate some compassion and does not kill everyone he encounters. He helps some people afflicted with humorous problems, as he did not in Mead's version. In one incident he separates people attached back to back, and in another opens a hole for people who had no orifice for defecating (neither of these incidents is included in Mead's or Fortune's version; what happened to the women who were attacked by birds is not clear in Fortune's text). Despite the young man's assertion that he was Satan, another informant called him the "number one trickster" of all time. It seemed that people were fascinated by and admiring of his ambiguity.

Although these specific changes are not necessarily meaningful and it would be an error to derive too much from them, the fact that the myth is still told and labeled significant is important. People in 1981 believed that anyone who ate a piece of Bilishoi's body died (in their version, his meat did not go soft) and that power still resided in his bones. Anyone eating scrapings from these bones, still kept in Kambambveut, even in 1981 would die immediately.

What happened to the skull piece and carved wooden body is also interesting. The wooden body was eaten by insects, and people had to bury it and carve another, an activity they performed several times. Finally, a priest from Marienberg, the story goes, came and took away the actual skull of Bilishoi. The informants I talked with wanted this skull returned so that they could feed and take care of it.

The Story of Gorinjime

Another myth equally compelling was that of Gorinjime. Mead recorded this myth from Omblean in 1938 and entitled it "The Time When There Was No Death." Mead's version, with her parenthetical comments, goes as follows:

Their names, this married couple, were Gorinjime (the wife) and Sumbiatume (the husband).[34] They went to work sago. Sumbiatume went back to the village while Gorinjime and their two children stayed to wash the sago. Then one group of bush people came; they called them Wolimba, these men from Wolimba came (this place no longer exists). They killed Gorinjime. Gorinjime said [first] to her children—"You go and hide." One child . . . she had no name (shakes his head in disapproval), this girl went and hid at the base of a sago palm. Then the men came and killed her mother. They killed her, made her die completely, really cut her up. Then the blood which had run on the ground came back together again (the blood from her coagulated), and the child saw this. She watched as the woman's blood came back together, a head formed, a chest formed, two arms formed, breasts formed, legs formed, then her skin reappeared. And the child saw this and was very afraid. She remained hidden. The woman got up and sat down. Then she got up again and stood, but her legs were shaky, and she fell down again. Then she called for her child, "You come. Get some clay and give it to me. I want to put it on my skin." Well, the child was afraid. Very frightened. She said, "You're a ghost." "I am not a ghost—I'm your mother." But the child was convinced. "No, you're a ghost." Then the mother herself got up and got some clay. She rubbed it on her skin.

Meanwhile, the child had run away and gone home. She went and told Sumbiatume, "My mother, Wolimba came and killed her. Her blood came back together again, and she became a human figure. She called out for me, but I was afraid. She's a ghost, already a ghost. I really shivered [with fear]. She'll be here soon." The father asked, "Where is she now?" He ran off. He went there and saw her. Then he ran back to the *haus tambaran* and said, "A ghost!" He stayed in the *haus tambaran*. She, the ghost, made sago pudding and called for her husband [to eat it]. He was afraid (disgust face when fear is the subject). He said, "I don't want any. You're a ghost." He got up from the *haus tambaran* and came outside into the village. He told all the men in the place. He told all of the women too. Some readied slitgongs, others got ready with sticks. They then all went after her, chased her. They chased her—some beat slitgongs, some hit her house with the sticks. They all yelled at her; they said, "You're a ghost— get out! You can't stay here." They all chased her, and she ran away. Now part of this I don't know. She ran away completely and hid. Where she went to hide, I can't know.

In 1981 I sat in Kinakatem with a group of men and women, discussing what had and had not changed in the past 50 years. Many side conversations were in progress as I listened and talked and questioned. Several of the older men were holding a whispered conference, and the Biwat language is close enough to the Bun language for me to eavesdrop: they were discussing the story of Gorinjime in rather hushed tones, deciding whether or not to tell me and trying to figure out if they knew the story correctly and fully. Yosep Ruova, who was a 14-year-old resident of Kinakatem when Mead was there in 1932 but who had spent most of his adult life upriver in Bun, was my good friend and informant. When the men decided that I could be told this story and were only working out the details, he whispered to me, "They're straightening an important story to tell you. It is a story of very long-ago ancestors, when there was no river here, only grass. This ancestor died but came back just on her blood—they threw her out of all the places, and she went away, but where?" His tone told me that I was about to hear something very significant; he was almost reverent. Bun has a version of the same myth (as does the downriver group in Saparu-Kausimbi), and I knew how important it was there. The quiet and serious tones of the others confirmed my impression. Finally, they told me the story of Gorinjime. The first part of the 1981 version was substantially the same as Mead's earlier version, although it was more detailed (the daughters, for example, had names) and more elaborate, and Gorinjime and her family were clearly identified as ancestors. However, an entirely new outcome had been added. In Mead's version Gorinjime just goes off somewhere and seemingly is never heard from again. In the more contemporary version her activities after leaving are of far more interest. Informants in 1981 continued the myth this way:

She was getting ready to leave, then, getting all of her things ready to go. She got a post (for housebuilding), a branch of greens, sugar, croton, some grass skirts, a *tanget*, a banana shoot; she also got yams, taro, all kinds of things. Then she got up and said sadly, "Sumbiatume, you are chasing me away—alright, I'm going to hide now." She spoke out then. "Later, you people of this place will die, people everywhere, you can come and face me where I'll be hiding. I am sorry now that I came back from my blood. Why are you throwing me out? I hold the clouds above, the ground below. I will never return to you here; I'm going away forever now. I came back through my blood only because I was thinking of you. Sumbiatume, you'll see me later—when I want you. Just wait."

Gorinjime's brother, Kaviersala, was sorry for his sister and took some of the food she offered. She said to him, "You wait, and when everyone is asleep you come and see me in the house." When everyone slept, he went up, and she appeared to him as a star, she was shining brilliantly.[35] The brother saw this star, and he was afraid. But she told him not to fear and that she was going away forever to hide. Then she left by going down the house post.

She heard the slitgongs and hourglass drums nearby. She put all of her belongings in a canoe and left. She followed the waterways all the way to Manam. . . . She went to Manam and planted her housepost, but she still heard the drums, so she left there. Where did she go from there? We are not sure. We think she went to America, with you people, and that's why we refer to Americans as our matrilateral kin. That's all.

Near the end of the telling of this tale, the narrators were interrupted by a middle-aged man who was very angry that they were telling it. His ostensible complaint was that they did not know it well enough and that an absent relative of his was the only one who could adequately recount it. His concern seemed to be the accuracy of the story and not who had rights to tell it (and to whom), but I cannot be absolutely certain that he was not distressed that it was being told to me (many informants in Bun consider their versions secret). In any case his anger partly explains the rather abrupt ending to the tale. Other versions told on the river, including all Bun versions and the one Saparu-Kausimbi version I recorded, go on to tell of Gorinjime's life in America, how she brought some of her relatives to live with her, how she and they developed white skins (from the clay she used on her skin after resurrecting), how she was the origin of all wealth and would one day remember her kin in Papua New Guinea and return to share that wealth. People in Bun explicitly recognized that there were two levels to this story—the old one, in which Gorinjime just went off somewhere, and the newer part, in which she founded America and all material wealth. They phrase it as "finding out the truth" about where she went. The cargo ideology is clear in the Bun and Saparu-Kausimbi versions, and had the story not ended as abruptly as it did more indications of Mundugumor cargo ideology would have been apparent in their version as well.

It is also relevant that at least two adult male informants associated Gorinjime with Jesus Christ: "Talk of God came and we thought of Gorinjime. [When we] heard talk of coming back from the dead [resurrecting] on blood, that's what we thought about." If Bilishoi was associated with Satan, then Gorinjime was identified with Christ, and the Second Coming takes on a special Melanesian flavor in that her return will be accompanied by the distribution of European material wealth.

KINSHIP AND MARRIAGE $\boxed{4}$

Mead's notes contain more data on the topic of kinship and marriage than on almost any other subject, a curious fact considering that Fortune was supposed to focus on these topics. A number of factors or combination of factors may have led Mead to collect so much data. There was and to a significant extent still is (for good reason) a conviction among many anthropologists that kinship provides the framework for social organization in small-scale societies and that one must use it as the context for structuring other data and inquiries. Therefore, understanding the kinship system is a priority. Another possible reason is simply that access to such material is relatively easy. These data are often less sensitive and more public, and asking about the topic is not a threatening process. I suspect that in this case, however, access was easy because of the nature of the Mundugumor themselves. Here I am drawing upon my own experience in Bun: I went to study one topic but found myself spending much of my time untangling the knots of kinship and brother-sister exchange marriage transactions because these concerns dominated people's interest and were in the foreground of public debate. Not only was access to these data easy; I could not have avoided the subjects even if I had wanted to do so. Perhaps yet another factor affected the amount of data Mead gathered on kinship. Although Fortune was supposed to cover the topic, Mead notes (see chapter 1) that in talking with children she discovered a main clue to the system that he had missed. Perhaps this near miss encouraged her to pay more attention than she might otherwise have done.

I begin the chapter with kinship terminology and then examine the behavior that characterized various dyadic kin relations. Socialization is included under parent-child behavior. The discussion of marriage is divided into two sections: the first describes behavior between husband and wife and among affines: the second, marriage rules and structure. A short section on patrilineal descent groups (i.e., clans) precedes the final one on the nature of what Mead called ropes. This chapter differs somewhat from the previous two in that, although I do add some data that I acquired in 1981, I include little of my own interpretation. There is so much to be said about these data that I reserve my main interpretive and analytic remarks and present them separately in chapter 5.

KINSHIP TERMINOLOGY

The terminological system was a relatively simple one that did not differentiate between siblings, parallel cousins, and cross-cousins in ego's own generation, but it did distinguish mother's brother and father's sister from parents and parents' same-sex siblings in the first ascending generation (see diagrams 1 and 2.) Only four terms were used for this first ascendant generation:

avbang: F, FB, FFBS, FFZS, FMBS, FMZS, and so on. Ego applied this
  term to father and to anyone his or her father called brother (which included father's first and second male cross- and parallel cousins);
  MH, or any man married to a woman ego called *ume* (mother);
ume: M, MZ, MMZD, MMBD, MFBD, MFZD, and so on. Ego applied
  this term to mother and to anyone his or her mother called sister (which

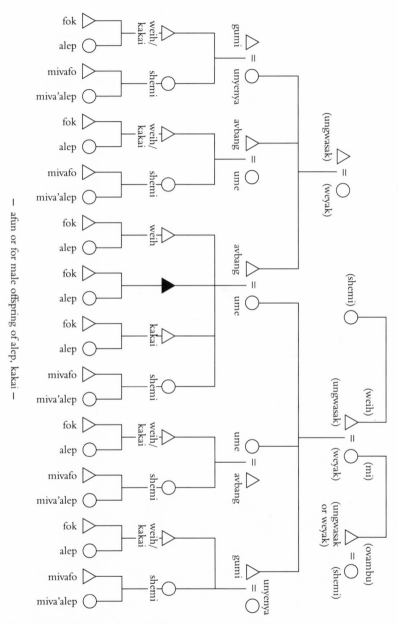

Diagram 1. Consanguineal kin terms (male ego)

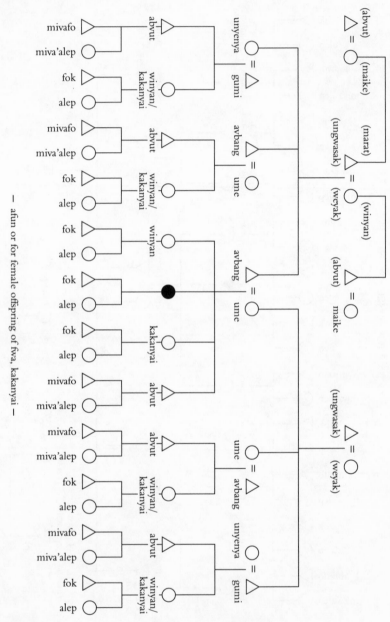

Diagram 2. Consanguineal kin terms (female ego)

included mother's first and second female cross- and parallel cousins);
    FW, or any woman married to a man called *avbang* (father);
gumi: MB, MMZS, MMBS, MFBS, MFZS, and so on. Ego applied this
    term to mother's brother and to anyone his or her mother called brother
    (which included mother's first and second male cross- and parallel
    cousins);
    FZH, or any man married to a woman called *unyenya* (father's sister);
unyenya: FZ, FFBD, FFZD, FMZD, FMBD, and so on. Ego applied this
    term to father's sister and to anyone his or her father called sister (which
    included father's first and second female cross- and parallel cousins);
    MBW, or any woman married to a man called *gumi* (mother's brother).

In ego's own generation only sex and relative age were distinguished. Siblings, parallel cousins, and cross-cousins were called by
the same terms:

abvut (female ego only): B, MZS, MBS, FBS, FZS, and so on. Ego ap-
    plied this term to all male siblings and first and second cross- and
    parallel male cousins;
shemi (male ego only): Z, MZD, MBD, FBD, FZD, and so on. Ego ap-
    plied this term to all female siblings and first and second cross- and
    parallel cousins;
weih (male ego only): elder B and any male first or second cross- or paral-
    lel cousins who were senior to ego;
kakai (male ego only): younger B and any male first or second cross- and
    parallel cousins who were junior to ego;
winyan (female ego only): elder Z and any first and second cross- and par-
    allel female cousins who were senior to ego;
kakanyai (female ego only): younger Z and any first and second cross- and
    parallel female cousins who were junior to ego.[1]

There were no special terms for cross-cousins, something of an odd-
ity given the fact that mother's brother and father's sister (the parents of cross-cousins) were terminologically distinct from parents
and parents' same-sex siblings. That mother's brother's wife and father's sister were terminologically the same (as were father's sister's
husband and mother's brother) is not remarkable because the Mundugumor practiced brother-sister exchange marriage, and mother's

brother was ideally married to father's sister, but that children of these unions were grouped with siblings and parallel cousins deserves note. There is little possibility of error here. Neither Mead nor Fortune recorded separate terms for cross-cousins, and no informants, young or old, remembered any in 1981 either.

Because different kinds of transactions occurred between first, second, and third cousins as well as siblings, it is also somewhat odd that all these relatives were lumped together. Mead's male informants did tell her that there were ways of distinguishing between close and distant sisters. *Shemi mepake* (pl. *shemili mapakate*) referred to a distant sister, and *shemi maketi* to a close one. There is no reference in the notes to a way of distinguishing other siblings in the same way, but this way certainly was a possibility (e.g., *abvut mepake* for a female ego's distant brother). The terminology for third cousins is not specified, but it is likely that sibling terms lapsed because according to the ideal marriage system, second cousins arranged marriages between their children, who were third cousins to each other. The application of sibling terms to both first and second cross- and parallel cousins was similar to the prohibition on first and second cross-cousin marriage because having sexual relations with such a relative, a sibling, was incest.

Only four terms were used in the first descending generation:

fok: generally, S and S of a sibling of the same sex. Specifically, for a female ego: S, ZS, and so on. A woman applied this term to her own male offspring and to any male offspring of women she called sister *(winyam, kakanyai)*;
   for a male ego: S, BS, and so on. A man applied this term to his own male offspring and to any male offspring of men he called brother *(weih, kakai)*;
alep: generally, D or D of a sibling of the same sex. Specifically, for a female ego: D, ZD, and so on. A woman applied this term to her own female offspring and to any female offspring of women she called sister *(winyan, kakanyai)*;
   for a male ego: D, BD, and so on. A man applied this term to his own female offspring and to any female offspring of men he called brother *(weih, kakai)*;

mivafo: generally, S of sibling of the opposite sex. Specifically, for a male
   ego: ZS, and so on. A man applied this term to any male offspring of
   women he called sister *(shemi)*. Its reciprocal was *gumi;*
      for a female ego: BS and so on. A woman applied this term to any male
   offspring of men she called brother *(abvut)*. Its reciprocal was *unyenya;*
miva'alep: generally, D of sibling of the opposite sex. Specifically, for a
   male ego: ZD and so on. A man applied this term to any female offspring of a woman he called sister *(shemi)*. Its reciprocal was *gumi;*
      for a female ego: BD and so on. A woman applied this term to any fe-
   male offspring of a man she called brother *(abvut)*. Its reciprocal was
   unyenya.

The second ascending generation terminology was somewhat more
complex. First, there were specific terms for grandparents:

ungwasak: MF, FF, and all males of this generation to whom kinship was
   traced;
weyak: MM, FM, and all females of this generation to whom kinship was
   traced.[2]

However, there was an alternative method of classifying grandparents based on an identification between alternate generations.
Terms for ego's own generation were used. A male ego called his
mother's father the term for elder brother *(weih)*, a female ego called
her father's mother by the term for elder sister *(winyan)*, and other
terms were applied logically from this starting point. Thus, a man
called his mother's father the term for elder brother, his mother's
father's brothers by the terms for brother, and his mother's father's
wife (actually his mother's mother) by the term for wife. A woman
called her father's mother the term for elder sister, her father's
mother's sister the terms for sisters, and her father's mother's husband (or father's father) the term for husband. Mead specifically
applies this method to a man's maternal grandfather and a woman's
paternal grandmother and implies that the same practice did not
necessarily pertain to a man's paternal grandfather and a woman's
maternal grandmother. Some diagrams of the practice do indicate
that it did pertain for grandparents other than a woman's father's

mother and a man's mother's father despite the fact that the notes suggest otherwise. This ambiguity is impossible to resolve (and is discussed further in the next chapter). If an individual used own-generation terms for a grandparent, terms for son and daughter might be used for parents' siblings. Thus, if a man called his mother's father elder brother, that might mean that he called his grandfather's children (including mother's brother) by the term for son. However, according to the notes, the male ego's father's father's mother's brother was called father, but there was no further skewing of generations.[3] These own-generation terms were used mostly by children and young people; adults, after the death of the grandparents' generation, tended to refer to them with grandparent terms only.

The second descending generation was a reflection of the second ascending one. A term did exist for use specifically for these relatives:

afun: grandchild or SS, DS, SD, DD; a reciprocal for *ungwasak* and *weyak.*

However, if the grandchild used own-generation terms to refer to mother's father (male ego) or father's mother (female ego), these relatives would reciprocate logically and use the terms for younger brother and younger sister and so on.

A variety of terms were used to distinguish affinal relatives (see diagrams 3 and 4):

marat (female ego only): H, ZH, and so on. A woman applied this term to her own husband and to any men married to women she called sister *(winyan, kakanyai)*, again including her first and second cross- and parallel female cousins;

mi (male ego only): W, BW, and so on. A man applied this term to his own wife and to any woman married to men he called brother *(weih, kakai)*, again including his first and second cross- and parallel male cousins.

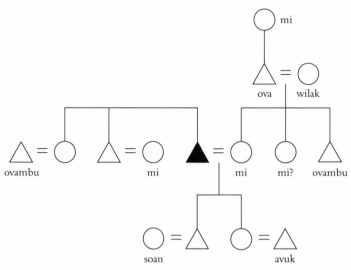

Diagram 3. Affinal kin terms (male ego)

Mead's listings of kin terms do not specify what a man called his wife's sister or a woman her husband's brother. However, it is a reasonable assumption that these terms were reciprocal, as were others. Because a woman called her sister's husband *marat* (husband), he probably referred to her as *mi* (wife). Similarly, a man called his brother's wife *mi* (wife), and thus it is likely (but again speculative) that she reciprocated by calling him *marat* (husband). Further affinal terms were as follows:

ovambu (male ego only): WB or any man ego's wife called brother; ZH, or any man married to someone ego called sister *(shemi)*; thus, a reciprocal term between brothers-in-law;

maike (female ego only): HZ or any woman ego's husband called sister *(shemi)*; BW or any woman married to a man ego called brother *(abvut)*; thus, a reciprocal term between sisters-in-law;

wilak: for a male ego—WM, anyone ego's wife called mother *(ume)*, and all of ego's wife's female relatives (maternal or paternal) in the first ascending generation;

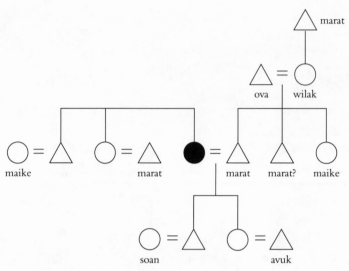

Diagram 4. Affinal kin terms (female ego)

for a female ego—HM, anyone ego's husband called mother *(ume),* and
all of ego's husband's female relatives (maternal or paternal) in the first
ascending generation;

ova: for a male ego—WF, anyone ego's wife called father *(avbang),* and all
his wife's male relatives in the first ascending generation;

for a female ego—HF, anyone ego's husband called father *(avbang),*
and all of ego's husband's male relatives in the first ascending generation.

These terms, *wilak* for mother-in-law and *ova* for father-in-law,
lump together relatives distinguished by the intervening spouse.
Specifically, a woman's mother's brother is lumped with her fathers
by her husband, and a woman does the same for her husband's relatives. Similarly, father's sisters were included with mothers. Thus,
spouses did not always make distinctions that consanguineal relatives did.

There were two additional specific affinal terms:

avuk: DH or any man married to someone ego called daughter *(alep);*
soan: SW or any woman married to someone ego called son *(fok).*

There were no specific affinal terms for the second ascending or descending generation. The identification of alternate generations was used as a guide. Thus, if a woman called her father's mother *winyan* (elder sister), her husband followed and called the woman wife *(mi)*, the appropriate term for wife's sister.

A few additional terms are mentioned in the notes. *Wokasa* was an alternate term for *weih* (elder brother), but when each term was appropriate is not noted. Sometimes near affinal relatives were differentiated from distant ones, and females were called *angela* and males *ya*, whereas *ovambu* was reserved for distant in-laws (whether this applied to female ego as well as male is not specified). *Mangap* was the term for an inherited wife, *mandamvon* for an inherited husband. Kinship terms were also used to refer to nonkin. Co-wives used the terms for sister to refer to one another. If one wanted to refer to a spirit, one used the same term that one used for the spirit's ward.

The Mundugumor differentiated true from classificatory relatives by adding an adjectival form to the kin term, but neither Mead nor Fortune indicates when this addition might occur or whether it was a common practice. Own mother was *mamandau ume* while a classificatory mother was *ume longwonga*, and thus for all other relatives. In the notes referring to this practice is also the statement that own father would be called *mamandau geun*, and it is difficult to know how to interpret this. Why not *mamandau avbang*? The translation of *mamandau geun* (own rope) makes the statement even more problematic. Mead wrote that ropes were a form of descent in which women joined their father's groups and men their mother's; if this was true, it would make sense only for a woman, not a man, to refer to her own father as *mamandau geun*.

The term *barangi* is also difficult to place. Mead clearly notes that *wa barangi* is an image, photograph, or drawing. But she also made note of the term *barangi* in two other contexts. In one it was a collective term for trade friends in other villages, and in the other it was a collective term for affinal relatives. If the term possessed all these meanings, it would certainly be rich for symbolic interpreta-

tion. In many Melanesian societies trade partners in other villages
are affines, and affinal exchanges allow for the development of more
elaborate transactions; indeed, arranging marriages with particular
groups is sometimes motivated by trade and exchange considerations. Mead herself (1970:26–27) recognized that a tie between affines and hereditary trade friendships was a common Sepik theme.
The use of *barangi* as an affinal term is not mentioned in the original notes of 1932 or 1938, only in Mead's beginnings of an interpretation in 1971; did she remember that the term applied to affines
although she had not noted it originally? Because there is much
room for doubt here, this term too remains a puzzle.

Finally, there are two additional terms that are difficult to interpret—*kamain* and *wareun*. Both refer to kinds of exchange partners, and because Mead did not include them in her listings of kin
terms, I do not discuss them fully here. However, they must be mentioned in this context because they played a significant role in marriage rules and transactions, and even if Mead was correct in excluding them from the realm of kin terms, they did affect kinship
and marriage.

Kinship terms were rarely if ever used as a form of address. Personal names were used to address someone directly, and kin terms
were used primarily for reference. *Ume* (mother) was used as a form
of address by very young children, however, and kin terms were
sometimes used in contexts of mourning and sorcery, although neither Mead nor Fortune speculates why. When a man was bitten by
a snake or pierced by a piece of bamboo, he called out "mother" (a
woman would call out "father," "brother," or her brother's personal
name). But these few contexts were the only ones in which kin terms
were used for anything other than a form of reference.

Mead makes interesting observations about the use of kin terms
in her notes. Most particularly, she recognizes that kin terminology
is not an inviolate template that is applied to unequivocally defined
relationships. A flexibility, a lack of conviction that the terms need
be consistent, infused the system. Mead located the flexibility of
kinship terminology in the fact that conceptually the people distin-

guished between "real" or "close genealogical connection" and more distant or classificatory kin. One should not change the term applied to a mother, father, mother's brother, or father's sister, for example, and by extension probably any close biological kin. But classificatory relations were different—and manipulable. Mead wrote that "with their insistence of [close consanguineal relationships] for all important matters, they feel as if [classificatory] kinship were in a sense another set of categories . . . something sufficiently un-intimate to be shifted about at will." (Mead also noted that "closeness and nearness of feeling are rather independent of kinship classification. . . .") Nor did the Mundugumor feel compelled to be consistent in the use of kin terms. One could call a man grandfather and his wife sister, for example, and apparently people frequently did just that.

Mead tended to view this flexibility and inconsistency negatively, as examples of how the system did not work. But what she construed as confusion and mixing up of kin terms can also be viewed as a significant source of flexibility (see McDowell 1978b for an example). This is especially apparent in the context of what Mead called "mixed relationships" or those in which two different kin terms might both be applicable. Such relationships can occur in any society, of course, but what occurs when they do varies. Unlike the Arapesh, who resolved the confusion by labeling the relationship "this or that," the Mundugumor reckoned the tie to be half of one and half of the other, and "act as if the personality had been split into two categories, weakening each, but each remaining." With two possible relationships open and consistency not required, people were free to shift between the two at will despite feelings of awkwardness.

What is especially interesting about these ambiguous relations is that in addition to being manipulable according to political and social context, they also presented a field for expressing and communicating personal sentiments, particularly hostility. Even teaching children kin terms provided an opportunity to score points against others. Children were taught what to call each relative separately and were never given systematic schooling. There was no use of what Schieffelin (1976) calls determining a relationship by "relative product." Men tended to teach specific terms to their daughters while women taught other terms to their sons. Each would teach the terms from his or her perspective, and there was ample room to insult a spouse or other relative by teaching children terms that would embarrass or offend the other. A man tended to use his mother's terminology in preference to his father's unless his mother's line had been very confused by incorrect marriages. Daughters were scolded by their fathers if they used their mothers' perspective.

Two examples illustrate the possible confusions and how people used the occasion of a mixed relationship to express an opinion. First, a man married his son's distant classificatory or joking sister (joking is discussed later). The son continued to joke with this sister-mother, thus refusing to regard her as mother (joking of this kind with mother was very inappropriate). He and his father fought over this issue. Second, Alemi married the daughter of his wife by a previous husband. His sons refused to call her mother and insisted that she was their wife (one of their sisters had been used in exchange for her). His daughters had called her sister (because she was a mother's daughter) and also refused to change to mother.

Many mixed relationships, however, did not cause such embarrassment and shame, and people chose which term to use or alternated depending on the context. In one genealogy recorded by Mead, a young man placed 13 of 71 names in a "this-and-that" category, and many of the unequivocal names were those of young children who might later become mixed-relationship relatives. Thus, a large number of the young man's relatives were not terminologically clear and straightforward.

KINSHIP BEHAVIOR

Most people could, if pressed, use a kinship term for almost every other person in the village, and so in a sense kinship behavior encompassed most interpersonal interaction. However, the Mundu-gumor treated presumably all classificatory relationships somewhat differently from nearer or "close blood" relations, and these exhibited a wider range of flexibility than the closer ties.[4] Personal preferences and situations were more important than precise genealogical connection in determining how one person behaved toward another. There were, nevertheless, both ideal rules and typical patterns of behavior (and sometimes patterned deviance from the ideal), and these are described here. I begin with a description of socialization to set the stage for the kin ties between parents and children.

Socialization, Child Rearing, and Childhood

Most of the data Mead gathered on socialization and child rearing as well as her interpretations are presented in *Sex and Temperament* (1963), and there is no need to repeat these here. However, it is important to present some of the information to serve as a backdrop to the discussion of parent-child ties.

Children were not especially prized. The reasons for infanticide, usually accomplished by throwing the infant into the river (either alive or already strangled), reveal that the value of children was low. If a man had not copulated frequently enough with his wife to cause pregnancy, he knew the baby belonged to another man, and such a newborn had little chance to survive. Not only did the husband desire the death of another man's child; he also shamed and berated his wife, the mother, so much that she too would want the offensive offspring killed. Infanticide was also a way to avoid the postpartum sex taboo, an end desired by both men and women.[5] Such a statement, on its own, appears extreme and perhaps is an exaggeration of the people's hostility to children; although the desire to avoid taboos was possibly a major motivation for infanticide, more likely it was an added factor in cases in which there already existed some doubt about the future of the newborn.

The actual cases of infanticide Mead recorded reveal parental motivations. One day Mead observed a bark packet floating by in the river. An informant told her that it contained a dead child from another village. Its mother discarded it because she felt such "anger and desolation" that her husband was in jail. (Later another informant maintained that only the afterbirth was contained in the bark.) In a second case a young woman who was betrothed to a man away at work became pregnant while living with her mother and father. Some informants said that the father of the baby was unknown, but others maintained that her father was the father. She bore twins, and both were killed. In a third case a Kinakatem woman visited relatives in Biwat, was seduced while there, and became pregnant. Her husband refused to take her back and demanded that she be replaced. When the child was born, she killed it. In a fourth case Fortune noted that one man seduced his wife's daughter and his brother's daughter, both in his care; both became pregnant and killed the infants.[6]

Often babies were rescued by someone willing to adopt the child. Sometimes the adopter literally rescued the child from the river still alive, and at other times, suspecting that infanticide would be attempted, he or she was close by at birth and simply took the child. Of the three specific cases of this sort that Mead recorded, one child from an unidentified place was rescued from the river and remained in Kinakatem, one was given to bush villagers (this child was fathered by a woman's first husband—she was pregnant when she went to her second husband—and her second husband wanted the child killed), and the third, whose father simply did not want it, was rescued by a Kinakatem man and raised in the village. The completed infanticides all involved the emotions of shame, anger, or both, but at least two of the three unsuccessful ones did not. It is tempting to speculate that children who were the focus of serious shame or anger succumbed while children whose parents just did not want them were more easily adopted by others.[7]

Mundugumor adoption seems to be on the far end of a continuum in which almost all—if not all—rights to the child were relinquished by the natural parents at adoption. Adopted children were as completely removed from their biological parents as possible; the child did not continue to have significant social or emotional ties with his or her natural parents. If the birth parents showed signs of interest in the child, the child was told that his or her real parents were bush spirits.

Adoption was relatively common. It provided a way for parents to avoid pregnancy and postpartum taboos. When the child was first adopted, the mother was required to avoid her husband for two days (thus imitating birth seclusion), but the new father was subject to no restrictions. Another motive for adopting a child was to acquire an equal number of males and females and so to facilitate brother-sister exchange marriages. (Facilitating such marriages was also the motivation for the institutionalized "feeding" of a sister's child by a man or a brother's child by a woman. A person provided food for a specific child and thus acquired the right to use that child in a future marriage exchange. But this custom was neither adoption nor fosterage; the child remained with the natural parents.)

Mothers were the primary caretakers of infants and young children. A father rarely even held a child (Mead noted only four such occasions). Although people recognized that a danger of strangulation existed, they frequently carried babies in the armpit. As children grew older, they learned to sit astride their mother's neck and shoulders and hold fast to her hair, and they developed a propensity to play with any hair near them (see figs. 3 and 4). After four months babies were not carried in the arms or in a basket but were expected to hold on for themselves. Even when seated mothers rarely held their children, and if a child fell asleep it was simply placed on the ground or in a basket. Only very small, usually female babies were ever carried or held for pleasure, and then only by small girls of other mothers. Mothers were certainly not places of refuge: they laughed at their childrens' fears, hit them for crying when they fell down or got hurt, and joined older children in teasing younger ones. The characterization of a child in panic was that he or she "crawled into the sleeping basket. Darkness represents safety to these children although it represents danger to ours." Frequently a fearful child sought its mother as a place of refuge, but her typical response was not nurturing, and mothers tended to regard their children's fear as amusing. A mother might reassure a child verbally but usually did so laughing. The typical act to comfort a frightened or fretful child, even as old as five, was not to offer the breast but to raise it to the shoulders, and, despite the rather mocking attitude on their mother's part, children were reassured by being lifted in this way.

Suckling behavior reveals much about mother-child interactions, and Mead's own words provide a description of the style:

. . . children are definitely fed here, just as if they were given the bottle. The breast is not to stop tears, comfort terror, and [is] never used playfully. Mothers suckle children in a thoroughly businesslike way, and often in uncomfortable positions—[they stand up], supporting the child awkwardly on raised leg . . . or sit and let the child approach, or bend down and let the child hold the breast like a bottle. No [saying] please, no dallying, no caressing is permitted. When a child is not suckling busily, it is hoisted on the shoulder. . . . Note also that women walk about a great deal, and when elder children cry, they don't sit down to suckle them but they give a perfunctory trickle from the breast only.

Mead did note one case in which a woman tried to use the breast to comfort a child. She had adopted a child and had no milk to give it, so it was suckled by others. She gave it her dry breast to appease it, but the infant took no comfort in this action and continued to wail.[8]

When a nursing infant's mother left the village, she deposited her child with another woman. When the mother returned, she gave the woman part of anything she had acquired while away (e.g., sago or fish). One woman became something of a specialist in nursing babies while their mothers were away. She had no husband to pressure her to wean her own child or become pregnant again and was as "strong as a horse." She made a not inconsiderable material gain from this activity. (Mead highlighted this woman as a deviant in *Sex and Temperament* [1963:230]). Older children who did not require suckling were watched for nothing.

Mead noted an interesting pattern among several women who

were divorced or whose husbands were away for an extended period. If one of these women had a three- or four-year-old child, weaned or about to be weaned, she would sometimes start nursing young infants who belonged to other women or adopt a new child of her own. The woman mentioned earlier, who cared for babies while their mothers were away, had a three-and-a-half-year-old child who was almost completely weaned when she adopted a daughter (one of twins).[9] Another woman, with an already weaned three-year-old daughter, spent time and energy suckling the adopted child of another dry-breasted woman.[10] The first of these women was divorced, and the second's husband was absent from the village. Thus, there was a tendency for relatively independent women to perpetuate the flow of milk in order to suckle the children of others. Women who helped suckle an infant were later given small food gifts at feasts and ceremonies associated with the child's rites of passage.

Children were ideally weaned at about age two on sago soup, and if a child had difficulty making the change, sometimes its mother smeared her nipples with a salt made from burned sago ribs. If a woman became pregnant before weaning, she occasionally nursed the child through the pregnancy, but this resulted in an abrupt transition for the elder nursing child when the newborn arrived. These older children tended to feel rejected in general and might "howl" when any nearby woman nursed her child. The fact that several women, not just the natural mother, would suckle a child also set such children up for what Mead called "group rejection"; that is, the child felt rejected by all lactating women.

Children were made independent very early, and Mead connected independence and lack of fear with weaning. It was not that older children showed less fear but that children weaned in favor of a younger sibling were less fearful, so that a five-year-old who had not been weaned in favor of a younger sibling would exhibit much less independence and more fear in general than a three-year-old who had.

The people's response to Mead's presentation of a doll for the first time is interesting in this context because it reveals a relative fearlessness among children. The predominant response was one of "glee"—people shouted, clapped their hands, and showed very little fear. Small children were frightened only if the doll was presented to them in an unfriendly or threatening way; they showed no fear whatsoever if it was given to them in a friendly fashion.

Mead thought that "remnants of the weaning trauma" were present in only a few cases of violent temper tantrums, which were rare. Mead often described children as "cheerfully disobedient" and noted that they rarely cried, even when they were hurt. Only a few children characteristically had temper tantrums, and in fact Mead recorded few tantrums—six about food (not including many tantrums concerning a mother nursing another child) and four about abandonment or threatened abandonment. Although food-related concerns prompted crying fits, they were not "extended and ramified" as they were among the Mountain Arapesh to harsh voices and refusals of requests. Mead noted only one tantrum that did not involve food or separation themes: the most tantrum-prone child in the village had a crying fit when his mother spanked him for defecating on the ground.

The notes contain few specific references to toilet training. One incident involved a small female toddler, dressed in a "huge fluffy grass skirt," who defecated on the ground in the village. Her mother scolded her in a good-humored way and cleaned up the mess. As punishment (which the child did not understand), the child was deprived of the skirt. The second, more general comment was that children who defecated or urinated in improper places were "shouted at." A man shouted early one morning because his seven-year-old son had defecated in a canoe. The man screamed for someone to come and clean it up. The father "could not beat the child, but he could make a public disturbance and shame him." (Fathers were not supposed to beat their sons, although some did.)

The notes indicate that respect for the property of others was directly taught. One man told his seven-year-old son to come down from another person's unfinished house, which contained some personal items: "Come down, come down, that is the house of another."

When Mead recorded a lengthy text from Omblean in which he describes the significant events of his childhood, one highlight was his theft of bananas from a neighbor's garden and the consequences of that theft (his mother began to beat him, but the neighbor stopped her and said that boys always do such things).

Children slept in the houses of their parents. Sleeping arrangements centered around mats and mosquito nets or baskets. Infants slept with their mothers, separate from fathers, although older children sometimes slept with fathers. One net or basket could accommodate three people. A childless couple might sleep together, and a sick man may have had his wife sleep with him to make him perspire more. It was taboo to share a basket with an affine; this rule effectively prevented a married son or daughter from sharing with a parent because the child's spouse was "conceived to be present." A father could sleep at the mouth of a teenage daughter's basket so that, if she left during the night, he could awaken and follow her to ensure that she was on a natural errand and not meeting a lover. Brothers usually did not share sleeping baskets.

Children tended to eat at home, although if they wandered into a neighboring house, they might be given food. But "mothers dislike having small children running about to other people's houses as it is so much work to look for them." They also feared that young children would drown, so they frightened them into staying close by telling them that their mother's brothers and father's sisters had "long teeth" and would eat them. Children early became sensitive to slights and teasing and avoided places where they might encounter trouble. Children of three or four years wandered about the village but rarely went into other houses. Families usually ate together, with visiting or resident affines at a distance. A child might go to another relative for food, but personal relations rather than kinship category or distance were more important. As soon as he or she was old enough to realize proper avoidances, a child avoided sisters if a brother-in-law was present. In a polygamous household, the first wife was obligated to offer food to all her husband's offspring, but other wives did as they pleased.

Mead brought a group of children together for drawing and recorded what happened. They needed some leadership to begin the project—especially the girls, who only giggled at first and were eventually led away from the boys by one of them—but not for the specifics. There was no copying except for a general tendency to produce a standardized lizard or crocodile design. All the children worked "seriously and quietly" on their drawings, and none exhibited much interest in the work of the others. Some did realistic drawings while others produced more abstract designs. The only criticism that emerged was directed at those who did abstract designs by those who drew more realistically.

Much can be learned by the ways in which children interacted with one another. Although they never played house or played at being married, some of their play was imitative of adult activities, especially ritual and subsistence activities. Sometimes the imitative play was elaborate and involved more than 20 children in coordinated activities. Rarely did boys and girls play together. Mead described children's play as basically fun, unorganized, physical, and noncompetitive. She wondered about

the purposeless nature of the horseplay and the lack of resentment and quarreling found among children. Only one near quarrel witnessed in two months. Elders teasing of youngers is patterned. Lack of resentment over robberies and physical license is patterned. Result is a children's group which ripples and sputters, throws things about, breaks up, reforms, chases, giggles, throws seeds, throws sticks, without any other theme and without quarreling. Plentifulness of food and lack of other material possessions also diminish quarreling.

In all play groups of mixed ages the older children provided the leadership, which often devolved into bullying. Despite the relatively aggressive and certainly physical nature of the play, it rarely turned into serious fighting, and if it did it was usually between "children of very disparate ages, when elders will bait youngers. Young children never see a fist fight, only the playful hitting of joking relationships which they imitate among themselves. . . ." It is difficult to tell whether children were ever seriously injured in these games. Fathers watched to be sure that the weapons, seeds, and fruits used were not too large. A child's response to injury varied according to his or her personality; some made a scene about a minor injury while others weathered serious pain with fortitude.

Adults were easily able to characterize good and bad children. A good boy was one who listened to his parents, quickly fetched items requested, came when called, and worked quickly. Good girls helped their mothers work sago, helped gather food, stayed near the hearth, and did not play with boys. Bad girls ran around, were lazy, played with boys, and only thought about men (not their parents) when they grew up.

Mothers and Adult Children

Much of the interaction between a woman and her children has already been described. Mothers were the primary caretakers and socializing agents of children. But children grow up—what kind of relationship did women have with their adult children?

There are no specific notes on the relationship between a mother and her adult daughters, but several observations allow a glimpse of the content of the relationship. It appeared that mothers and daughters were relatively distant from one another: fathers scolded daughters who used kin terms appropriate to mother or wife; women joined their fathers' ropes as well as patrilineal clans. In *Sex and Temperament* Mead presents a clear picture of a woman's preference for sons over daughters.[11] And yet, mothers and daughters spent much time together, especially working together, while the girls were growing up. In fact, Mead's Daily Events Diary reveals that adolescent girls were frequently in the company of their mothers, and young married women sometimes continued to work with their mothers (e.g., processing sago) after marriage. Interaction with married adult daughters probably waned as the younger women turned their attention to their own husbands and children.

Unlike their sisters, boys and adolescent males spent little time with their mothers, but a strong affective tie existed between mother and son that was inculcated by the mother and her close kin. Mothers defended their sons' interests first and attempted to allocate goods and property to sons rather than daughters. If a woman spotted a large tree appropriate for a big house post, she reserved it in the name of her son. Adult daughters, however, seemed to assist mothers more frequently than adult sons did. For both son and daughter, the relationship with mother was informal and not hedged with taboo, avoidance, or strict respect.

If a woman was widowed or divorced, there was apparently no rule or ideal that stipulated with whom she should live. An examination of the five such women in Kinakatem reveals no pattern, but the sample is not definitive because the choices the women had were restricted: some had no adult living children, and thus we cannot know if they would have preferred to live with a son or daughter.

Fathers and Adult Children

Fathers and daughters were relatively close. Men preferred daughters and sometimes continued to share a sleeping basket with a daughter until her betrothal. Fathers taught kin terms to daughters, and daughters were in the same ropes as well as patrilineal groups as their fathers (but see chapter 5). Fathers defended their daughters' interests in preference to their sons in inheritance and attempted to allocate more goods and property to them. The content of the relationship between a particular father and his daughter depended to a large extent on his motivations concerning her marriage arrangements. Women were supposed to be used in exchanges to acquire wives for their brothers, but men sometimes used their daughters to acquire wives for themselves. In sum, fathers and daughters were close and often allied against mothers and brothers, but the relationship was tinged with some formality; they were, for example, not allowed to joke with one another. Fathers did sometimes beat their daughters, especially for sexual misconduct.

The relationship between men and their adult sons was pervaded by formality; distance as well as respect and avoidance characterized the relationship. Grown sons were forbidden to sit near their fathers "for fear that they would step over something of theirs" and make their fathers sick. Fathers were ashamed to beat their sons. The actual relationship between a father and son depended to an even greater extent than for a daughter on the father's intent and actual activities in regard to arranging the son's marriage. Sons had to be vigilant to ensure that their sisters were not used to acquire more wives for their fathers. This element introduced additional mistrust and increased the tension between father and son.

Siblings

The brother-brother relationship was, like that of father-son, one of formality and respect. Brothers were ashamed in one another's presence and could not sit side by side. Full brothers were required to avoid one another, but a man was obliged to send part of his kill to his brothers. These men were forbidden to enter one another's houses, to ask one another for things, to talk casually or informally, to joke or jest, and to touch one another. If they wanted to speak, they stood a long distance apart. They did quarrel and fight. Unlike a parent and child, brothers could eat from the same plate but not at the same time. Some solidarity existed between brothers, and a term existed to describe a group of brothers. They were also members of the same patrilineal clan and, if brothers of the same mother, the same rope. But, again, competition for wives and the use of sisters to acquire wives introduced an element of hostility and competition. Brothers and indeed patrilineal kinsmen in general almost never cooperated with one another. Writing in 1973 Mead pondered the tie between brothers and, I think, exaggerated the distance between them by saying that "there is a taboo against two brothers who are full brothers ever speaking to each other except in anger." The issue here is a tricky one. Nowhere in the original notes is such a taboo recorded. But what ethnographer writes literally everything in a notebook? Did Mead recall something when she was preparing her monograph? Is this statement an exaggeration, either unwitting or for effect? The notes contain examples of brothers cooperating and coordinating events, so I suspect that the statement is an unwitting exaggeration.

Almost no data are available on the relationship between sisters. Some continued to work together even after marriage, which indicates a close and informal relationship between them. No avoidance rules or taboos applied to sisters, and they exhibited none of the competition that characterized close male kin. Mead did write in *Sex and Temperament* that sisters were more amiable than brothers.

The relationship between a sister and brother was of central social and cultural significance. This importance derived largely from the marriage system, in which brother-sister exchange was the ideal form. Marriage tied a sister and brother together in a special way, and it was through his sister that a man acquired important affines, including his wife. Mead repeatedly notes that there were strong ties between brothers and sisters. Women frequently visited their brothers in other places. Brothers could always go to their sisters for food. No joking was permitted between sister and brother, including cross- and close parallel cousins. Sister and brother could share the same plate of food, but as with brothers they could not eat from it at the same time. As an indication of the strength and closeness of this relationship, Mead noted that young boys, when they were first confronted with a doll (presumably female), cried out, "Sister!" in contrast to the Mountain Arapesh, who typically called out, "Wife!" The relationship between elder sister and younger brother was particularly important, and younger brothers often helped their elder sisters, especially in processing sago. It must also be noted that the brother-sister tie provided the pivot upon which other very significant relationships depended, especially those between mother's brother and sister's child and between father's sister and brother's child.

Mother's Brother and Sister's Child

The frequent references made to the mother's brother–sister's child relationship indicate its significance. Mother's brother played an important part in initiation; he or sister's child (especially sister's son) was an important actor in mortuary rites; and the crocodile-yam feast was specifically an event between these two. Mother's brother and sister's son also performed a central role in the manufacture and launching of the war canoe.

The relationship between mother's brother and sister's son or sister's daughter was basically one of cooperation and friendliness. One could ask one's mother's brother for any item and expect to receive it. One could take things such as food, tobacco, and betel directly from his net bag. Jesting, but only of a nonobscene and asexual nature, characterized the relationship. A man could call his mother's brother or sister's son a bloody fool, take his things, playfully burn his skin, or pretend to be angry, but this banter could not include any sexual references.

There are indications that own mother's real brother was treated with some respect and that informality and jesting were more appropriate for a classificatory mother's brother. Real mother's brothers were "too close" to receive a child's first-achievement offerings, which were given to a distant mother's brother. If a young woman was sexually wayward, presumedly her real mother's brother might join her father and brothers in beating her, and small boys typically did not play with real mother's brothers their own age because they were "ashamed" in their presence.

The mother's brother–sister's child relationship was crucial in a variety of exchange transactions. Some of these have been described in the context of ritual (e.g., the crocodile-yam feasts and initiation rites). Others, such as the all-important skull-pig exchange, are discussed later in the context of marriage and intergenerational exchange.

Father's Sister and Brother's Child

Like the relationship between mother's brother and sister's child, the tie between father's sister and brother's child had significant ritual components. It was father's sister who assisted at birth, initial taboo releasing, and ear and nose piercing and to whom feasts were given by the father on these occasions. Girls gave first-achievement offerings to distant father's sisters. These women were also important in intergenerational exchange transactions (as will be discussed later).

The relationship between father's sister and brother's child was also one of easy informality and jesting. The banter did have limits: there was no sexual joking, father's sister could not be called old, and neither could refer to the attire of the other. They could take each other's food, betel, and tobacco and pretend to fight and quarrel. Mead described the behavior between them as "roughhousing" that included pushing, poking, thrusting, and pulling.[12] This kind of jesting behavior was more likely to occur between father's sister and brother's son rather than brother's daughter.

If the ideal marriage process had taken place, father's sister married mother's brother, and the relationship a person had with father's sister was inextricably related to that with mother's brother. Furthermore, the relationship a man had with his sister and her husband (his child's father's sister and possibly real but at least classificatory mother's brother), and the exchanges that took place between these kin and their descendants also colored the whole complex of kin ties surrounding the father's sister–brother's child relationship.

Classificatory Siblings

Kinship terms for brothers and sisters included at least first, second, and perhaps third cross- and parallel cousins, but the Mundugumor differentiated distant classificatory siblings from close ones and behaved differently toward them. It is not possible to draw a precise line between close and distant siblings because there were shades of behavioral variation rather than distinctly demarcated categories. The phrase *shemi mepake* (pl. *shemili mapakate*) referred to a distant sister, whereas a close sister, usually including first cross- and parallel cousins, was called *shemi maketi*.

There is evidence that distance was reckoned by generation even though all these cousins were called by the same basic terms. First cousins were not permitted to joke with one another, nor could they marry; second cousins, particularly cross-cousins, could joke with one another, but they too could not marry; third cousins also joked but were allowed to marry (indeed, specific third cross-cousins were the ideal marriage partners). Certain kinds of cross-cousins had ritual and exchange obligations toward one another's children. Distant classificatory siblings, in addition to providing a pool of potential marriage partners, could also be ritually transformed into special kinds of relatives, called *kamain*, who also could not intermarry. Joking seems to have provided the mediating means by which close relationships, to which the incest taboo applied, were transformed over time into distant relationships, those between whom sex and marriage were not only possible but also desirable.

The joking that took place between classificatory siblings, unlike that between mother's brother and sister's child or father's sister and brother's child, was primarily sexual, and the relationship was characterized by few if any elements of respect. Distant brothers and sisters could not make reference to one another's genitals, but a man could say to his classificatory sister, "'Your grass skirt is rotten, your ass is no good, you never wash, your grass skirt is really filthy. Your ass is full of shit, it stinks.'" A sister replied to her classificatory brother with similar comments.

The joking between two distant brothers was almost the opposite. There were no anal jokes, and the teasing centered almost exclusively on the genitals: "'Your cock is too big. I think it is always in a woman. You have no shame. You are always using it. Your balls are too big.'" Similar but sexually appropriate content characterized the joking between classificatory sisters: "'Your cunt is too big. It's covered with hair. I think your lover drinks milk from your breasts. I think you screw around with lots of men, and now your cunt is rotten.'" Along with this joking went playful behavior similar to that described between a person and his or her mother's brother or father's sister, including thrusting, poking, and pushing. Joking with the spouse of a distant sibling ceased on the death of that sibling.[13]

Neither Mead nor Fortune speculates on the unusual pattern of joking here, that intergenerational relatives (primarily mother's brother–sister's child and father's sister–brother's child) could not joke about sexual matters, that the jokes between same-sex siblings referred to the genitals while those between opposite-sex siblings contained anal references. Without much more detailed data, especially about the context in which these jokes occurred, one can only speculate on the meaning of this pattern. It is possible that intergenerational relations required more respect or were less ambiguous than those between distant siblings—no mediator over time was required here; the lack of any specifically sexual elements in the actual relationship between same-sex siblings allowed the expression of ambivalence through sexual references, whereas the sexual tension between opposite-sex classificatory siblings may have required the muting of sexual references. It is also possible that Mead was not in the field long enough to obtain a random sample of this behavior; the notes contain only examples, not normative statements from informants about what should happen. Perhaps Mead's sample of joking was simply biased.

All joking ceased if marriage occurred between classificatory siblings (i.e., third cousins). Mead suggests that joking was a way to create distance between these relatives: "It is all obscene . . . and may be interpreted as an attempt to break down the last vestige of kinship feeling in these distant cases."

Grandparents and Grandchildren

The relationship between grandparents and grandchildren was one of friendliness and cooperation. Grandparents were typically kind to their grandchildren and rarely angry with them. A grandmother helped her daughter's son by urging her own son (the grandson's mother's brother) to get busy and kill a pig for his sister's son. Unlike other ties, cooperation was especially important in this relationship.

It is something of an anomaly that a grandfather, who was treated with warmth, friendliness, and little formality, was sometimes terminologically transformed into an elder brother, a relationship characterized by a measure of avoidance and always respect. Mead indirectly suggests two explanations for this. The first is that the grandparent might have been conceived to be a distant, not close, sibling, and thus joking behavior was appropriate. The joking was in fact like that between classificatory same-sex siblings in its content—that is, primarily sexual. The notes do not clearly state that such joking occurred between an actual grandparent and grandchild but suggest that it was typical behavior with a classificatory grandparent, especially with one related affinally.

The second possible component in the resolution of this anomaly involves the concept of helping. The jesting, especially with classificatory grandparents, was viewed as a way of helping the grandparent: ". . . a small boy is said to 'help' his grandfather, and so he can call his grandfather's wife, wife and his sister, sister."

Despite the anomaly, the behavior that characterized the relationship was clearly one of familiarity, cooperation, and friendliness. The terminological equation of a woman's father's mother and a man's mother's father with an elder sibling occurred only during the child's youth; adults usually referred to their grandparents with the terms specifically for them.

The notes are not clear whether all grandparents or only those in the child's rope were subjected to this terminological switch, but all grandparents were treated with friendliness and cooperation, which they reciprocated. There is no indication that the actual behavior was different toward a man's mother's father or a woman's father's mother, although the possibility certainly exists that the helping by jesting may have been more significant in the relationship to these two particular kinds of grandparents.

Kamain

An additional relationship should be mentioned here, although there is some question as to whether it legitimately belongs under the rubric of kinship. More than anything else it was an exchange partnership, but it was based on kin ties and had a significant impact on kin relations. Mead did not list it as a kinship tie and occasionally contrasted the two.[14]

Extracting the data on this relationship from Mead's notes presents two problems. The first is a confusion of terms. At times she referred to the tie as *kamain*, at other times as *wareun*. These are two separate types of relationships, but which label goes with which is not clear. The confusion comes from the fact that the pidgin term *pren* is used for both, and because Mead was working primarily in pidgin the distinction is not always apparent. I use the word *wareun* to refer to the nonkin trading partners who usually lived in distant villages and the word *kamain* for the kin-based relationship described here. The Bun use the term *wareum* for trading partner and *kamain* for this special part-kin, part-exchange relationship, and it seems more than likely that the same was true for the Mundugumor. The nature of the relationship in these two places seems to be very similar if not identical, and in 1981 informants certainly described a *kamain* as similar to the tie in Bun.

The second problem in describing the *kamain* relationship is one that does not frequently arise because Mead was a thorough and methodical ethnographer: the relationship was apparently so memorable that she used only brief phrases and short descriptions in her notes, probably assuming that she would remember. The detailed data were perhaps in her head but not in the notes. The descriptions are cursory and sometimes enigmatic, such as a reference to the fact that a *kamain* was able to perform the "falling down feast," but nowhere is there a description of what the "falling down feast" is. Because I am familiar with the *kamain*-related "falling down feast" in Bun, the reference makes some sense to me, and the temptation exists to fill in the gaps with Bun data. Although the Bun assert that the Mundugumor do exactly as they do, this assertion must not be accepted as fact (see especially McDowell 1976). I have resolved this problem and, I hope, kept the data in their proper contexts by first giving Mead's statements and references and then Fortune's and, finally, briefly describing the relationship in Bun. This procedure will provide at least some sense of what the *kamain* relationship is all about.

The following are the only substantive comments made by Mead about the *kamain* relationship. "Note that . . . kinship obligations can be translated into a *kamain* or can initiate a kind of *kamain.*" Marriage with this kind of person (and his or her close kin) was forbidden. A *kamain* was called by that term, and his or her relatives were treated terminologically as if he or she was a sibling. *Kamain* relationships were initiated only with distant brothers. If a *kamain* "were in progress and the child of one dies, the other will take the skull [to decorate]. This will then be [reciprocated] by the next death on the opposite side. . . ." The *kamain* relationship was "an exchange partnership" between two people for whom fighting was taboo. "The two *kamain* band together . . . against anyone who starts a fight, and this preserves the peace." Distant siblings (i.e., potential *kamain*) can repeat any mishap experienced by the other—such as falling down or capsizing a canoe—and demand a feast, which is later reciprocated. In a letter to Boas Mead wrote the following:

There is . . . a sort of inexplicit dual division in the existence of a relationship called [*kamain*], ceremonial friends. . . . These are inherited either patrilineally or [if] father's *kamain* group becomes depleted, a man may have as *kamain*, the sister's son of his mother's brother's *kamain*. *Kamain* anoint each other . . . in initiation and have to be paid heavily for ceremonially imitating each other's misfortunes. Both of these functions can also be discharged by father's sisters for girls and mother's brothers for boys.[15]

Fortune's observations on this topic are scattered and fragmentary, but the frequency of references does indicate something of the importance of the relationship. He did note that newly established *kamain* exchanged flutes as well as feasts. Some of his notes also seem to hint that making a *kamain* relationship was a significant way of establishing peace. He also noted that one man and his child had worked a garden together, and then the child drowned. The father tabooed his garden in mourning, and his *kamain* and the *kamain*'s wives removed the produce from the garden and gave it to the grieving father.

Although these references are indeed sparse, it is possible to draw some conclusions from them. First, although Mead contrasted this relationship with kin, it was in fact derived from the tie between distant siblings. (Mead always used distant brothers and did not mention whether women or sisters were involved; in Bun women are as concerned and active as men in *kamain* activities.) The second significant thing is the processual nature of the relationship— it was created by those who initiated and participated in it. A kinship relation was purposefully turned into that of a *kamain*, basically an exchange relation. The behavioral elements were respect, some avoidance, and a taboo on fighting, which could affect others if one chose to exercise his or her ability to sanction a *kamain*. Finally, a *kamain* could begin a feasting sequence with the other by imitating a misfortune.

These few clues indicate that the relationship between *kamain* among the Mundugumor was very similar to that in Bun. In Bun people transact in three mutually exclusive modes: they can share (close kin), they can exchange marital partners (affines), or they can exchange goods *(kamain)*. The *kamain* relationship is based on a ritual transformation of the cross-cousin relationship (in Bun cross-cousins are terminologically distinct from siblings), and the relationship once begun is inherited. Cross-cousins joke with one another (much like distant siblings among the Mundugumor) until the ambiguous nature of the relationship is resolved either through marriage or transformation into *kamain*, when joking ceases and respect becomes prominent. The behavior between the two is characterized by respect and avoidance. They cannot sit near one another, mention sex in the presence of the other, quarrel, or be familiar in any way. Name taboos are strictly observed. If any of these strictures is violated, people feel a sense of profound shame, and the Bun often use the word "shame" to describe the basic nature of the tie between two *kamain*. An important aspect of the relationship is the reciprocal giving that takes place. Any significant event is marked by a feast, and the largest portion of goods distributed always goes to the feast-giver's *kamain*. Special feasts take place between the two even after the series of reciprocal transactions that began and established the relationship. Ideally, exchanges are always balanced and equal; the tie is not one of competitiveness but of distant equality. In Bun, too, *kamain* possess a ritual means of stopping quarrels. The reduplication of misfortune, especially falling down, also could initiate a feasting sequence. (For further data on the *kamain* relationship in Bun, see especially McDowell 1976, 1980a.)

MARRIAGE

Arranging marriages was a serious focus of concern that consumed much time and energy. In addition to its other functions—economic, political, reproductive, and psychological—marriage was also a pivotal mechanism in ordering the social structure and the system of intergenerational exchange that gave shape and form to interpersonal relations and, over time, the society itself. I devote three sections here to marriage. In the first I discuss courtship and sex, then move on to behavior in marriage (including husband-wife relations, polygamy, co-wife interaction, and divorce), and behavior among affines. The second section concerns marriage rules, and the third describes the marriage process and illustrates the complexity of marriages and the transactions they entailed.

Courtship and Sex

Mundugumor marriages were ideally arranged by parents and other relatives, but young people frequently had their own ideas that they were sometimes able to realize. After a sexual affair lovers might convince their parents to assent to and arrange an exchange that included their marriage. Women objected more than men to marrying a person of their parents' choice. That women were not always passive pawns in men's games is illustrated in a case recorded by Fortune. Because it also shows that quick thinking and the preferences of the wife givers for a particular affine could deprive the rightful man of his wife (and that quarrels had serious repercussions), it is worth quoting. The main characters are depicted in genealogy 2.

Mashamba's mother's brother's daughter, Ivandu, was [designated to be the sister used] for a wife for her father's father's younger brother's daughter's son, Kombokata. . . . [But] Ivandu ran away to Kuainvoh. Kombokata [was angry with those who had helped] . . . Ivandu to elope. . . . Mashamba came running, got here first, and [said] to Kuainvoh that he wasn't [angry, although it would be appropriate to be angry], but he didn't want to be. He had come alone. He suggested that he would . . . marry Kuainvoh's sister [in exchange for Ivandu; the sister should have gone to Kombokata]. They said alright. They tell him, "You stay here now. Don't go back." The [resulting] quarrel [between Kombokata and those who helped Ivandu elope] lasted a long time.

Girls were ideally virgins *(avonalep)* when they married. Their husbands were aware that first intercourse should produce some blood,

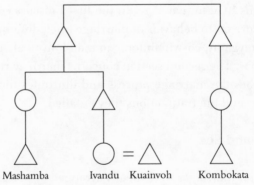

Genealogy 2. Kuainvoh marries Ivandu

but a man did not tell others if by this criterion his new wife was not a virgin; he was too ashamed and simply said nothing. It was the public knowledge of the fact that was troublesome rather than the woman's previous sexual experience. Mead suggested that the term *avonalep* be translated as "social virgin" or one not disgraced by public scandal. A woman who had eloped, borne an illegitimate child, or had an affair that became public knowledge was called *depiak* and theoretically could not be used in an exchange for a virgin. Although neither Mead nor Fortune indicate so, it is probable that powerful men such as Alemi and Mongova were able to force others to accept a *depiak* in exchange for a virgin, and it is certainly possible that others did so as well to execute exchanges.

It is safe to say that observance of this standard was not strict, as the marital histories given later illustrate. Girls were taught that sex was important and pleasurable. From childhood on they were taught to make their own sentimental choices and to take the initiative in their relations with boys and later with men. Although boys were warned about the potential sorcery involved in playing with many women, they also used love magic to seduce desirable women. The notes do not include any reference to the polluting or debilitating effects of sex other than that (1) the use of the mouth during the sexual act was forbidden for fear that sexual fluids might get into food and that (2) young men grew tired if they copulated too frequently. Young men were especially interested in beautiful girls and women—those with good eyes and long, straight noses.

Women were very active sexual beings. Some of the advice young men received from older men was not to hurry or the woman would not like it. Groups of girls masturbated with pepper catkins in their urinating places. A woman's sexual feeling was localized in her clitoris. "Women whose husbands are away are said to feel their clitorises get up and to go about . . . looking for a new man." Despite the advice young men received, women spoke of their preferences in terms of a long penis over a short one rather than the duration of intercourse. Women talked among themselves and were critical of men who did not meet their requirements, but men did not appreciate such talk. "Women who complain of not being satisfied are asked, are you stone or wood? As for us, we are flesh (i.e., can't last forever)." A husband thus criticized might be angry enough to attempt to catch his wife in adultery. Women who were excessively demanding were "reproached, 'you are like a hole in a tree, always wanting a long penis while we are content with short ones.'"

Sexual foreplay, which usually included biting the shoulders, was violent and aggressive. Mead noted a "lack of diffuse cutaneous sensation, lack of [foreplay involving the] breasts. . . ." The position for sexual intercourse was the "missionary" position.

Behavior in Marriage

The relations between a husband and wife depended upon a variety of factors. How the marriage was established—whether desired by the man and woman or arranged as a sister-brother exchange or by the levirate—influenced its character and the partners' behavior. Polygyny was also a factor. And, as is true everywhere, the personalities (see Mead 1963) and personal attributes such as physical characteristics or village of origin also affected the nature of the tie. Despite these variations, one cannot escape the general impression that marriages were typically stormy affairs and that peaceful domestic relations seem to have been exceptional.

Marriages were particularly fragile during their early stages, especially before the birth of children. Young people were often somewhat shy, hesitant, and ashamed about having a spouse. The character of this settling-in period depended to a large extent on how the marriage had been established. If the two people had already been lovers and had desired, even insisted upon, the union, then relations were relatively smooth.

Arranged marriages in which the partners did not care about each other were different. These marriages were prone to failure, and recognizing this people often refrained from completing the exchange until they were sure that the initial marriage was secure.

When a young wife returned to visit her kin, often her counterpart or brother's new wife returned to visit her family as well, thus reflecting a lack of confidence in the arrangements. Young wives avoided their new husbands in public until the marriage was firmly established. The case of Numba, a 16-year-old son of Alemi, and his potential marriage is illustrative. A marriage was arranged for him, and he slept with this new wife for two nights and then decided that he did not like her and threw her out of his mosquito net. She remained in Alemi's compound while Numba was scolded and berated about his behavior. Although Mead listed these two in her census as married, nothing was resolved during her stay in Kinakatem. (Informants in 1981 reported that she had married someone in Akuran, so the marriage with Numba never did take place.) Young males were not alone in rejecting spouses provided by their relatives. One of Mongova's daughters was grown but refused to marry. Her father arranged marriages for her and sent her off to new husbands, but she always returned. Mead suggested that elder daughters were more able to resist arranged marriages because they could argue that their younger sisters were still available. No such option was available to the younger girls, who thus felt the pressure to conform more than did their older sisters.

Marriages based on leviratic inheritance were somewhat less fragile for two reasons. The first is that participants were older and more mature. The second is that at least to some extent they were based on mutual affinity. A widow was unlikely to join the household of a man she did not like. Most leviratic marriages were between a widow and her deceased husband's classificatory brother.

Once the initial uncertain stage of the marriage was past and the union firmly established, a variety of factors influenced the behavior of wife and husband. One of the most significant and complicating of these was polygyny. Only strong and forceful men married more than one woman at the same time, for only such a man could handle several women and the affinal obligations inherent in each marriage. Although the ideal for a man was to have many wives, only

Alemi and Mongova successfully achieved the ideal. (Polygyny was still practiced in 1981, and informants indicated that only important and strong men were able to have more than one wife.)

Men had favored wives and unfavored ones. In some cases the favored wives were simply younger and more attractive, but in others they were older, more mature and reliable women who worked hard to produce tobacco and other items their husbands needed (the garden labor women provided was a major motivation for polygyny). In some cases wives would be so out of favor that they seemed not to be married at all. In a note about sleeping arrangements Mead wrote that "Kunisi, aged nine, sleeps alone with his widowed mother in her sleeping bag." The word "widowed" was crossed out, and there immediately followed this addendum: "Note the fact that I wrote widowed here is significant. Although she is the *luluai's* wife, she might just as well be a widow; she depends entirely upon her children for food and affection."

Although there were occasional examples of cooperation, the relationship between co-wives was almost always a stormy one. Competition for the husband's resources and attention, for their children as well as for themselves, and jealousy were usual. Established wives objected to the addition of new ones, and co-wives regularly quarrelled with and insulted one another.

The complications of polygyny were not the only source of quarrels and strife in marriage; other issues brought a wife and husband into conflict. Many couples argued over the fate of a newborn child, while others disputed the marital exchange arrangements of their children, especially if the husband wanted to use one of his own daughters in exchange for an additional wife for himself or if he wanted to marry the daughter of his wife by a former husband. There were two cases of the latter situation, both involving important men. Alemi was successful in marrying Neneminah, the grown child of his wife Orendena, but the marriage caused considerable conflict between Alemi and Orendena. In the second case Mongova married a widow named Sangofelia, and she bore him two children. When she was in her third pregnancy by Mongova, he announced that he wanted to marry her adolescent daughter from her first marriage. She refused to permit the marriage and sent the girl to live with her deceased husband's brother. Sangofelia herself took her children and left. Eventually other marital arrangements were made for the girl, and her mother lived with her and never returned to Mongova.

A wife's absence was a frequent reason to quarrel, especially when the wife was from a nearby village and often went to visit her natal family, sometimes staying for extended periods. One man angrily greeted his wife on her return, only to see her turn around again and go back to her brother in another village. Often quarrels between a wife and husband concerned food preparation, but sometimes quarrels between spouses were only manifestations of other conflicts and resentments. In one case a man beat his wife because he was angry with her brother over the rights to a stand of sago palm. Quarrels between a husband and wife could also affect other kin ties.

Mead noted that wives were "always running away." The main defensive response of women whose husbands abused them or who were fed up was simply to pick up and leave. If a woman did not like her husband, especially early in a marriage, she just left. Women usually returned to their natal kin, particularly their brothers, for shelter, and some never returned. If a man beat his wife, there were no formal payments to her or her kin for spilling her blood, nor were there any recognized procedures for getting the woman back. Husbands usually beat their wives with their fists and sometimes with sticks; only occasionally was a woman scarified with crocodile teeth. One strategy women used against their husbands was to cover themselves with white clay as a sign of mourning and cry ceremonially at the edge of the village when they were beaten.

In Fortune's notes are recorded the stories of women who did not fare well in their marriages, but it is not clear whether these are based on fact or are tales oft told by men. One is about a woman who did not like her husband and perhaps committed adultery; her husband threw her out. She searched for another husband elsewhere but found none. (The reasons for her lack of success are not given, unless it was the fact that she had pus-ridden sores around her eyes, but, given the penchant for adding wives to work in the gardens, this reason seems insufficient.) She went from village to village and in each was gang-raped. Some places tried to sell her as a captive to Anduar, but each time she escaped. One man did try to take her in, but she insulted him, and he threw her out. Finally, she was killed. Two other women ostensibly met a similar fate.

Divorces were messy but not infrequent. They caused extensive conflict because if the marriage had been an arranged brother-sister exchange, the other intermarrying pair was left with no corresponding reciprocal exchange. The husband in the continuing marriage was under pressure to replace his sister (the divorcing or divorced woman). If marriage payments had been made instead of an exchange, demands for the return of the goods were made.

It is difficult to calculate a reliable divorce rate because so many arranged marriages never became established: should they be included as a marriage and a divorce or not designated as a marriage at all? Numba, for example, slept with his wife for two nights and then discarded her—is this a marriage and subsequent divorce or not a marriage at all? Instability in the first year or two makes it particularly difficult to calculate any precise divorce rate. Established marriages may have involved partners who had tried out several others before settling down.

However, after children were born marriages did tend to be more stable. Among the 47 adult women who were pregnant or had borne a child, Mead listed only 5 of them as having previously been involved in a divorce (one of them had divorced two previous husbands). Two were not coresiding with their husbands, and divorce seemed imminent. Eleven of these women were remarried widows, and another was an unremarried widow. The remaining 28, as far as Mead knew, were still married to their first established husbands. Thus, if one looks only at established marriages and disregards the shaky initial first few years, the divorce rate is only a little more than 10 percent.

Affines

Although some joking did occur between distant classificatory brothers-in-law and female affines were permitted to delouse one another (males were not), the relationship between affines was generally one of respect and near avoidance, especially if the affines were of opposite sex.[16] A man could not address his brother's wife or enter her house if his brother was not present; if he remained outside and called out, she was supposed to remain silent out of shame. A woman avoided her husband's brother whenever possible. If she entered a house in which he was present, she would "sit down at the other end and hang her head," and if the encounter occurred outside, in a group or gathering, she would skirt the edges of the crowd. (Such behavior was sometimes exhibited by a newly marked wife and husband.) A man could not ask his son's wife for food or firewood because that might indicate his immaturity or dependence.

Respect and avoidance also characterized the relationship between same-sex affines. A woman and her son's wife, for example, were required to eat at a distance from each other. Children of both sexes were shy in the presence of a sister's new husband and hesitated to eat while they remained in his presence. The relationship between brothers-in-law was also formal and distant. They could not sleep together, nor could they ask one another for food, although it could be given voluntarily. Mead's notes contain a contradiction as to whether or not a man could request betel nut from his sister's husband or wife's brother, but it is clear that rummaging around in his net bag in search of betel was forbidden. A man could not sit near his brother-in-law or where his affine had recently sat. Affines of the same or opposite sex were never allowed to share the same mosquito basket.

Despite the respect and formality inherent in the relationship, affines were also a source of aid and assistance. These were the relatives who helped by giving their labor for major tasks such as house building. Brothers-in-law and sons-in-law were likely to assist and

were fed or given tobacco at the completion of the task. Affinal kin
from other villages, especially those from the Grass Country, were a
good source of labor if they desired to maintain the trading connections established or strengthened by the marriage. Alemi, for example, had several affines in Grass Country villages who were almost always in attendance when he undertook a major construction
task.

The relationship between brothers-in-law was particularly important, especially if the two men had married each other's sisters. The
ideal was for them to assist each other frequently and regularly. The
tie was one of friendship and support, and some men visited their
brothers-in-law in distant villages. However, this kind of close and
friendly tie was likely to develop only if the establishment of the
initial marriage and subsequent events had gone smoothly and
without conflict, an ideal not regularly achieved. A variety of factors
caused the affinal relationship to sour. If there had been a dispute
about the marriage, if a woman spent too much time with her natal
relatives, if there had not been a sister exchange, if payments at the
initial marriage had not been adequate, if conflict over resources
existed between the men, if the husband beat his wife too much or
without just cause and she obtained shelter from her brother—these
and a variety of other possible factors caused conflict between
brothers-in-law, and tension rather than cooperation was the norm.
If brothers-in-law were angry, their insults were restricted—ideally,
of course—to references to defecation, and no sexual insults were
permitted.

Sister's husband and wife's brother had significant obligations toward each other. A man was required to provide a feast for his wife's
brothers on the death of his wife. If a man had more than one wife,
he was obligated to feast all his brothers-in-law, not just the brothers
of the deceased wife. Many other exchange and feast obligations
between brothers-in-law were indirect ones in that they were
phrased as being obligations of their children. For example, many
of the obligations between a boy and his mother's brother were at
least partially borne by the boy's father and thus actually involved

brothers-in-law. These affines were central figures in the complex system of transactions that hinged on marriage, but to understand this system marriages rules and the structure of marriage must be examined.

Marriage Rules

The Mundugumor had a variety of marriage rules. One could not marry someone who belonged to one's own patrilineal clan or to the patrilineal clan of one's own mother, nor could one marry a *kamain* or a *kamain*'s affine. Marriage between close relatives was forbidden, as was marriage between any classificatory relatives except siblings.

The exogamy of totemic groups is unclear.[17] Some informants insisted that the rule of exogamy held, but others disagreed. Those who said that such unions were permissible had usually already contracted such a marriage. Given Mead's depiction of the Mundugumor in 1932 as people who were upset because no one ever followed the rules, it is interesting to note that informants in 1981 told me that totemic groups were indeed exogamous, that it was taboo to marry someone with the same totem, but also that now people just ignore the rules and do what they please.

The proper marriage was between two people who were of the same generation[18] and who were classificatory siblings but very distant ones. In fact, the ideal marriage partner was a third cross-cousin; second cross-cousins were reckoned to be too close for marriage. When third cross-cousins married, the feeling was that the originating sibling pair, the third ascending generation, should be dead (a likely event in any case). Nonkin were acceptable marriage partners, especially for big men who wanted many wives and might not be required to reciprocate, but the ideal was with a third cross-cousin.

Marriage rules were also inextricably related to the phenomenon of ropes because the ideal marriages between distant classificatory siblings were designed to reunite ropes after several generations. I postpone discussion of these until after the presentation on the nature of ropes. It must be noted here that although these rules existed, they were not always observed. The extent to which the rules were violated is evident in the cases presented here. Most significant is the fact that the ideal marriage with cross-cousins was easily ignored in order to execute an exchange marriage.

THE MARRIAGE PROCESS

Among the Mundugumor there was an additional rule that stipulated not only whom but also how one should marry; that is, there was a rule about the process of marriage. The ideal was unquestionably to marry by brother-sister exchange. Unions in which a man gave his affines goods instead of his own sister in return were permitted but not preferred. One informant, when asked why he could not marry his own sister, replied, "How would I pay for her? I must send my sister away to get a wife." That comment reveals a significant attitude about the centrality of exchange in Mundugumor marriage. The proper marriage was arranged by second cross-cousins for their children. A man arranged with his classificatory mother's brother's daughter for an exchange of their children. Mead's notes include the fact that this ideal marriage arrangement (i.e., between third cross-cousins of a particular kind) pertained only to firstborn children but that all children were supposed to marry by exchange even if it was not with the appropriate cross-cousin.

In 1981 this ideal still obtained: people were supposed to marry by brother-sister exchange, and parents tried to arrange such marriages. Exchange marriage was almost always mentioned by people when I asked what things remained from the past. Older informants said that one's partner also ought to be a distant cousin. They said that exchange is a good way to marry because it prevents a man from being wild and discourages divorce. If a man has no sister available, he could pay bridewealth; informants gave figures between 50 and 700 kina (in 1981 one kina was equivalent to $1.30 in U.S. dollars). Some couples marry in the church today.

Achieving the ideal entailed many problems, of course. The Mundugumor recognized that the first children of second cross-cousins were not always of the appropriate age and sex for a brother-sister exchange, and they had a way to rectify such demographic problems. If a person, especially a man, wanted to execute the proper exchange for his children but did not have ones the correct age or sex to exchange with his classificatory mother's brother's daughter, he could feed or provide general support for his sister's child and then use this child in the exchange as if he or she was his own. Ideally, the appropriate sister was the one he himself used in exchange for his own wife, and thus these children were also his wife's brother's children. The general rule was to feed the children of one's opposite-sex sibling to use in a marital exchange. Thus, from the perspective of the children whose marriages were being arranged, those who were being fed were cross-, not parallel, cousins (see diagram 5). In the diagram E (with his wife, F) could feed and then use the children of H (and her husband, G) to execute exchanges with the children of A and B. A (and her husband B) could feed and then use the children of D (and his wife, C) for the same purpose. A problem with this method of balancing imbalances was that those doing the feeding were too often in a hurry to lay their claims and began to feed and provide support before the child was born. By doing this they did achieve the proper age balance but often ended up laying claim to a child of the wrong sex.

The Mundugumor permitted the groom to send payments to his new affines in lieu of a sister. This method was more acceptable when the groom had no available sister or was an up-and-coming young man or an established big man or when the bride's male kin already had wives. In these cases the groom's family was obligated to provide a large amount of goods including rings, shells, and food. The woman's side gave pots, net bags, baskets, spears, bows, arrows, and sometimes slitgongs. The payment from the bride's side was part of a dowry that the woman brought to marriage regardless of

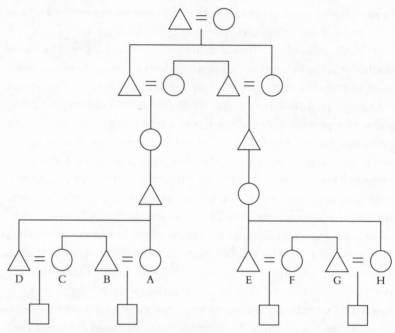

Diagram 5. Feeding another's child

whether it was by exchange or payment. It typically included pots, net bags, fish nets, ladles, and sago-turning sticks. A woman also brought to her marriage a crocodile flute, her most significant inheritance. When a wife was acquired by payment rather than exchange, the groom's family was supposed to give the bride's family one of these sacred items as well. (Two, one belonging to each bride, would be transferred in an exchange marriage; two were thus supposed to be transferred in payment marriage as well.) A significant attitude about marriage is revealed in the following note:

The whole idea . . . of paying for a woman with a [crocodile flute] may be just [as] a valued object, or might be, so to say, "by marrying your sister I have robbed you in a way in which I can not repay you. But here is such an object as my sister would have brought which you can have for your children." [In the original the entire quotation was in capital letters.]

Thus the equation of sacred flutes with women was expressed in both kinds of marital transaction.

A third way to acquire a wife was by the levirate, by which a man would acquire a widow as wife from a distant male relative, usually a classificatory brother but sometimes other relatives such as mother's brother (see Kelly 1977 for a discussion of different forms of widow remarriage). A man was not allowed to take the wife of a close relative, only a distant one. Widows, especially if they were strong and determined, had some choice as to whether they remarried at all and if so, whom. Fortune's notes include a case in which a woman refused to marry a man who had been born with no foreskin. She and other women were afraid of him, and despite the fact that she was his father's brother's son's widow and he wanted to marry her, she refused and was supported by others. Furthermore, there was some competition among eligible men for the right to marry a widow, just as there was competition among close agnates for the right to use a sister in a marriage exchange.

A final road to marriage was with strangers and nonkin from non-Mundugumor villages. Mundugumor men, particularly big men with many wives, did marry women from enemy communities. A few foreigners came from downriver groups (there were no cases of marriage with upriver groups), but most came from villages in the Grass Country. Mead suggested that there were two types of marriage between Mundugumor men and Grass Country women (few Mundugumor women married swamp-dwelling men). In one a woman was sent to an important man (such as Alemi or Mongova) to initiate or ensure a trade connection. Although Mead does not mention it, these generally one-way alliances surely had a political as well as economic function. Sometimes such wives were paid for. The second type of marriage was with women of the Grass Country who ran away from their homes to marry Mundugumor men. Typically these were women who were "regarded as unimportant and are given to no-account men. . . ." Grasslands women "are continually running away and only payment given." It is an indication of political hegemony that although grasslands villagers expected and requested women in return, they almost never received them. It took an unusual circumstance or situation for a Mundugumor woman to marry and remain in the Grass Country. Mead recorded only one case. When Biobi's father died, she married a man in Akuran, but he soon died. She married a second time but left this husband and went to stay with her classificatory brother who tried (or did) seduce her, whereupon she ran away and married a "Grass Man." When the people of Kinakatem demanded a woman in return, the grasslands villagers refused and said that one of Alemi's wives had never been reciprocated. They wanted Biobi to begin to rectify an already existing imbalance. The people of Kinakatem, however, did not accept this reasoning and continued to demand a return. If pacification had not already taken place and warfare and raiding ended, Kinakatem might have raided the grasslands village and just taken a return, but they did not. They lessened their demand by insisting that they receive at least one of Biobi's children.

These, then, were the recognized means of marriage: brother-sister exchange, payment, levirate, or paymentless marriage with a foreigner. Big men and successful polygynists such as Alemi and Mongova utilized all four means of acquiring wives, and Mead astutely noted that there was a pattern: "In cases of polygamy, the first two or three wives come from exchange, later ones are bought, inherited, or run away from the Grass." This makes sense in the context of the process by which a man acquired power. A young man needed a wife, and his first marriage was usually by exchange, but as he matured and gained a reputation, it was easier for him to acquire additional wives without sister exchange. His first one or two wives could also help generate the means by which he could acquire additional wives by payment. It was only after he had established himself as an influential man that he could easily activate leviratic rights to widows and pull foreign women without payment.

A detailed look at Alemi's marital history illustrates these processes. By 1932 he had had 13 wives in all. How he married 4 of them is not clear. Two he simply took—1 from an older relative, the other from a grasslands village. Two he paid for, and 1 he obtained through the levirate. He acquired 1 wife by sister exchange with Mongova. The remaining 3 he also got through exchange, but in these cases he used not a sister but one of his own daughters to acquire a wife for himself. In 1932 he had 14 living daughters and 9 living sons, so he did have spare daughters. He had made marital exchanges for his 4 oldest sons with daughters (their sisters), leaving 5 sons yet to have their marriages arranged. He allowed Omblean, who perhaps was a classificatory son, to use 1 of his daughters to finalize his marriage to Ndebami (Sangofelia's daughter, whom Mongova wished to marry while married to Sangofelia; as Alemi and Mongova were keen rivals, Alemi must have had some political motivations in doing this). Thus Alemi used 5 of his 14 daughters on sons, real and classificatory, and even though he used 3 for himself he did not squander all his daughters and leave his sons without sisters. The notes are not clear that these were conscious intentions, and perhaps he planned to use more daughters for himself in the future.

He did violate an important rule in using his daughters to get wives for himself. Two of these daughters were by his first wife, now deceased. They had no full brothers and were Alemi's eldest children, and perhaps it was easier to usurp these daughters than it might have been if they had had full brothers or had been younger and had half brothers of the same age. The two daughters were Molonda and Yesou, and their marriage stories are revealing. Alemi married Orendena, and she brought with her two children by a previous marriage—her daughter Neneminah and her son Mondamvu. Despite Orendena's protests, Alemi married her daughter, Neneminah. He had planned to use Molonda as an exchange for her, but while he was away Mondamvu took Yesou, and so the exchange was arranged as shown in genealogy 3. Alemi still used his daughter Molonda to acquire a wife (Makima) for himself, as shown in genealogy 4.

Finally, Alemi's reluctant wife Berangime was acquired by using another of his daughters, Kalifuvi. She married a man from Akuran and went to live there while Berangime was sent to Alemi. A feeling

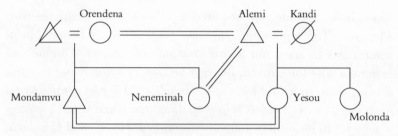

Genealogy 3. Alemi marries Nenemineh

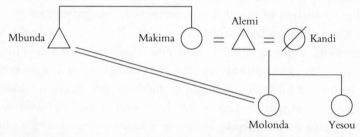

Genealogy 4. Alemi marries Makima

existed that men should use their full sisters rather than half sisters in exchanges, and even though Alemi's sons had an adequate number left to assure their marriages, some were distressed that their full sisters were not available. His son Afima, for example, had an exchange arranged for him. He was to use a half sister to acquire a wife, and the arrangements were set. However, Afima felt that he should have used his full sister, Kalifuvi, to get his own wife and that Berangime should have been his spouse, not his father's; and because of this shame he refused to call Berangime by any kinship term. The confusion of calling the reciprocation for his full sister by a term for the first ascending generation rather than wife was too great.

Although the data are not comprehensive and exhaustive, actual arrangements bear out the generalization that exchange was the preferred way to marry. Of the 67 women married or betrothed to particular individuals in 1932, it is impossible to discover the way in which 17 of them married. Of the remaining 50 women, 30—a full

60 percent—married by exchange. The notes do not include enough genealogical detail to determine how many of these marriages were with the correct third cross-cousin, but the data do substantiate the importance of exchange as the proper way to marry. Of the remaining 20 women, 6 were paid for. Three of the 20 were not reciprocated in any way: 1 was taken by Alemi from an older relative before his death, another was taken (again by Alemi) from a Grass Country village in revenge because the villagers there helped another of his wives run away, and the third was not yet settled. She was married to Omblean, had no children, and was afflicted with a serious case of ringworm; Omblean maintained that he did not sleep with her and implied that because no one would want her she was worth nothing. He clearly had no intention of reciprocating anything despite the fact that her relatives were complaining. The remaining 11 women were inherited from classificatory relatives. There are two points to be made about these inherited wives. The first is that the data are inadequate to determine how their first marriages were executed; they could have been exchanged, paid for, or married without recompense. Thus, it is possible that the percentages of women who married by exchange are even higher. Second, of these 11 inherited women, 5 were married by a male relative of the deceased husband, but the new husband of the other 6 paid for them as well. It is possible that the men who gave material goods to inherit a wife were more distantly related to the deceased husbands than men who did not, but again detailed genealogical data are lacking. It is also possible, of course, that those who paid simply had less political power.

Although brother-sister exchange was the preferred way to marry and the majority of marriages did conform, the actual execution of such transactions was far from simple. Demographic imbalances required manipulation that the feeding described above could not adequately handle. Individual choice sometimes entangled the arrangements because one or more of the participants was hesitant or refused the marriage outright, thus promoting conflict among kin and potential affines. But the arena for conflict extended beyond this: agnatically related men competed, overtly and covertly, for the chance to use their sisters to acquire more wives for themselves. The ideal was that a man used his full sister, but the reality was that men used their female relatives. Further, the rule that one should marry someone of one's own generation and use a female relative of the same generation to execute the exchange was not infrequently violated. Men used daughters to acquire wives for themselves before their sons were old enough or strong enough to complain. Powerful men tried to renege on exchanges once their wives were firmly tied to them. And rather than harming a man's reputation, such behavior seems only to have enhanced it by making him seem stronger and tougher.

Fortune recorded many cases illustrating that conflicts frequently arose because a man simply took a woman not designated for him. (Unfortunately, neither Mead's nor Fortune's notes reveal much about the women's attitudes in these examples.) Taking a woman sometimes resulted in making an exchange or payment after the fact, but more commonly it resulted in conflict, long-lasting enmity, and occasionally serious injuries and death. Fortune's notes also include a series of cases illustrating the conflicts that arose between agnatically related kin when there was a dispute over who had rights to use a sister or receive a wife from a sister's husband's people. These quarrels occurred between brothers, between father and son, and between more distantly related agnatic kin as well.

Various factors made brother-sister exchange a less-than-smooth process. To illustrate some of these problems and complexities I have chosen four cases from Fortune's notes. They are more elaborate than most exchanges, but they are not atypical and serve as excellent illustrations of various points about kinship and marriage.

Case A. This case illustrates the intricacies of kinship reckoning as well as how an unusual circumstance complicated marital arrangements. Genealogy 5 shows all the main characters.

Genealogy 5. Davimba's troubles

Lugum arranged that his daughter by Kakaravi, Nyenda, marry Ombieng-gen and that Ombienggen's sister, Davimba, marry Evandjong, son of a woman called Njoka, officially married first to Gavarian to whom she bore Vuon (Gafumbu). Then Gavarian [threw her out] for adultery, and all of the men [had sex with] her in the bush. In due time, officially without a husband, she bore Evandjong. [When] asked who was the father, she said other men [had sex with] her occasionally, but Lugum [did] daily so he was the father. So she proposed that Lugum marry her, but Lugum didn't want to. Finally Anagwa . . . married her, Anagwa being Kakaravi's father's sister's son. Anagwa adopted Evandjong. So Lugum arranged that Nyenda should be considered as sister of Evandjong, who was really her mother's father's sister's son's son, reputed to be her father's bastard. Lugum apparently agreed that he was his bastard, otherwise the relationship seems a bit tenuous. So Evandjong married Davimba, the return for Nyenda. This made Mongova and Yeshimba furious. They pointed out to Evandjong that he wasn't a brother of Nyenda, and Evandjong pointed out that he was reputed to be their father's son; therefore he was the brother of Nyenda on both sides, father's and mother's, which was more than they were. Yeshimba and Nangulesh threatened to marry Davimba themselves later. Evandjong gave a little female child called Vevenda to Yeshimba, Vevenda being the child of two men, Evandjong and Vangeda, by a woman named Vorunda, daughter of Nali and Mandjong. [When] asked for the father, Vorunda named both men. Evandjong renounced any claim to marry her; Vangeda married her and gave Evandjong their child. Yeshimba is now offering Ndelong Vevenda for Yemo.

Case B. The complexities of marriage transactions and the serious consequences of disputes arising from these transactions are apparent in this elaborate case. See genealogy 6 for the main characters.

Mblemok married Umbainda . . . and fathered Yowan. Then he married the younger sister Nyadime and fathered Gavima. Mblemok left Akuran because he had killed someone else's pig and came here [Kinakatem]. After Mblemok died, Nyadime went with the young Gavima to her father's, Yemou's, place, Ulevepele. Umbainda married Matambuna and stayed here with Yowan, her son, and Shengma, her daughter. Yowan married Lugum's daughter Yamena and ran away to Ulevepele. Gavima married Mbideleme, daughter of Alenganavat (son of Grok), and reciprocated her with his sister Kuainvove, who married Shivoma. Mbandemon,

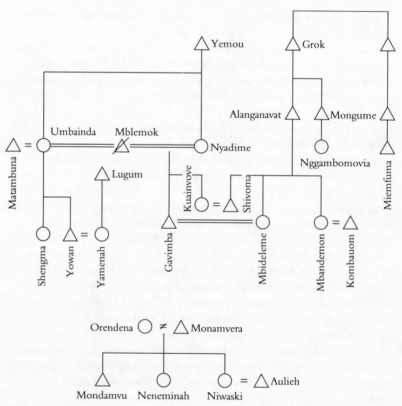

Genealogy 6. Quarrel over Mbandemon

Mbideleme's younger sister, was married without exchange or real payment by Kombavom who only paid a nosebone for her. Kombavom threw
her out, and she went and stayed with her father's father's elder brother's
son's son, Miemvumba, in Ulevepele. Gavima then pinched [stole or
eloped with] her. Miemvumba, Vuvutpa, Aulieh, and Nakwon came to
fight Gavima. Yowan planted his spear on the edge of the compound and
said he was not participating, but if anyone damaged Gavima he would
reciprocate. They all shot spears at the shields, and then Miemvumba and
Gavima came close to one another and cut each other's shields to bits with
knives, whereat Gavima's wife Mbideleme came out and helped Gavima.
They fought with the flats of their knives. Meanwhile Mbandemon, who
was being fought over, was hidden inside a mosquito bag. A woman sat in
the mouth of it. Mbandemon stayed with Gavima and went blind. Nakwon
and Miemvumba and Vuvutpa told Aulieh to get revenge by getting Niwaski, daughter of Monamvera, sister of Mondamvu. [Yowan and Gavima
were close kin of Monamvera, but the exact relationship is not clear.] He
did. So Gavima without a spear or shield came after Aulieh, and they
fought with flats of knives. Later because taking Niwaski cheated Mondamvu, they offered the [woman with ringworm] that Ombani
subsequently married to Mondamvu, but he declined her. . . .

Case C. The main characters in this rather elaborate case are presented in genealogy 7. The initial events are described by Fortune
this way:

Mbunda was born in Biwat, his mother having been [reciprocated] by To-
lenda, who married first Gavarian, and he gave her to Lugum. Gavarian

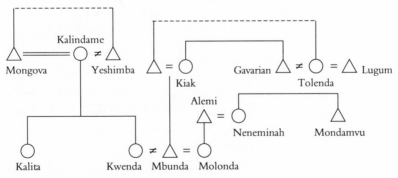

Genealogy 7. Mbunda and Kwenda

got Mbunda and reared him. Gavarian was his mother's brother. His own mother, Kiak, reared him to the stage of walking about, then Gavarian got him. When Gavarian died, he stayed around, first with Lugum, then Komeaka, and later with Mongova, and finally [stayed] with Mongova. Mongova had married the mother of Kwenda, Kalindame. (Yeshimba had married her first but didn't like her and gave her to Mongova.) (Kalita is a sister of Kwenda.) Mbunda went along to Mongova, saw Kwenda, and [took off] with Kwenda. They ran away to Biwat. They came back, and Alemi had gone to a government feast at Ambunti. Mbunda and Kwenda stayed with Yeshimba because Mongova was angry. Mbunda then ran away to Fundukwa with Molenda. . . . Alemi was very angry at Yeshimba. Alemi took Kwenda and the child. Alemi wants to marry her. Kwenda got up in the night and with her child followed Mbunda to Fundukwa. Alemi was cross all the time at Yeshimba [for harboring Mbunda]. He threatened Yeshimba's women, and they lived in a state of siege in the houses. Alemi [stole] Neneminah, sister of Mondamvu [classificatory sister of Mbunda and daughter of Alemi's wife Orendena]. Mbunda stayed in Fundukwa a year. A half-caste Biwat living there warned him that he was to be killed and eaten, so he and his two wives better leave. They went to Andafugan, then to the river where he saw a recruiter's pinnace and ran away to work, leaving Kwenda and Molonda to find their own way home. They arrived back at the place. Alemi took back Molonda, and Kwenda stayed with Yeshimba. Mondamvu, angry with Alemi for pulling his sister, went to Madang to work. Three years later Mbunda came back and found Alemi's daughter [Molonda] pregnant. Everyone questioned her, but she refused to answer [who the father was]. Mbunda went to Biwat with Kwenda. The first *kiap* then came up with a doctor, and the doctor persuaded Mbunda to go to Ambunti to be trained [as a *doktorboi*]. He left Kwenda in Biwat, and came back three months later and found Kwenda pregnant. He ran back to Kinakatem. Here he found that Molonda has thrown away her child, and his devotion to her was increased by hearing that Kwenda begot twins. . . .

Mead's notes provide data on subsequent events. Mbunda clearly wished to divorce Kwenda, and because he had given a substantial payment for her, he demanded a replacement woman from her kin. Because someone supposedly in Biwat had seduced her while she was there among her father's people, the European patrol officer sided with him in his efforts to get a different wife to replace

Kwenda. Her relatives gave him another woman but she refused to remain with him and cook, so Mbunda tried to acquire the daughter of the Biwat *luluai* instead. Mead wrote that when Mbunda was satisfied with the arrangements, Kwenda would return to Biwat and marry the man there who seduced her. In the meantime she lived with Yeshimba, her classificatory father.

Case D. This example is really a complex series of interrelated cases that illustrates many aspects of the volatile nature of arranging marriages as well as something of the substance of various kin relations (such as brother-brother). It also shows how quickly tension can escalate to violence. The political motivations of men in arranging and executing marriages are clear here, as well as the political consequences.

Kombevom of Kinakatem died suddenly and without apparent previous sickness. . . . It not being known who was responsible for the sorcery . . . Mongova suggested and even insisted that Yopou of Vroang [a hamlet], a woman, was guilty. . . . She had married into Dowaning, borne two daughters, and then her husband had died. She had come back to Vroang with her two daughters for awhile to stay. . . .

At this juncture Mongova had demanded one of her daughters in marriage to wipe out the fact that a man of Kinakatem had been killed by a man of Vroang, a fact that had not been wiped out by any former act of vengeance. . . . Yopou had declined to accede to Mongova's demands and had married her two daughters off to Dowaning men. . . .

[So] Mongova [was angry] and said that Yopou had sold Kombevom's dirt. . . . Thereat [many] got up, ready to kill Yopou. Godva, one resident of Vroang, directed Mongova and the . . . avenging party on the road to find Yopou. Kaindzhin, the father of Godva, had adopted Mokasinda as his sister. . . . Mokasinda married Lugum . . . and bore Mongova and his brothers. Kaindzhin, treating Mokasinda as a sister, treated Mongova as a sister's son. . . . Godva and Mongova hence were fairly close "brothers" [cross-cousins]—so Godva seconded Mongova against Yopou.

Alemi was another intermediary. He had married [a woman from Vroang]. . . . He agreed . . . to deceive Vroang. Men of Biwat, Branda, Akuran, and Ulevepeli [a hamlet] came as allies . . . to kill Yopou by stealthy approach. . . .

Alemi went to his brothers-in-law . . . and advised them to keep to their houses—they were not to be killed—but if they showed up to fight, they'd be exterminated by a vastly superior force. He then told Yopou the crowd was coming for her, so she'd better run (having taken care not to tell her until the place was surrounded). She got out the back of the house through the hole for throwing out rubbish, met the armed enemy at the edge of the village, was wounded, ran back into the house and was killed there when they came in after her.

Before this Mongova . . . ignored a close relationship and married Godva's sister . . . and Godva ran away to Vroang. Some time later Godva came back from Vroang and stayed with his sister's husband Mongova, worked with him, etc. During this interval Godva helped Mongova kill Yopou. Then waiting for his opportunity, he ran away with Mongova's [adopted] daughter Vaianyada. . . .

Mongova [was furious and gathered up his brothers] . . . and they went to fight Godva. They succeeded in killing Vaianyada. . . .

Thereat Vaianyada's mother's brothers . . . got up in a rage with Godva for causing the death of Vaianyada. They raised half of Vroang and half of [another hamlet], saying "Come now and get revenge for Yopou." . . .

One man met the brother of Godva . . . and threatened him . . . told him to clear out—a killing expedition was after his brother. . . . The brother . . . [fought] with the man, snapped off his spear and got wounded. . . . He ran away and returned at dusk to hear "all have killed Godva." (Note: Godva had been surprised in his house . . . so his brother had not been particularly brave in not getting warning to him [as he was] already surrounded.)

Godva had many spears deep in him, but he was not dead. Yeshimba, Mongova's brother, took him into his house and cared for him. . . . Yeshimba disagreed with Mongova about Godva. He remembered that Godva's father had fed both Mongova and himself and was their mother's brother. This disagreement grew. . . . Godva virtually recovered in Yeshimba's house. . . . They thought him sure to die and had not worried about him. [But when they learned of his recovery], they came and finished him off, making sure this time. Yeshimba and Mongova, younger and elder brother, thereafter fought each other on sight.

The deep enmity between Mongova and Yeshimba continued and spread as their siblings were forced to take sides. Divination revealed that Mongova himself had had a hand in the original sorcery death and had accused Yopou only to divert suspicion from himself. A variety of complex economic and marital exchanges was involved in the attempted resolution of this complicated series of events, and a Biwat woman was killed to avenge the death of Yopou. But bad feelings remained among many of the participants.

CLANS

The Mundugumor had patrilineal descent groups that Mead labeled clans. These groups were called *maikua* (pl. *maikundu*), but the particular groups themselves were not named. (The way in which these groups articulated with totemic groups is unclear.) Occasionally one was referred to by the name of the hamlet in which many of its male members resided. These groups were exogamous and usually localized. Mead described them as "foreshortened" and said that they were regarded as "short and fat" (as opposed to the "long and thin ropes"). Informants compared the clan with the rope by saying that the clan is a short, insignificant group, but the rope is very long.[19] No long genealogies were kept to trace membership, and the group was typically composed of a relatively small number of patrilineal kin. (These groups would probably be called lineages in contemporary anthropological usage.) Several possessions were inherited patrilineally in the clans: land, old sago patches, old *barets*, house sites, some ritual objects, and bush spirit names. These groups were also associated with the spirits that lived on their land.

Mead stressed throughout her notes that these kin groups were relatively unimportant. The clan never engaged in concerted cooperative activities. In fact, competition among men for rights to their female kin as well as the respect and hostility inherent in the relationships between agnatic kin kept these male patrilineal relatives apart. Land was plentiful, so even access to it through the clan was not a precious right. Mead noted that "there is a concept of a patrilineal group, but it is a term hardly ever used, almost impossible to get, and without social bolstering." Mead believed that the social system she observed in 1932 was a "broken down" one that had previously functioned differently, and she speculated that at one time the Mundugumor may have had stronger and more functional patrilineal groups. Their significance was certainly minimal in 1932.

In 1981 descent was still relatively unimportant, and in fact there was actually confusion in the minds of people about the descent rules. Some informants were not clear as to whether they joined the clan of their fathers or mothers. At first a few people intimated that matrilineal descent might be the case. But as our discussions continued, it became evident that ideally children affiliated with their mother's group only if father had not been able to provide a sister exchange; the "mother's group" was her patrilineal group, however, so the rule of patrilineal descent seemed to hold. (The principle, related to me by male informants, was phrased thusly: if a man gave his sister but also received a wife, he cannot ask for his sister's children back; but if he gave a woman and did not receive one in return, then he should expect to get his sister's children back for his own group.) Individuals had begun to take on the surname of their fathers, but whether this was a natural evolution, the imposition of Western colonialists, or a combination of the two is uncertain.

The naming practices of the Mundugumor are not clear. In one note Mead states that names were associated with the spirits of a patrilineal clan and were inherited within the clan, yet in another she remarked that names were inherited down ropes (from male to female to male and so on).[20] It might be possible to reconcile these two statements with a third note: women bequeathed their own clan names to their children, and in fact it was more appropriate for a woman to hand down the names of her "family" (Mead did not define this term) than for a man. In this way a man could receive his mother's father's name as the rope system suggested. Exactly how a woman received the name of her father's mother, however, is not clear. Mead further noted that one did not receive the name of either parent and that "great uncles' and aunts'" names were preferred to grandparents'. Every individual bore several names, each received from a different relative.

ROPES

Much of Mead's data on the rope *(geun)*[21] as well as her interpretations are included in her discussion of the Mundugumor in *Sex and
Temperament*. In this section I first present Mead's view and include
quotations from her published work and then supplement these
with additional details from her notes as well as from Fortune's material. Because I make much of exactly what Mead and Fortune
wrote about ropes, it is important to quote them precisely and at
some length to substantiate the reinterpretation in the next chapter.

Mead sets out a basic description of ropes in *Sex and Temperament* (1963:176–77):

> ... Mundugumor social organization is based upon a theory of a natural
> hostility that exists between all members of the same sex, and the assump-
> tion that the only possible ties between members of the same sex are
> through members of the opposite sex. Instead therefore of organizing
> people into patrilineal groups or matrilineal groups, in either one of which
> brothers are bound together in the same group as either their father or
> their mother's brother, the Mundugumor have a form of organization that
> they call a *rope*. A rope is composed of a man, his daughters, his daughters'
> sons, his daughters' sons' daughters; or if the count is begun from a
> woman, of a woman, her sons, her sons' daughters, her sons' daughters'
> sons, and so on. All property, with the exception of land, which is plentiful
> and not highly valued, passes down the rope; even weapons descend from
> father to daughter. A man and his son do not belong to the same rope, or
> respect the same totemic bird or animal. A man leaves no property to his
> son, except a share in the patrilineally descended land; every other valu-
> able goes to his daughter. Brothers and sisters do not belong to the same
> rope; one is bound in allegiance to the mother, the other to the father.

After describing the constellation of affective ties within a large po-
lygynous household, she goes on to comment that the brother-sister
marriage system ran counter to the rope system in that strong structural ties were set up between brother and sister, members of different ropes. In discussing how men usurp their sons' claims and use

their own daughters to acquire wives for themselves, Mead (1963:179) adds that

the father has already a strong sense of possession in his daughter. She belongs to his rope, not to her brothers' rope. She gardens with her father, works in the bush with her father, uses kinship terms calculated through her father when she talks, bears the name of one of her father's female ancestors.

The conflict between rope and the prescribed marriage system is clear. Later Mead (1963:202–3) describes how the rope system complicated kin behavior and terminology, and the discussion illuminates kin usage:

It will be remembered that along one rope are ranged together a man, his daughter, and his daughter's son, and that his wife, his son, and his son's daughter belong in another rope. These rope organizations are partly defined by the possession of names which help to identify a woman with her paternal grandmother and a man with his maternal grandfather. In the theory which underlies this structure, a man is socially identical with his maternal grandfather and may apply the same kinship terms to his grandfather's generation that his grandfather himself uses; this includes calling his maternal grandmother "wife." Such use of kinship terms is congruent with the ideal marriage that reunites the ropes [to be discussed later], but is so meaningless in the present disorganized state of Mundugumor society that the people now phrase this tendency to identify members of alternate generations by saying that a boy is permitted to joke by using his grandfather's terms. They thus convert a formal structural point into a point of licence. . . . As a girl is supposed to take over the social identity of her paternal grandmother, she has to learn the details of kinship from her father, who knows it better than would her mother, and the same thing holds for a boy—it is his mother who can instruct him in his rope relationships. But here again what is in form a simple point of structure the Mundugumor phrase as a girl's helping her father and a boy's helping his mother.

Mead mentions in *Sex and Temperament* (1963:181) that particular items were inherited down ropes, especially sacred objects such as flutes. (Fortune noted that flutes went from a man to his daughter to her first-born son.) She also mentions (1963:208) the possibility that rope membership may have had something to do with the relative lack of animosity between sisters:

There are several features of the social structure that are favourable to girls' maintaining more comfortable relations among themselves. This does not mean that sisters are always friendly; the general atmosphere of struggle, competition, and jealousy is too great for that. There is no insistence upon sisters behaving formally and distantly to each other, and half-sisters belong to the same rope.

Mead does not address the issue of why brothers who would belong to the same rope are not allied because of it.

Mead's most important data on ropes are contained in the following lengthy quotation (1963:182–83), to which I will refer frequently in my own later analysis:

The religious cult is thus as powerless to integrate the group permanently as are the lines along which descent is organized. The Mundugumor did, at some period in their past history, as is demonstrated by the existence of maxims and rules that are mainly honoured in the breach, make some attempt to intertwine the intractable ropes into some sort of co-operative society. This was done by the establishment of mutual obligations between the descendants of an inter-marrying pair of brothers and sisters [see diagram 6]. The son of the sister scarified the grandson of the brother, who in turn scarified the grandson of his scarifier, and in the fourth generation the children of the two lines were supposed to marry. This elaborate and impractical system of preserving obligations through five generations, and expecting to have at the end of the process two brother-and-sister pairs of the right age to marry, is never carried out in practice.

The only consequence of the existence of such a traditional system is to intensify the conviction of every Mundugumor that he is doing wrong and that he is being wronged by others. The right to scarify a boy is financially profitable; the scarifier receives pigs and rings from the novice and the return on this investment comes when the one-time novice, now grown to adult years, is called upon to scarify the grandson of the man who performed the operation on him a generation before. Similarly, when a woman pierces a girl's ears and receives gifts for it, it is expected that some day that girl will pierce the ears of the granddaughter of the woman who is now being paid, and in return receive handsome presents. But this meticulous observance of obligations through three generations is too difficult for the aggressive individuality of Mundugumor. Quarrels, removals, the desire to pay off debts by asking someone else to perform the lucrative ceremony—all of these interfere. As a result a great number of people are always angry because someone else has been asked to perform the ceremony that they have inherited the right to perform. As for the proper marriages that should reunite two ropes after four generations of reciprocity, these never take place They are remembered in phrase and maxim and are invoked by those members of Mundugumor society who rebel against the disorganized state of its social life.

Later, in describing one such "misfit" named Kalekumban, Mead (1963:228) says that "daydreamers like Kalekumban are quite capable of perpetuating and elaborating the legend indefinitely, the legend of the time when everything was 'straight,' when ropes and patrilineal groups were woven together, when people cooperated with each other and kept the rules."

One of the most interesting aspects of Mead's raw field notes is that they include very few half-formed ideas, statements or observations and little speculation. The earliest notes include very few gropings or apparently incorrect interpretations. That Mead did correct early mistakes is certain because notations exist that were meant to revise earlier notes (and all are labeled "correction"). This is all the more remarkable in the context of ropes, a rather aberrant phenomenon and certainly not described for any other society at the time Mead and Fortune were in Kinakatem. (That Mead showed no surprise at this seemingly strange arrangement probably best illustrates both her open-mindedness and the wonder at the range of human diversity that was characteristic of American anthropology at this time.) There are no notes that indicate a struggling to understand the concept, no evidence that small bits and pieces of information were gradually assembled, each of which ultimately contributed to comprehending the concept. Because of the theoretical importance of ropes and their somewhat controversial nature (some anthropologists have, at least in private conversation and communication, skeptically questioned their existence), I have chosen to present here all references to ropes contained in Mead's notes as well as Fortune's and, whenever possible, in their own words. What follows, then, are raw data with some interpretation by the ethnographers. Mead's full interpretation was presented in *Sex and Temperament*. Fortune seems not to have worked with the material beyond his beginning summary (included later.)

It is difficult to determine when the first reference to ropes appears in the notes because one narrative is not dated. The undated references are made in the context of describing totemism and say little substantive about ropes. The first dated reference, from November 23, does indicate that Mead had not quite formulated the image of ropes presented in later published works: "*Ashins* or *maindjimis* can descend along a rope, *geun*, either male or female or mixed. So for all property." Sometime after this date, however, the ambiguity of just what a rope was is gone, and except for the enigmatic comment "*Kamain* is a form of reciprocal amenities with distant brothers who belong to a straight male rope or a straight female rope," as well as the comment cited earlier, the assumption is that the rope was a descent phenomenon in which the tracing of the line went through alternating sexes:

... this rope system produces an equivalence between grandfathers and their daughter's sons. These have the same *ashins*, the same emblems, etc. It is possible to say that the Mundugumor are unilateral, but a change of sex occurs in each generation. So a rope consists of a man, his brothers, his daughters, his daughters sons, and if the blood descent in direct line were not so insisted upon to the exclusion of all collateral lines, it would include also his brother's daughters and their sons.

Some notes are additions to or clarifications of terminology. Mead defined rope, or *geun*, as a "rope of alternating sexes." In another note the translation of *geun* is made clear:

A *geun* is literally a rope; [it] is also used to signify string with which fishing nets are made—note that this is a two-strand twine—and also the two sides in children's games. In social organization each individual starts a *geun* so that one can speak of father's *geun*, father's sister's *geun* and father's brother's *geun* as all distinct.

Some of these references, however, are not at all clear. *Papakala* was a term that referred to the rope of a grandparent, but it is unclear whether this term was restricted to the ropes of grandparents other than that to which ego belonged. "The ropes of the sisters of grandparents are called *papakalandi ke shemilu*." Similarly, there is some ambiguity in Mead's statement that the phrase *shemi lukan geun* referred to "sisters of half rope (*geun* same name but far line)." The last statement is especially problematic because the notion of "half rope" was never clarified (Fortune does have one reference in his notes, describing a relationship as one of a "half rope"), and there are no other references to the idea that ropes were named.

A page of handwritten notes that could belong to either Mead or Fortune addresses the question of terminology. It confirms that *shemi lukan geun* referred to "sisters of half rope," but it translates *papakalandi ke shemilu* as "sisters of *tumbunas* (ancestors)" rather than ropes of grandparents' sisters. This is a significant discrepancy: Mead's note indicates that the phrase referred to the ropes of grandparents' sisters, whereas the other note indicates that it referred to the actual sisters of ancestors and did not include rope as a part of its meaning. It is relevant that the phrase does not contain the word *geun*. Another discrepancy arises from the information on this page because it contains a notation that *papakala* (which Mead translated as "rope of a grandparent") meant line of *ungwasak* (grandfather), thus deleting references to ropes and specifying grandfather and excluding grandmother. The term *wiyakpapakala* referred to both the lines of *ungwasak* (grandfather) and *weyak* (grandmother), and again rope was not included; yet one must wonder if the term is a combination of *weyak* and *papakala*.[22]

This particular page of handwritten notes contains more terms that evoke confusion. *Ngu ke shemilu ke geun* referred to the line of a particular relative (which relative is unintelligible; *shemilu* is, of course, plural for sister, and *ke* is, I believe, a possessive suffix, but *ngu* is not clear); the phrase does contain the word for rope *(geun)*. Finally, the author translated the phrase *owambo papa ke geun* as "father's line and grandfather's line." The problem here is that *geun* refers to rope, and the phrase makes little sense if father's and grandfather's ropes are referred to by the same term, for father and father's father or mother's father were not members of the same rope. The translation also may be questionable. It is possible that *papa* is the pidgin term for father, and *owambo* a form of *ovambu* (brother-in-law), and then the phrase would mean rope of brother-in-law's father. Apart from these problems of translation, there is a more general problem here. Some phrases contain the word for rope while others do not. Even if one assumes that phrases containing the word *geun* do in fact refer to a rope, there is confusion about the remaining terms. It is not possible to determine whether these various words and phrases actually do refer to the rope of a particular relative or whether they are intended simply to designate his or her general line of descendants. Thus, according to Mead, *papakala* refers to a grandparent's rope (which meant descent with alternating sexes), but according to the note on the handwritten page it could have meant the line or general descendants of a grandfather and could have been totally unrelated to the phenomenon of ropes.

Many of the references to ropes relate to what was inherited "down the ropes"—that is, from father to daughter to daughter's son or from mother to son to son's daughter and so on. The following items all followed rope inheritance: *ashins* and other sacred flutes, *maindjimi* (objects but not names, which were probably inherited patrilineally), some names, slitgongs, bows and arrows, spears, and large sago storage pots. In the following passage Mead distinguishes between rope and clan inheritance:

Things which belong to the [clan] and so can be inherited patrilineally are: garden land, old sago patches, *barets*, and some sacred objects. But newly planted sago, yam seed, new *barets*, newly planted coconuts, new betel palms, if [the] major part of the work is done by mother, go to [her] sons;

[if the major part of the work is done] by father, [they go] to [his] daughters. If [the work] is done by both parents working together, [these] are divided. Mother is represented as always speaking up and claiming for her son, while father continually allocates to his daughter.[23] All [varieties of] yam seeds are [rope] inherited. House sites belong to the [clan] and even sister's sons of [the clan], but [these] are not regarded seriously. [Large] house posts are [rope] inherited; if mother sees them first, [she] reserves them for [her] son. . . . Canoes are insignificant. [Slitgongs], spear and bow and arrow, tomahawks, and large sago storage pots [are also rope] inherited.

Rope . . . inheritance is used here to mean mother-to-son, father-to-daughter. If a girl elopes without her family's consent, her brother will try to calaboose [withhold] all her inheritance. This is the context for stealing [a flute], and also sanctions against elopement. Shields are only inherited by men. Houses go to sons, or brothers who inherit [the] widow and young children. . . .

In another contrast between kinds of inheritance, Mead wrote that

maindjimis are inherited down ropes, preferably always with the change in sex [note the use of "preferably" here]. *Ashins* and *yakats* [two kinds of sacred objects] are similarly inherited. The *maindjimi* and *pelevas* [other sacred objects] are associated together in one initiation ceremony . . . but *pelevas* are inherited patrilineally as are *ngaungaus* also. All the other three follow ropes. . . . Names, like the ritual objects, descend along a rope [with exceptions; see earlier discussion].

Some of these items, especially flutes, were very significant:

When Orendena ran away, she did not take her [crocodile flute] and her husband's small [classificatory] brothers . . . broke it, so by Orendena's act, Mondamvu [her son] lost his inheritance. Connect this with his great bitterness to his mother, and the bitterness with which he was brought up to regard her. A son's sentiment for his mother's line must be inculcated by his mother or her sisters.

Here Mead also added this: "Note: if polygamy were always with sisters, the [rope] would go straight, i.e. brothers would always belong to the same [rope]."

Totemic emblems, according to many (but not all) of the notes, also were determined by rope affiliation: "Inheritance of emblems follows the usual rope pattern, a woman receives hers from her father, a man from his mother. In making *tangets* for anger, or death, etc., the leaves of both the father's and mother's and sometimes more remote ancestors may be used." When Mead goes on, it is clear that there is some phenomenon involving primary and secondary totems here.

Each animal or bird and each plant has a [slitgong] call, of which there are sometimes several varieties. The [slitgong] calls actually used are arranged to avoid ambiguity within the community. Different combinations of the *four inherited emblems* are used, and sometimes a wife's or husband's is added [emphasis added].

In 1981 people still used these signals to call others via the slitgong.

Malep (pl. *malefuh*) was a term that translated as "the totemic leaves of the *geun*," and *ip* (pl. *ifuh*) the "totemic living thing [e.g., pig] of the *geun*." In a summary statement Mead noted that

in addition to those emblems which they had for longer than they can remember, marriages with [outsiders] are occasionally bringing in new ones. They are not primarily totemic, but may be regarded as emblems, or signatures of ropes of alternating sexes, as a woman receives her "bird" and her "plant" from her father, a man from his mother. . . . There is no prohibition against the intermarriage of people who have the same emblem [but see earlier]. When the emblems are used in plant form, as in anger or at death, not only the father's and mother's but those of other two grandparents, mother's mother and father's father, may be added if it is desired. However the primary inheritance is final.

These totemic emblems were slightly different from inherited physical objects. If a rope died out, "if the alternation fails, the same sex can inherit in default as far as valuable objects are concerned, but the totem would die out." Finally, "when a rope ends [dies out], its sago is cut for a feast, coconut and betel and breadfruit cut down, and its [crocodile flutes] are broken. Land and *barets* revert to collateral lines." (The last sentence is of course problematic: ropes did not own land, patrilineal clans did. It is also important to note that in other places Mead intimated that totems were affiliated with patrilineal clans, not ropes. The small evidence I gathered in 1981 indicates that such was the case.)

The way in which ropes articulated with the marriage system was noted in *Sex and Temperament*, but the purpose of the description there was not to present the complexity of the phenomenon, and it did not include many of the details and data about the significant exchanges that ideally took place among descendants of an intermarrying pair for four generations. The main point was that the rope descendants of a couple—the founders of two distinct ropes— were supposed to marry five generations later. Diagram 6, taken directly from Mead's notes with slight modifications, illustrates the ideal pattern of marriage.

Mead explained the diagram in this associated narrative comment:

As will be seen from the diagram, the pattern of relationship between two ropes was, in the first generation, marriage; in the second generation, siblingship in which the sister is exchanged for a wife for the brother; in the third generation, cross cousinship in which jesting is forbidden but in which the male cross cousin cuts the son of his female cross cousin and gives him a skull of an enemy, and the "sister's son" reciprocates with pigs; the female cross cousin can pierce the ears of her male sibling's daughter and in return receives rings. In the fourth generation, there is cross cousinship in which jesting is permitted, and marriage forbidden, but *kusak* (arranged marriage for children) can be made; ideally this marriage should not be consummated until the related grandparents in the third generation are dead, and the man in the fourth generation can cut the child of his *kusak*-making female cross cousin, and she can pierce the ears of his female child, thus returning the economics set up a generation before. In the fifth generation, the two can marry, and the brothers-in-law can cut each other.

This ideal marriage scheme applied only to first-born children (who also inherited the *maindjimi*). In diagram 6 one must assume that

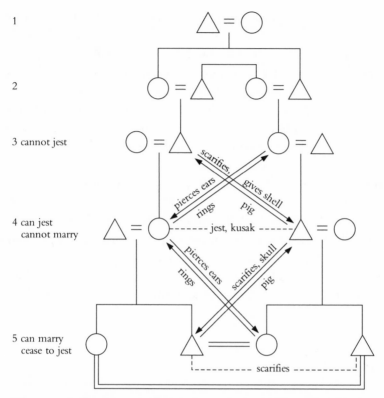

Diagram 6. Intergenerational exchange and reunification of ropes

in the fifth generation, the marrying pair in the center of the diagram were both elder children. Neither Mead nor Fortune ever comments on the fact that because marriage was by exchange the other marrying pair were not reuniting ropes. In another version of the diagram Mead labeled the reciprocal gift from a woman to her classificatory father's sister pigs instead of rings. Finally, Mead noted that she based this diagram on facts received from Omblean, who gave her his own genealogy (see genealogy 8) to "illustrate proper marriages—which don't take place." The genealogy also indicated that the children of Ashue could marry the children of Gisambut, but such marriages were not regarded as ideally proper. I have reproduced genealogy 8 just as it appeared in Mead's notes.

The concept of ropes seems to be violated here—the line from Bilishok down does not alternate sexes. However, if the diagram is rearranged and the entire first and second generations are included as they are in genealogy 9, it does conform to the pattern. It should also be noted that because this system did involve repeating associations of totemic affiliations, identity of kin terms, and so on, Mead inquired about reincarnation, but the response was negative: "They flatly deny all ideas of reincarnation, but the ideal marriage plan is arranged to make a perfect repeat in the fifth generation of the personalities—name, leaves, etc., of the pair of ancestors who were the progenitors of the split rope."[24]

One further explanatory comment is required. Mead noted that in the third generation (see diagram 6), "the male cross cousin cuts the son of his female cross cousin and gives him the skull of an enemy" or a classificatory mother's brother scarifies and presents the skull of a slain enemy to his classificatory sister's son. The cut-

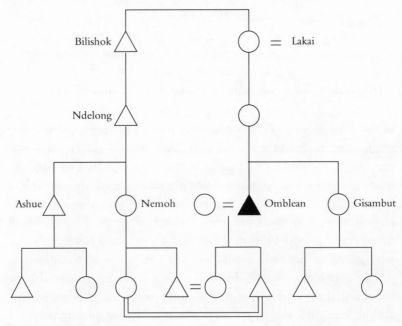

Genealogy 8. Omblean (A)

Genealogy 9. Omblean (B)

ting during initiation is described in chapter 3, but the skull gifts need further elaboration. A sister's son could acquire his mother's brother's enemy skulls during the mortuary rites for the mother's brother, but the mother's brother sometimes chose to present the skull or skulls during his own lifetime. Mead included diagram 7 to explain the transaction.

The skull taken in war may be given to the [sister's son] before the [mother's brother's] death or afterwards. If given before death, it constitutes a pig exchange. [In diagram 7] #1 kills an enemy and gets a right to a certain number of homicidal emblem feathers. Then he gives this skull—which he [is] especially likely to do so if he has more than one—and the right to decoration which goes with it, to his [sister's son] who is supposed to fasten [mark, promise, and give] a pig for it. Then the [sister's son], #4, when he kills an enemy must return the skull to the grandson of his [mother's brother] or #5, who will give him pigs. If this skull were given without reciprocation, as it may be if given to a [sister's son] after the

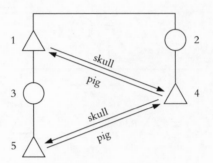

Diagram 7. Skull gifts from
mother's brother to sister's son

death of the [mother's brother], then a skull is returned and no pigs demanded. Old skulls are [decorated] and set out whenever a new skull is
taken by the village. Skulls, like [crocodile flutes] can not be inherited by
sons, only by sister's sons, and returned to daughters children.

The ideal marriage (see diagram 6) was for a man, an eldest sibling,
to marry his MFMBDSD, and a woman, also an eldest sibling, to
marry her FMFZSDS, both third cross-cousins. However, because
the ideal was also a sister-brother exchange in each generation, including generation 2 (in diagram 6), a man who married appro-
priately would also marry his MFFZDSD because his MFMB married his MFFZ. (Omblean's genealogy, as Mead recorded it,
indicates that Omblean was using this second means of reckoning.)
This is clearly bilateral cross-cousin marriage with third cousins. It
is interesting to remember here that a man was identified with his
mother's father even to the point of assuming his grandparent's kin
terminology and a woman was identified with her father's mother.
Mead sometimes used the word "equivalence" to describe this identification. This practice is consistent with the marriage system, and
in effect the two identifications collapse these third cross-cousins
into first cross-cousins. In an "identificatory" sense, then, the marriage is between first bilateral cross-cousins as well (diagram 8).

Many of Mead's notes about ropes are concerned with the way in
which this ideal marriage pattern reunites ropes after four genera-

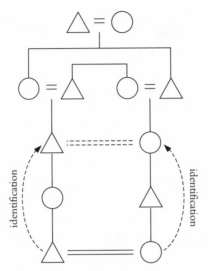

Diagram 8. Identification between alternate generations

tions. These data underscore her view of the importance of the phenomenon.

If the ideal marriage scheme is followed, the same marriage will recur in the fourth descendant generation. However it is a simpler scheme to regard the whole society as based on ropes, with all descent except land, following this plan. So [crocodile flutes], names, *maindjimis,* birds and plants [totemic emblems] are inherited in the ropes, and the economic arrangements for cutting, ear piercing, inheritance of skulls of enemies, rings, the personal property which is placed by the corpse, all are a form of reciprocity between ropes which culminates in the fourth generation in inter-marriage, the forming of two strands again, and these two strands may but of course not necessarily reunite again after four generations or more.

... *Kusak* is a form of reuniting ropes. ...

The system is based upon ropes which intermarry as above, and control all inheritance except land, *ngaungau* and *peleva; maikua* are localized, unnamed patrilineal clans (exogamous), with a provision against marrying into mother's clan also, a rigid endogamy of generation, and the suggestion of at least one dual division which kept *kamain* and *kamain*'s affinals and mother's brother's *kamain* and *kamain*'s affinals from intermarriage with one's own group. Possibly there may have been a four part division.

This is speculative. What is clear is the form of the arranged marriage and the identification of a woman with her paternal grandmother and a man and his maternal grandfather.

The system of rope inheritance ensured that special objects, such as sacred flutes, were passed down to the person with whom one identified in the alternate descending generation, for example, from a man to his daughter's son. "So the whole [rope] system may be regarded as passing [sacred flutes] down to one's namesake, or the equivalent." If *maindjimi* flutes were brought to a marriage—that is, if the woman brought such an inheritance to bequeath to her eldest son—a special procedure sometimes took place whereby the objects were adopted into the clan of her husband and son.

Note that this means the adoption of the *maindjimi* into the [clan] of its next male possessor [i.e., the woman's son], so a consonance is established between the bush and the *maindjimi* objects. . . . *Ashins* and *yakats* don't have their names changed and have no equivalents in the bush but can be exchanged for *maindjimis* if they exist. If only one side to an exchange has one [*maindjimi* flute], it goes just the same; in other words, it is not an exchange but going down the rope, regardless of the rope it meets.

"The whole idea of affinal exchange [of objects] is lacking." Adopting apparently meant renaming the object so that it fit with the patrilineal group. "So although they pass down the *geun* as objects, they would in name always correspond to locality [and its associated patrilineal group], and thus renaming would be a sort of adoption into the *maikua*, assuring a son of [some] solidarity with his father's bush and his father's *maindjimi*." Thus the intertwining of ropes was not only with one another through eventual remarriage but also with patrilineal clans through the transference of sacred objects.

While in the field Fortune began to organize some of his data, and he wrote the following description of social organization. Because it is his only substantive statement on the nature of ropes, which both agrees and disagrees with Mead's portrayal of them, it is important to quote it directly and at some length.

The Mundugumor . . . were organized into six villages, into patrilineages and families. They recognized pairs of descent lines of alternating sex with successive generations coming from families and distinguishing the children of brothers from those of sisters. This recognition also distinguished some cross-cousins by exclusion from all parallel cousins. The Mundugumor conceived marriage with [a] metaphor taken from the manufacture of fish line, netting, cord or rope as the interweaving of pairs of descent lines of alternating sex with successive generations as if such lines were the plies of a two-ply cord or rope. In their theory of the conduct of relatives between themselves, a marriage should be arranged between members of a pair of the descent lines of a *geun* or two-ply rope once every fifth generation. The form of their theory is this [diagram 9].

This form should be repeated with the next marriage between a pair of members of these descent lines being arranged in the ninth generation, and the next again in the thirteenth generation and so on. The man represented in generation III should be invited to initiate his cousin's son represented in generation IV into religious secrets at his coming of age, and the latter should be invited to initiate his cousin's son represented in generation V. In a similar way the woman represented in generation III should be invited to pierce the ear lobes of the girl represented in generation IV and the latter in turn invited to pierce the ear lobes of the girl

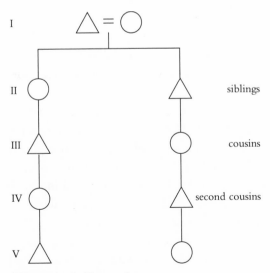

Diagram 9. Fortune's ropes

represented in generation V. In each of the plies or descent lines of the *geun*, names, personal signal calls on slit-gong drums and bamboo flutes decorated for use in men's initiation ceremonies are received by each generation from the preceding generation. Such bamboo flutes are secreted from women in other tribes in the area and their sound given out to be a voice of a divinity. Amongst the Mundugumor, however, a daughter takes a flute owned by her descent line within the *geun* with her at her marriage and hands it on at his coming of age to her first born son. When a man initiated his cousin's son into a religious fraternity he was expected also to give the young man a skull of an enemy, and he expected to be given a pig for his services.

In practice the Mundugumor arranged marriages by exchange of women given in marriage—their affinal relationships were dual and reciprocal. No marriage between third cousins who were members of the two descent lines of a rope had been arranged within living memory. The handing down of personal names, personal signal calls on slit-gong drums and initiatory bamboo flutes in the two lines of a rope was maintained, and second cousins were sometimes invited to initiate or to pierce the ears of third cousins in the way which was prescribed by their theory of the conduct of relations between themselves.

In other notes Fortune made several further observations about this pattern. First, the man in generation 3 was supposed to initiate only the first born of his cousins. (There is no mention in Mead's or Fortune's notes about the appropriate relative to initiate later-born sons.) This rule held throughout the pattern. For example, the woman of generation 3 performed the ear piercing for her cousin's first-born daughter only. Second, these ceremonial functions were not performed by an actual mother's brother or father's sister but classificatory ones only. Third, for these ceremonial tasks the actor received a pig and in return gave a shell bracelet or armband. Fourth, some initiatory flutes were inherited patrilineally. Fifth, a special relationship existed between a boy and the mother's brother who was to initiate him and between a girl and the father's sister who was to perform her ear piercing. It was to these relatives that youngsters gave their first products—the first game killed in the case of a boy, the first fish caught and first sago worked in the case of a girl.

Fortune also mentioned that the proper relative was not always the one to assume the role. If, for example, the woman in generation 3 married against her father's wishes, her father's sister's son might not initiate her son. In another note he presents a different mechanism for identifying the initiator: "The mother of the son [to be initiated] picks her 'brother' who is to initiate her son . . . by sending a killed pig to him." Fortune also added here that parents and their "blood" siblings prepared a feast for the initiators, and the latter did so as well for the former. (Fortune also noted that if a woman left her husband for another man before their son went through initiation, the boy's father's brothers might locate and destroy the flute she was to pass on to her son.)

These, then, are the data Mead and Fortune acquired about kinship and marriage among the Mundugumor. A variety of questions and puzzles remains, however. Although I cannot solve all the puzzles and answer all the questions, I can, using these data, offer an alternative interpretation of kinship and marriage, especially of ropes. This is the subject of the next chapter.

KINSHIP, EXCHANGE, AND ROPES: A REINTERPRETATION |5|

Margaret Mead's keenest talent was her ability to observe and record. In this chapter I use her observations and records (and some of Fortune's) to offer an interpretation of kinship and social organization at variance with the interpretation she herself put forward. The fact that I can reanalyze her data only underscores her ethnographic skills and the quality of her data-gathering ability. There is no definitive means of deciding which interpretation is the correct one, but the one I propose is more logically satisfying, elegant, and coherent.

The significant philosophical and epistemological issues here require analysis in greater depth than is possible in this context, but we must at least acknowledge their existence. Is there a "correct" interpretation? Is there only one? How can it be recognized as "correct"? It is easy to give facile answers—for example, the best interpretation is the one that fits the facts better than any other—but then one is left with other problems, such as defining "fit" and identifying "facts" (and ultimately reality itself). A significant and deeply embedded issue is the artificiality of the distinction, at least in anthropology, between fact and interpretation. Although I write here as if Mead collected facts and interpreted them and then I looked at the same facts and interpreted them differently, the process is not that simple: disentangling observation and interpretation is often impossible because both go on simultaneously in the ethnographer's mind and experience. Mead interpreted as she processed her own sensory data and images; hence the materials I worked with to reinterpret were far from some unbiased record of reality.

Mead recognized the centrality of exchange in Mundugumor life, a phenomenon I believe to be the key to understanding the society's social organization.[1] Several quotations from her notes and writings already cited indicate that she saw that the process of exchange in its myriad forms pervaded the society, but she did not go far enough. For example, in *Sex and Temperament* (1963:178–79), she wrote that

the existence of polygyny as an ideal of power means inevitable conflict between brothers, no matter how many sisters they have, and when there are fewer sisters than brothers, this conflict is sharpened. Rivalry is complicated further by the fact that old men can marry young women. In theory, individuals are not permitted to marry out of their generation, but the Mundugumor respect none of their own rules, and the violent social personality that has been fostered in both men and women breaks out in direct sexual rivalry between father and son. The son can trade his sister for a wife; with his sister he can buy a sexual partner. But so also can the father.

The significance of this statement lies not only in the picture it paints of the rivalry between men but also in the fact it underscores that rules of all sorts were frequently violated or broken except the one stipulating that to obtain a wife a man had to provide a woman. Exchange, ideally of sisters but also of daughters, was not easily cast aside within the community despite the apparent frequency and ease with which other rules were circumvented or ignored.[2] Reciprocity and exchange simply took precedence.

Reciprocity in marital exchange was central, but it must be added that the *kamain* relationship also was one of balanced and equal transactions. These two synchronic exchanges—marital and *ka-main*—were similar even if the first involved marriage partners and the second goods and services: ideally, both were egalitarian, relatively simultaneous, and between people of the same generation; the behavioral correlates included formality, distance, name taboos, and respect.

The exchanges that marked a variety of ceremonial occasions contrasted with those of marital and *kamain* exchange—that is, ceremonial occasions such as birth feasts, first-achievement offerings (which sometimes evolved into the more elaborate crocodile-yam feasts), initiation rites, the ritual of release from taboos, enemy skull gifts, and mourning rites. All these significant events in the life of a person were marked by feasting, exchange, or both. Furthermore, all the transactions on these occasions shared certain characteristics that contrast markedly with those of affinal and *ka-main* exchanges: First, formally they were between people of different generations, although if one of the central figures was still a child, parents acted on his or her behalf. Second, the main transactors were always either mother's brother and sister's son or father's sister and brother's daughter,[3] relationships not characterized by a great deal of formality, distance, or respect, especially when classificatory (as was usually true for the major exchanges). Third, the items exchanged were not the same or identical—that is, one did not give a woman and get a woman in return, as in marital exchange, or give a feast of sago grubs and receive a feast of sago grubs, as a *kamain* might; if one gave pigs, he or she was likely to receive yams in return, and so on. Fourth, although the goods exchanged between any particular dyad (e.g., mother's brother–sister's son) were not the same, there was always a delayed balancing out: if, for example, a man received yams from his mother's brother in return for a pig, he would later act as mother's brother and give yams to a descendant of his mother's brother (his own classificatory sister's son), from whom he would receive pigs.

Although these transactions took place on a variety of occasions, they all had the same structure, involved the same people, and continued through generations. From a male perspective all were in a sense matrilateral exchanges, with mother's brother or sister's son. From a woman's point of view they were with father's sister and brother's daughter. If one looks from the perspective not of the transactors but of the intervening relative, a woman observed and mediated exchanges between her brother and her son, a man between his sister and his daughter. On some occasions the sex of the younger generation participant was not relevant, and the exchanges were between mother's brother and sister's child and between father's sister and brother's child.

There were thus two contrasting modes of exchange: intragenerational (e.g., affines and *kamain*) and intergenerational (e.g., mother's brother–sister's son and father's sister–brother's daughter). The first was basically a synchronic exchange of identical items between persons of the same structural positions or equals, the second a diachronic exchange of disparate items between unequals or those in different structural positions. Respect and formality were required in the first, informality and perhaps jesting in the second. Thus, the two modes contrasted in several ways:

intragenerational	*intergenerational*
formality, respect	informality, jesting
same goods	contrasting goods
equality, symmetry	inequality, asymmetry
synchronic	diachronic

However, because the diachronic transactions continued for more than two generations, there was an eventual balancing out at the end; in this sense even these were balanced and equal.

What is especially significant is that ideally a whole complex of exchanges united both modes: an exchange marriage in one generation was followed by diachronic transactions among the descendants of those unions, and the whole series of transactions ended with another exchange marriage, thus at the same time bringing the series to closure, balancing and equalizing the unequal diachronic-disparate exchanges, and beginning another series.[4] Indeed, this was the schema by which the Mundugumor conceptually ordered their society and which embodied all significant values and precepts. Understanding the detailed nature of this intergenerational exchange will also allow us to unravel the puzzles of ropes, their nature and meaning.

INTERGENERATIONAL EXCHANGE

We must begin by looking in detail at the nature of these intergenerational exchanges. To do so requires that we look again at the diagrams of Mead and Fortune (diagrams 6, 7, 8, and 9) and reassemble the various data pertaining to them. The basic and essential relationships are shown in diagram 10.

These 12 people represented the core of Mundugumor social organization and process. Among them were both modes of exchange, intragenerational and intergenerational. The first mode (intragenerational), here basically marriage exchanges in generations 1 and 4, has been amply discussed in chapter 4 and need not be examined in detail again.[5]

There were two kinds of intergenerational exchange, which complemented and in some senses opposed one another. The first was centered on males, particularly on the mother's brother–sister's son

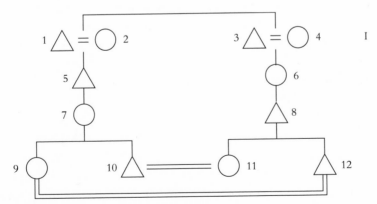

Diagram 10. Reunification of ropes

relationship (although occasionally sister's daughter entered in), while the second focused on females, particularly the father's sister–brother's daughter relationship (although, similarly, sometimes brother's son was also relevant). In this section I describe first the basically male transactions and then the fundamentally female ones. It is important to underscore at the beginning that each of these did not exist in isolation; male and female here opposed and complemented each other, and each was inextricably related to and intertwined with the other. Indeed, the relation—perhaps tension—between female and male was one of the key threads in Mundugumor conceptual thought and was deeply embodied in the social organization.[6]

Although there was no terminological differentiation, there was a behavioral difference between actual and classificatory mother's brother and sister's son.[7] Real mother's brothers were treated with some measure of respect and formality (but nowhere near the formal behavior apparent toward male agnates), and they were "too close" to receive a boy's first-achievement offering. Classificatory mother's brothers, however, were treated with informality, and relations were generally easy and friendly. Nonsexual joking and light horseplay were also typical. Thus the relationship between 3 and 5 in diagram 10 was somewhat formal and respectful, whereas that between classificatory mother's brothers and sister's sons (5 and 8, 8 and 10) was more relaxed and informal. It is very significant that almost all intergenerational exchanges between mothers' brothers and sisters' sons took place between classificatory, not true or close, relatives.

These relatives exchanged on a variety of occasions, including ritual events. Initiation provided the context for significant transactions between mother's brother and sister's son. The mother's brother scarified his classificatory's sister's son (in diagram 10, 5 scarified 8), and in return for this service he received a pig. (As most boys were mere youths when they were initiated, the boy's father was likely to be the actual donor of the pig.) However, in the following generations the directions were reversed, and the boy, 8, now an adult, acted as mother's brother to his classificatory sister's son. But it was not any classificatory sister's son who played the role: the appropriate partner for the exchange, the boy who was scarified and returned a pig, was the grandson (daughter's son) of the man who scarified his mother's brother. Thus, in diagram 10 if 5 scarified 8 and received a pig in return, it was the obligation of 8 to play the role of mother's brother to his classificatory sister's son (daughter's son of 5), who was 10. In this way the exchange was eventually balanced. It is crucial to note here once again the terminological identification between a man and his mother's father (see chapter 4). Because of this identification, 10 was identified with 5, and thus in one sense the exchange was completely reciprocal. If 5 scarified 8 and received a pig in return, then later 8 scarified 10 (identified with or as 5) and received a pig in return.

The same pattern of reciprocation held in the ritual to release initiates from the breadfruit taboos and perhaps other taboo-releasing feasts as well. (There seem to have been no elaborate exchanges on these occasions, but perhaps this observation reflects a lack of data rather than a lack of activities.) One phase of the ritual required a mother's brother (presumably classificatory) to give his sister's son (and perhaps his sister's daughter as well) tobacco and betel nut on a shell ring; later, when the recipient was mature, he was obligated to reciprocate when his mother's brother's daughter's child was initiated. Thus, again looking at diagram 10, if 5 gave goods to 8, then 8 reciprocated when 10 (and perhaps 9) was released from the taboo imposed by the initiation. The same two elements are critical here: matrilateral transaction, especially, but also identification with mother's father.

Here it is necessary to recall a relatively aberrant feature of Mundugumor initiation rites: girls were given the choice of being initiated or not, and if they so desired were initiated along with the boys. Far more data are available on the interaction between mother's brother and sister's son than between mother's brother and sister's daughter (father's sister seems to have been irrelevant or, not surprisingly, identified with father in these contexts). In one place

Mead noted that not only was the nature of the experience different for girls (they were not scarified) but also they were not involved in any economic exchanges. However, in the detailed description of the ceremony to release initiates from the taboo on breadfruit, she noted that an adult woman appeared with a ring "which had been given to her by her [mother's brother], when she saw the *tambaran,* and which she was now returning to the mother's brother's daughter . . . who was not present nor has she been initiated." An adult man (not her mother's brother) took the ring, presumably to deliver it to the appropriate person after the ritual. There is no way of knowing whether this exchange was typical or a voluntary flourish on the part of the participants. It is interesting to note, though, that when the sister's daughter went to reciprocate the ring given to her by her mother's brother, she did not follow the pattern of skipping a generation but apparently gave it directly to her mother's brother's daughter, the classificatory sister with whose son her own brother would transact in the future.

The inheritance of enemy skulls was sometimes incorporated into initiation transactions. A man's own children never received his skull trophies; only his sister's children were allowed to do so. The pattern of this inheritance also continued down generations in exactly the same way as rights to scarification and the reciprocation of a pig. If a man scarified his classificatory sister's son in initiation, it was to this sister's son that he gave his enemy skull; in return the sister's son gave him a pig. (It is not clear in the notes whether the pig given in return for these services during initiation was the same pig or whether an additional animal was required.) Thus, in diagram 10, 5 gave his enemy skulls and the rights to homicidal decoration to 8 and received a pig in return. But the same pattern then continued: when 8 matured, he acted as mother's brother and passed on these enemy skulls to his classificatory sister's son, again not any sister's son but the grandson (daughter's son) of the man from whom he had received them—10, his classificatory sister's son but also his classificatory mother's brother's daughter's son. The skull inheritance pattern was thus completely isomorphic with the scarification during the initiation pattern, having the same matrilateral substance and the same significant identification with mother's father. A man's trophy skulls were thus inherited only by his sister's children and then returned to his daughter's children.

If this transfer of enemy skulls did not take place during initiation, then when the mother's brother died the sister's son inherited them. No reciprocation of a pig was necessary, but later the inheritor did transfer a skull to his mother's brother's daughter's son. A man's sister's children also inherited his net bag, bows and arrows, and spears. If a joking relationship had developed with a particular set of classificatory sister's children, then these relatives took precedence in inheritance. It is important to note that when a man died, it was also possible, if unlikely, that these items were inherited not by a sister's son but by a mother's brother, a fact that fits well with the pattern of identification between a mother's father and a daughter's son.

A sister's son (or mother's brother if the deceased was a child) performed several services at the death of his relative. He put totemic leaves on the roof of the house (along with the accompanying ghost of the dead), he made the initial skull decoration, and he ate the final feast and escorted the ghost from the village. Unfortunately the notes are not clear whether these actions were performed by real or classificatory relatives or whether any sort of reciprocation or payment for items inherited was perceived to be necessary.

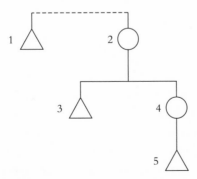

Diagram 11. Matrilateral exchange

One fact about transactions during mourning rituals presents a puzzle. If a sister's son, for whatever reason, did not inherit the enemy skulls, spears, and so on, then the sister's daughter did. This fact does fit well with the established pattern of matrilateral exchange, but Mead noted that the sister's daughter then passed these items on to her son. In diagram 11, 1's possessions would ordinarily have gone to his classificatory sister's son, 3, but in exceptional circumstances (such as 2 having no sons), these then went to classificatory sister's daughter, 4, who gave them to her son, 5. In one sense this is strict matrilateral inheritance, for the items went *as if* from mother's brother to sister's son, as if 3 had inherited them and passed them on to his sister's son, 5. By now this matrilateral inheritance is no surprise. The problem and potential puzzle is that if 3 had inherited, he should have passed on at least the enemy skulls to his own classificatory sister's son, not his real sister's son, or to his classificatory mother's brother's daughter's son (not shown on diagram 11). There are two possible explanations for this anomaly: (1) it may be an alternative way to pass on enemy skulls, a different procedure altogether even though it is still fundamentally and essentially matrilateral; or (2) Mead and Fortune, who were frequently imprecise about whether relatives referred to were real or classificatory, may have been so here. It is possible that the goods were given not to 3's real sister but to a classificatory one, who then passed them on to her son. Or it is possible that 4 acted as if she had been her brother, 3, and passed them on to his classificatory sister's son—that is, her own classificatory son. Unfortunately, there is no definitive way to determine which of these alternative explanations is the better one.

Significant transactions also took place between classificatory mother's brother and sister's son in the context of first-achievement offerings. Boys presented their mother's brothers with their first kills of pig, cassowary, cuscus, and bandicoot. The notes do not indicate whether the mother's brother reciprocated these first prestations immediately, but clearly this exchange ideally developed into a more elaborate one between these two kin in which the mother's brother reciprocated with what Mead called a crocodile-yam feast. The sister's son presented his first kills (and, by extension, meat in general) to his mother's brother, and the latter reciprocated with a predominantly vegetable feast. The mother's brother built a large model crocodile, adorned it with a large triangular palm spathe painting, and filled it with yams. Unfortunately, there are no data to indicate whether sister's son behaved as mother's brother for his mother's brother's daughter's son, as was the case in initiation.

Finally, not all interactions between mother's brother and sister's son involved transactions of a material and complementary nature. On some occasions (e.g., initiation) they shared food rather than exchanged it. During the ceremony to launch a war canoe, they were opposed and even in challenging and antagonistic positions vis-à-vis each other, and there are no data to suggest that the event included material transactions.

This brief survey of the mother's brother–sister's son relationship and the transactions inherent in it indicates that it was central in the pattern of intergenerational exchange. Furthermore, the survey highlights the critical role of matrilateral exchange among the descendants of intermarrying pairs of siblings. The fundamental significance of the identification between a man and his mother's father is also apparent. But these transactions, basically matrilateral, are only half the story of intergenerational exchange: there is another whole side that revolved around the tie between father's sister and brother's daughter (and brother's son), and it is to this phenomenon we must now turn.

The behavioral components of the relationship between father's sister and brother's children were basically friendly and informal. Nonsexual joking was a significant aspect, especially between classificatory father's sister and brother's child. More jesting occurred between father's sister and brother's son than between father's sister and brother's daughter.

Neither Mead nor Fortune paid as much attention to the transactions involving father's sister as those involving mother's brother, but the significant role she played is evident from their diagrams (see diagrams 6, 7, 8, and 9 in chapter 4). These diagrams highlight a reciprocal transaction between father's sister and brother's daughter in the context of ear piercing: a woman acting as classificatory father's sister was in charge of piercing the ears of her brother's daughter. In the next generation the girl, now grown, acted as father's sister and pierced the ears of her classificatory brother's daughter, the original father's sister's son's daughter. In diagram 10, 6 pierced the ears of 7, her classificatory brother's daughter, and in the following generation 7 pierced the ears of 11, 6's son's daughter. According to Mead's and Fortune's diagrams, this series of transactions was the exact mirror image of that between mother's brother and sister's son. Although one probably would not describe it as matrilateral, it did concern the opposite, or cross-sex, relative. Furthermore, the same identification with grandparent was central: a woman (e.g., 11 in diagram 10) identified with her father's mother; again, in an identificatory sense the exchanges were between the same structural positions and thus balanced.

The narrative textual description of ear piercing supplements the information provided by the diagram. It is clear that father's sister was central in this context, especially for brother's daughter but also for brother's son. Father's sister received a feast in return for her services, and it was the child's father (the brother of the woman acting as father's sister) who actually provided the feast. A man thus paid his sister for services rendered. (Mead also notes that sometimes father himself actually did the piercing; what this means and what it says about the actual role of father's sister is impossible to determine, but it is true that father and father's sister were often structurally equated.) Finally, although the details are sparse, it must also be mentioned here that on the occasion of nose piercing, father's sister received a feast as well, so it is likely that the structural and transactional alignments in nose piercing were the same as in ear piercing.

There is something odd about Mead's diagram (diagram 6) and subsequent description of the ear-piercing ceremonials. She clearly stated, as well as indicated on her diagram, that brother's daughter gave shell rings to her father's sister. The direction of this transaction, from brother's daughter to father's sister, or younger generation to older generation, is the reverse of the same transactions (described later) in the context of birth and taboo-releasing ceremonies, during which the father's sister gave rings to the brother's daughter. All other intergenerational exchanges are consistent: if the elder generation gives a particular item to the younger generation, then the younger relative never gives back the same item in return, in the same or any other context. I think that Mead made an error in the direction, and Fortune's cursory notes on ear piercing confirm it: father's sister gave rings to brother's daughter in all of these ceremonial contexts.

Father's sister also played a significant role in the process of birth. She cared for the newborn child (her brother's child) and the new mother (her brother's wife), cooked for them, and so on. Usually a classificatory father's sister of the newborn assumed this role, and in return she was given a feast (which included pork) to "wash her hands" from the birth. This feast was provided by the baby's father, her classificatory brother, and she reciprocated the feast by giving rings; whether these rings were officially given to the new baby or the father is not clear.

The same pattern appeared in the context of performing taboo-releasing activities for a child. Remember that newborns and toddlers were subject to a variety of food taboos (including their totemic animals); it was the child's father's sister who released her or him from these restrictions by ritually passing the food under her armpit (then either the child ate the food, or, if he or she was still too young, the father's sister touched it to the child's lips). When describing this event, Mead noted something that probably applied to all situations involving father's sister: if a man was lazy, he would ask his real sister to perform the activity so that he would have few obligations to reciprocate.[8] Ideally, however, a classificatory father's sister performed the ritual, which then became an important feasting event. The child's father gave a large feast (including meat) to this classificatory sister, and she returned, again, rings.

Young girls also made first-achievement offerings (e.g., their first fish caught, their first sago processed) to their classificatory father's sisters, who reciprocated with "small, private feasts." There was no escalation of these transactions comparable to the crocodile-yam feasts between mother's brother and sister's son.

The notes do not indicate whether birth, taboo-releasing, and first-achievement transactions continued on into the next generation. It is possible that they did, as did ear-piercing exchanges, but not certain.

Finally, there is some confusion about *naven*-like behavior on the part of father's sister. The confusion stems from the fact that it is not clear whether father's sister or mother's brother's wife was the central character, as this narrative related by Omblean in 1938 illustrates:

> If I do something, like killing an enemy, *unyenya* can do something. Or if I go and kill a pig. . . . She can *singsing*. . . . She gets up and doesn't really sing, she said, "Good *mivafoh*, bring him here." Alright, she dances, bends the palm bark floor of the house. She goes and holds him, holds him tightly and says, "You're very good. You learned to kill. You'll always kill successfully. It won't be long before you kill again and we will eat. Later kills your brothers and sisters will eat. But now it is just us." (All the relatives of this line of *gumi* and *unyenya*, they meet and eat together.)

Here, *unyenya* could refer either to father's sister or mother's brother's wife. This may seem an irrelevant distinction to worry about,[9] but it is analytically relevant because the young man's main interaction may have been with mother's brother (and, by association, his wife) rather than with father's sister (and again, by association, her husband). If these activities involved real rather than classificatory relatives, then the problem is not as apparent because father's sister was more likely to be married to mother's brother. Unfortunately, there are no further details.

In any case the transactions between classificatory father's sister and brother's daughter (and brother's son) were basically consistent. Father's sister performed services for her brother's child, and in return her brother (and his child) gave her feasts, predominantly of meat. In at least one ritual context (ear piercing), this pattern continued into the next generation, as did that between mother's brother and sister's son. This second intergenerational exchange pattern, predominantly but not exclusively between women (father's sister and brother's daughter, with brother, father or sometimes brother's son mediating), acted as a complement and counterbalance to the first intergenerational exchange series between men (with mother or sister mediating).

At the core of social organization were these two series of intergenerational exchanges. In both, a central task of the elder generation relatives (mother's brother or father's sister) was to provide ritual services (scarification, taboo releasing, and so on); they also gave items of value (e.g., skull trophies and shell rings). On only two occasions did they give food: mother's brother gave yams to sister's son in the crocodile-yam feasts, and father's sister reciprocated brother's daughter's first-achievement offerings with a small feast. The second generation—sister's son and brother's daughter—reciprocated these services and prestations predominantly with gifts of food, especially meat (never garden produce). There were only two exceptions to this general rule, both somewhat expectable. Brother's daughter gave first offerings to her father's sister that were appropriate to her sex—for example, fish and sago pudding (not red meat). Sister's son performed services on the death of mother's brother, when he inherited mother's brother's personal possessions (spears and so on). In general, then, both series of exchanges were similar in that senior kin provided services and gave items that were reciprocated with food, especially meat. The two series were also similar in that they continued for at least two generations, and both employed the significant identification between grandparent and grandchild (father's mother with son's daughter, mother's father with daughter's son).

These two series, then, were in some ways opposed but in other ways similar. One of the most significant ways in which they were structurally the same was that cross-relatives were profoundly significant. In each case of transaction, if we trace through the mediating kinsperson, we find that the official transactors are of the same sex but are connected by a member of the opposite sex (a male connects father's sister and brother's daughter; a female connects mother's brother with sister's son). (The exceptions may be insignificant; e.g., a father's sister would attend to the birth of brother's daughter or brother's son, but see later discussion.) It is also interesting to note the same pattern in the identification with the grandparental generation—again, those who were identified were of the same sex, but the intervening link was of the opposite sex.

Despite the fact that these two series of exchanges are in an essential way opposed to each other, they are also structurally equivalent and involve a directionality and content of prestations that are also similar. Furthermore, they form complementary parts of one entire complex that begins with brother-sister exchange marriage in the generation before the transactions begin and ends with a second brother-sister exchange marriage that completes the old cycle and begins another.

But the relationship between these two series was inextricable not only because they were structurally similar yet conceptually opposed or complementary parts of the same whole. If one looks predominantly at the formal arrangements, the transactions "in name," then the pattern appears to be the binary zig-zag down generations, as in diagram 6. However, if we shift attention to who was actually doing and producing and giving, then another highly significant fact emerges: the central and overriding importance of the brother-sister tie. The two cases of brother-sister exchange marriage in the total complex are obvious, but it is also true that in the generations intervening between the two marriage exchanges (in diagram 10, generations 2 and 3), the classificatory brother and sister in each are actually performing ritual services (which are reciprocated) for each other's children. It is not the child who reciprocated with a feast or meat on these ritual occasions, but his or her parents. Only in the case of first offerings (which, in the case of boys, might have continued into adulthood as crocodile-yam feasts) does the junior generation member actually assume the responsibility for producing the goods (he or she does, however, reciprocate in the next generation, when he or she becomes the senior relative). In generation 2 in diagram 10, 5 and 6 (classificatory brother and sister) reciprocate ritual services for each other's children, and these children (also themselves classificatory siblings) do the same in the next generation. It is the brother-sister relationship that continues down the generations and provides the pivot on which all other exchanges hinge. Finally, affines are brought into the picture as well—the spouses of 5 and 6 are also involved (e.g., when 8 "gives" a pig to his mother's brother in return for initiation services, it is surely his father, 6's husband, who actually produces the pig). Thus, in another sense these two series of exchanges are further intertwined because in generations 2 and 3 these classificatory siblings are exchanging with one another.

I wish to stress two further points about this whole complex in diagram 10 before going on to examine the concept of ropes. The first is the significance of the identification with the grandparental generation. If we begin in generation 2 (diagram 10), 5's significant possessions (e.g., skull trophies and so on) are first given to 8, who then gives them to 10. The same pattern obtains with 6: she gives rings to 7, who passes rings on to 11. There are two remarkable aspects here: first, the goods eventually end up with the grandchild who is identified with the grandparent who began the transactions, and thus in one way they end up where they began. Second, if one was to ignore the intervening transactions, the inheritance of these objects would appear to be through alternating sexes (a fact of central importance in later discussion). It is also worth mentioning again that because of this identification with a particular grandparent, the marriage between third cross-cousins 10 and 11 in generation 4 (diagram 10) is, again in this identificatory sense, between first cross-cousins.

The second major point is the behavioral distancing that occurs down the generations. The classificatory brother-sister pairs in generations 2 and 3 are, in Mundugumor thought, too close to marry, but the behavioral components of these ties change down the generations and generate enough distance to allow the marriages in generation 4. Remember that the classificatory brother and sister in generation 2 are too close—they not only may not marry but also may not jest with each other. The classificatory brother-sister pair in generation 3 are more distant from each other; ideally, they too were not to marry, but they did joke with each other. Finally, in the last generation (generation 4), the relatives were distant enough for marriage to occur, and ideally these were the most proper marriages. But note that if they did marry, all joking ceased. Here it is apparent that jesting was either a force for or a reflection of distance, and it was opposed to the intimacy of marriage (a common occurrence cross-culturally). The transactions of the intergenerational exchange system certainly helped generate the necessary distance by defining these kin as structurally opposed and apart so that they could operate as separate identities and exchange goods and services.

AN ALTERNATIVE INTERPRETATION OF ROPE

I presented Mead's and Fortune's analysis and interpretation of rope *(geun)* in chapter 4. All the written data in the notes on which Mead based her analysis are given in full, basically without comment. It is now time to look more closely at ropes and to reexamine the data. What I suggest here is an alternative interpretation based on the notes and the system of intergenerational exchange described earlier. Briefly, I maintain that ropes were not related to descent at all but were a metaphor for this complex of intergenerational exchanges in which strands of the descendants of intermarrying pairs of brothers and sisters were woven together and reunited in the fourth generation. Like most anthropological interpretations, this one cannot be unassailably proven, but it is more logically satisfying.

If all one had to work with was the published data on ropes, there would be little or no reason to attempt an alternative interpretation (and of course no additional information with which to do so). Although anthropologists have wondered about the system, we know that human groups have created a great variety of ways in which to organize themselves, and there is no reason that the Mundugumor could not have incorporated a form of descent based on alternating sex links. Indeed, complex organizations are common, especially throughout the Sepik area (see, for example, Thurnwald [1916] on the Banaro; see also Williams [1932] on what he called "sex affiliation" elsewhere). However, given the analysis in *Sex and Temperament* (which was never meant to be a description of social organization) and the raw notes, a variety of problems and contradictions leads one to question the interpretation offered by Mead.

The best place to begin a new understanding of the concept of rope is with the literal meaning of the word *geun*. Both Mead and Fortune agree that it actually referred to a real, physical rope. Mead noted that "a *geun* is literally a rope, [it] is also used to signify string with which fishing nets are made—note that this is a two-strand twine—and also the two sides in children's games." Although Fortune couched the literal meaning of the word *geun* in the context of alternating sex links in descent, it is clear that he recorded the same basic meaning: "The Mundugumor conceived of marriage with [a] metaphor taken from the manufacture of fish line, netting, cord or rope as the interweaving of pairs of descent lines of alternating sex with successive generations as if such lines were the plies of a two-ply cord or rope." There are several important points in these two quotes: (1) *geun* literally meant rope or cord; (2) the rope or cord was two-ply; (3) the word was sometimes used metaphorically to represent two sides (e.g., in children's games); and, most important, (4) Fortune noted that it was used metaphorically for marriages that interwove two "lines" back together. Fortune believed that the lines were of descent based on alternating sex links, but he did not clearly state that these separate lines themselves were ropes; hence, a possible ambiguity exists. His statement quoted earlier does indicate, however, that rope referred metaphorically to the interwoven strands together, not each separate strand or line. Mead also wrote that the ideal marriage was one that repeated "in the fifth generation . . . the personalities—name, leaves, etc., of the pair of ancestors who were the *progenitors of the split rope*" [emphasis added], thus indicating that both lines down from the original intermarrying pair were included in the whole rope (in diagram 10, 2–5–7 was not a whole rope but part of one; 3–6–8 was the other part). These are essential clues: *geun* was a metaphor for the entire complex of exchanges that wove together the descendants of a brother-sister pair and eventually came to fruition in the repeating marriage. The alternating female-male-female line of relatives itself was not the rope but only one of two strands that comprised the *geun*.

In 1981, when I visited Kinakatem, I asked several men what the word *geun* meant. Their reply was straightforward, quick, and unanimous: it meant rope, simply a rope. I explained that Mead had noted that it had something to do with kinship, and they were clearly puzzled. Their knowledge of traditional kinship forms was in some ways sparse indeed: men in their thirties were unable to recall kin terms because they had been using pidgin terminology most of their lives and told me to ask old men who might remember (they did know terms for the nuclear family but completely failed to recall second ascending and second descending generation terms). They pondered the question of kinship and ropes for awhile, and finally one man thought he had the answer (and the others agreed that although their knowledge was sparse, this sounded correct). He said that rope could refer to "all of these ropes, all of us together— pig, cassowary [I assume these refer to totemic or clan names]." He continued by saying that if you left, if you cut your ties with your kin, you "broke the rope."[10] Someone desiring to cut his or her ties could literally attach a woven armband to his or her arm and then cut it off, saying, "I cut the rope, I am no longer with you, I am alone."

These additional data are interesting for two reasons. First, the information validates Mead's and Fortune's literal translation of *geun* as rope. Second, when people were asked to place the term in the context of kinship, what emerged was a metaphor, not a descent group or any specific kin ties. I am not suggesting that this information is sufficient to undermine completely or even substantially Mead's interpretation of ropes; although older men (some of whom were nearing adulthood in 1932) were present, one cannot rely on data gathered almost 50 years later. The changes that occurred during this time were in some ways dramatic, and by their own admission many of these men simply did not know much. However, we cannot totally discount these data; they provide one clue that when added to others is significant.

My main contention, then, is that ropes as described by Mead were not descent groups at all but that the word *geun* was used as a metaphor to describe the complex interweaving of relationships and ties between classificatory brother-sister pairs and their children over time, ties that began and ended with brother-sister exchange marriage. Instead of seeing the alternation of male-female-male and so on down generations as the organizing principle of this complex set of transactions and relationships, I suggest that this sexual alternation was a by-product of the system stipulating that descendants of a brother-sister pair, themselves classificatory sister and brother, engage in transactions with each other and their children until enough distance had been created to allow for reunification through intermarriage.

Forget for a moment Mead's definition of a rope and look only at the descendants of intermarrying pairs of sister and brother (diagram 12). We know that brother-sister exchange marriages were supposed to occur in generation 4, but sibling sets 1 through 4 are all third cross-cousins (i.e., appropriate marriage partners) to sibling sets 5 through 8. Who is supposed to marry whom? Here we can invoke the rule that these marriages are supposed to reunite two "lines" that have been performing ritual services for or exchanging with each other for two generations, and these exchanges were always between a classificatory brother and sister and their children. Of the 16 possible marriages in generation 4 (diagram 12), only two would permit the fulfillment of these rules. To demonstrate this it is necessary to examine all 16 possible marital exchanges (diagram 13).

Diagram 13a represents the eventual marriage between sibling sets 1 and 5. According to the exchange rules, this marriage would not reunite lines that had been transacting for the previous two generations because in generation 2 both people (E and F) are male, and therefore the appropriate exchanges could not have taken place. E and F, for example, have no sister's sons to scarify here, G has no mother's brother, H has no father's sister, and so forth—so the marriages in generation 4 would not reunite the appropriate relatives; the marriages would not be the culmination of intergenerational exchange and therefore not proper marriages. The same observation can be phrased in a different way: E and F should each scarify their classificatory sister's sons, but these men of generation 3, not shown on the diagram, are not the ascending relatives of the sibling sets in generation 4.

Similar reasoning obtains to rule out other possible combinations. Diagram 13b illustrates the marriage of sibling sets 1 and 6; again, the two males in generation 2 preclude the correct exchanges from

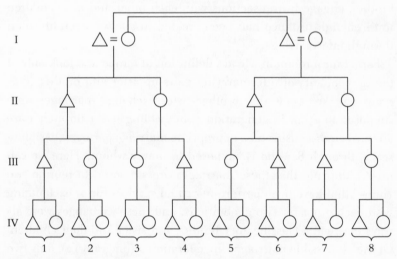

Diagram 12. Descendants of brother-sister exchange

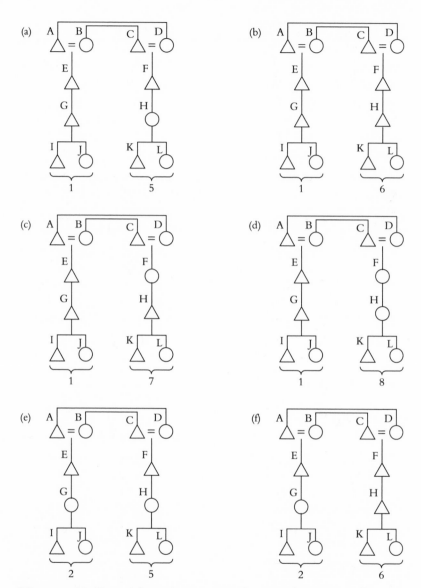

Diagram 13. Potential marriage partners (*continued on next page*)

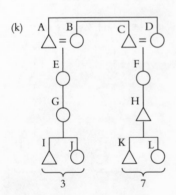

Diagram 13   *(continued)*

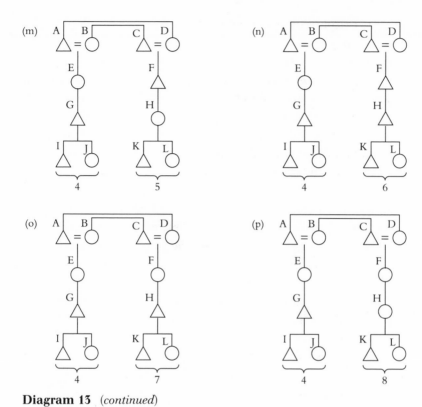

Diagram 13 *(continued)*

ever beginning. In fact, wherever two males appear in generation 2, we can exclude the resultant marriage in generation 4; all such marriages are incorrect. This is true not only for the two cases already mentioned but also for the potential marriage between sibling sets 2 and 5 (diagram 13e) and sibling sets 2 and 6 (diagram 13f). Thus 4 possible sibling-set marriages of the 16 must be excluded because both people in generation 2 are male, and the transactional pattern necessary would be violated. However, the same problem—the inability to execute the appropriate transactions—occurs if both people in generation 3 are male. Thus, we can also rule out marriages between sibling sets 1 and 7 (diagram 13c), between sibling sets 4 and 6 (diagram 13n), and sibling sets 4 and 7 (Diagram 13o).

(For this reason a marriage between sibling sets 1 and 6 [diagram 13b] is doubly excluded.)

Of course, the same reasoning applies if both people in generation 2 or generation 3 are female. They would not represent the kin with whom the correct transactions occurred. We can thus also exclude as inappropriate the marriages between sibling sets 2 and 8 (diagram 13h), 3 and 5 (diagram 13i), 3 and 7 (diagram 13k), 3 and 8 (diagram 13l), and 4 and 8 (diagram 13p). Sibling sets 2 and 5 (diagram 13e) and 4 and 7 (diagram 13o) are thus also doubly excluded.

We are left, then, with only four possibilities for executing the appropriate culminating marriages. First examine diagram 13d, which represents the marriages of sibling sets 1 and 8. Both generations 2 and 3 contain classificatory brother-sister pairs, so the first problem encountered is not relevant here. However, the correct transactions still cannot take place between these people. E does have a sister, but his sister's son is not among this constellation of kin, and F has a brother but no brother's daughter. The exchange transactions that culminate in third cross-cousin marriage are not between these relatives, and therefore the marriage of sibling sets 1 and 8 is also inappropriate. For the same reasons the marriage between sibling sets 3 and 6 (diagram 13j) is also wrong.

Finally, we are left with two possible marriage exchanges, both of which do fulfill all the requirements for the culminating marriage transactions. A marriage between sibling sets 2 and 7 (diagram 13g) is perfect: E scarifies his classificatory sister's son, H, who in turn scarifies his classificatory sister's son, I; F pierces the ears of her classificatory brother's daughter, G, who pierces the ears of her classificatory brother's daughter, L, and so on. For the same reasons the marriage between sibling sets 4 and 5 (diagram 13m) is also a correct marriage.

What makes these marriages "correct" and the others "incorrect" is simply that they represent the possible culmination of transactions between classificatory brother-sister pairs and their children as both Mead and Fortune describe as necessary (logically necessary—in fact, these marriages rarely took place). For this to occur two things are required in generations 2 and 3: (1) the people in each generation must be classificatory sister and brother—that is, they must be of opposite sex; and (2) both people in adjacent generations (e.g., E and G, I and H in all of diagram 13), related as parent-child, must also be of opposite sex. In other words E and F must be of opposite sex, as must also G and H, but E and H must be the same sex (so that they are related as mother's brother–sister son or father's sister–brother's daughter), as must also be F and G (for the same reason). If either of these two conditions is not met, then the intergenerational exchange pattern is broken.

The reader will no doubt have noticed that diagrams 13g and 13m look familiar: they are essentially the same as diagrams 6, 9, and 10. That is because the alternation of sexes is required to fulfill the exchange pattern, and in this way what Mead called a rope is really only a by-product of the transactions of intergenerational exchange. If one subscribes to the desirability of elegance in models, one begins to wonder just why and how this alternative interpretation is in any way better than Mead's. There are two separate but related reasons to prefer this alternative: (1) it seems to correspond more closely to the conceptual system of the Mundugumor themselves, in which exchange was more central than descent; and (2) Mead's data and her interpretation of those data contain contradictions that are significantly resolved if the alternative interpretation is accepted.

One of the most obvious problems with Mead's interpretation of ropes is in generation 4 (diagram 10), where the reunification of two ropes is supposed to occur. Because of brother-sister exchange marriage there are two unions (between 9 and 12 and between 10 and 11), not one, but only one of these marriages (between 10 and 11) conforms to the rope rule as presented by Mead. The other, between 9 and 12, does not: 12 would not be a member of his father's rope, nor would 9 be a member of her mother's. And yet there is no doubt that this is the correct marriage exchange in this generation. Ropes as Mead envisioned them are not relevant. What is important is that

third cross-cousins marry and that second cross-cousins (the classificatory brother and sister, 7 and 8), who are involved in significant
exchanges, arrange a marital exchange between their children.
There can be no doubt that brother-sister exchange marriage was
required as well. If the reunification of ropes as described by Mead
was the dominant concern, ideally 12 would certainly not marry 9.
The requirement of exchange marriage, then, necessarily violated
the rope reunification principle; these two were simply contradictory.[11]

Another problem is that both Mead and Fortune underestimated
the importance of the brother-sister relationship in general. Mead
did note (in *Sex and Temperament* and in the notes) that it was a
significant force, especially in the context of arranging marriages,
that ran counter to the rope arrangements, but logical evidence exists that the tie was an integral part of the whole complex rather
than an opposing force. The interpretation I have offered stresses
the significance of the relationship, especially between classificatory opposite-sex siblings, but further support is contained within
the pattern of ideal marriages itself. If one begins with two intermarrying pairs of brothers and sisters (diagrams 12 and 13), one
ends up with two sets of brother-sister exchange marriages in generation 4, but these are not the ones indicated by Mead (in diagram
6) and Fortune (in diagram 9). Both of these conform to the rules of
exchange and appear to follow Mead's rope pattern. The reason one
ends up with two marital exchanges, not one, is that one began with
two sets of siblings. In fact, it is the descendants of a single brother-
sister pair who reunite in the fourth generation; the exchange marriages shown in generation 1 in diagrams 6, 9, and 10 are not logically necessary to accomplish the required result. If we look again
at diagrams 13g and 13m, this becomes obvious. In diagram 13g,
the sibling set A and D could be deleted without changing the pattern, and the same would occur if we deleted sibling set B and C
from diagram 13m. Thus, the simplest schematic representation of
the rope phenomenon would be as shown in diagram 14. The central significance of the sister-brother tie is clear.

There are reasons, however, to examine both sets of descendants from two intermarrying pairs of brothers and sisters (i.e., to combine diagrams 13g and 13m into one). One motivation is simply that the exchange marriage was of critical importance in social organization and social life, and so including it in the first generation is a more accurate rendering of how the Mundugumor conceptualized their system. A second reason is that doing so reveals a fundamental principle of the marriage system that has not yet been brought into prominence although it has been lurking in the background of this discussion: the marriage rule was, in fact, that of simple bilateral third cross-cousin marriage.

Diagram 15 combines diagrams 13g and 13m to show the total pattern. First examine the marriage of M. Following Mead's conception of ropes, he marries his MFMBDSD (female T), but because of the sister-brother exchange marriage in generation 1, the woman T is also his MFFZDSD (traced this way, it is a violation of Mead's ropes; see also Omblean's genealogies [genealogies 8 and 9] in chapter 4). If we look at it from the perspective of the woman T herself, she too conforms to the rope idea if we trace her relationship to her husband as FMFZSDS but not if we trace it as FMMBSDS. The same relationships are involved in the marriage of

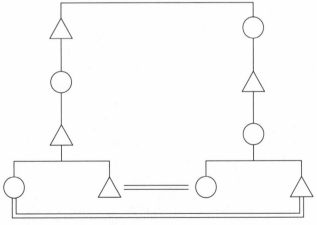

Diagram 14. Ropes, simplified

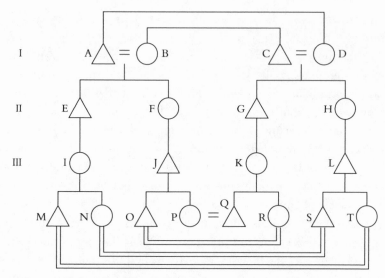

Diagram 15. Marriage pattern

Q and P. Q marries his MFMBDSD, who is also his MFFZDSD, and P marries her FMFZSDS, who is also her FMMBSDS. The other two marriages, those between O and R and between S and N, however, in no way conform to Mead's idea of ropes, although they do conform to all the other ideals and are in fact third bilateral cross-cousin marriages. O marries his FMFZSDD, who is also his FMMBSDD, as does S; R marries O, her MFMBDSS, who is also her MFFZDSS (as does N when she marries S). Thus, the real pattern of the ideal marriage system was third bilateral cross cousin marriage with brother-sister exchange; not only did the descendants of a sister-brother pair reunite in marriage in the fourth generation, but also the descendants of the marriage of A and B married the descendants of C and D.

The interpretation of rope that I am proposing here has its problems as well, the most serious of which has to do with inheritance. Mead clearly states that a variety of items was inherited "down the ropes," and by that she meant from mother to son to son's daughter or from father to daughter to daughter's son and so on. My assertion that *geun* is a metaphor for this whole complex does not accommodate this kind of inheritance within what Mead believed to be descent relations (the nature of descent will be discussed more later). I cannot resolve this problem completely, but a close examination of this inheritance will introduce sufficient doubt to allow my alternative at least equal plausibility. The suggestions that follow, then, are speculative.

In various places in her notes and in *Sex and Temperament*, Mead listed all the following items as being those that were inherited "down the ropes": all property (including weapons), sacred flutes, slitgongs, some names, bows and arrows, spears, large sago storage pots, new sago patches, seed yams, new *barets*, new coconut and betel nut trees, large house posts, axes, totemic emblems, and trees and land. When they are listed together in this way, the ambiguities and contradictions become apparent.[12] First of all, in many other places and contexts Mead made it perfectly clear that ropes did not own any land—only patrilineal descent groups did; so we can exclude land from this list. The list also includes the general term "weapons" as well as specific items (bows, arrows, and spears), but elsewhere Mead maintains that these were inherited by sister's son at the death of mother's brother; they were not inherited by a man's daughter or a woman's son. These items were a part of the pattern of intergenerational exchange already described. It is interesting to note that the reference to all property (even weapons) descending from father to daughter is not in the field notes but in *Sex and Temperament* (1963:176). It is possible, then, that the statement that all property, even weapons, was inherited down the ropes was a generalization without support from Mead's own data. That trees and *barets* in general were inherited "down the ropes" probably refers only to newly planted trees and recently constructed *barets*, not older, established ones that were owned patrilineally. However, I suggest that the passing of these new items to children of the opposite sex was not a structural imperative but a choice based on sentiment. The fruits of one's own personal labors were perhaps free to be given to whomever one chose because they had not yet been incorporated as group property; and because of the close tie of affect between mother and son and between father and daughter, it appeared that formal inheritance went from parent to child of opposite sex. This is admittedly only a guess. The only support, indirect at best, is that large house posts were also supposed to follow the "rope" pattern. However, this applied only to trees that would make good posts; a woman who spied such a tree marked it for her son, a man for his daughter. Houses once constructed and house sites were patrilineally inherited. It is also possible that a woman assisted her son whenever she could in order to strengthen the exchanges between her son and her brother (the son's mother's brother), with whom he transacted; a man assisted his daughter to support the exchange she had with her father's sister. Doing so enriched his or her classificatory sibling.

The inheritance of sacred objects was not as unequivocal as Mead asserted. First, in her first dated reference to ropes in the notes she wrote that "*ashins* or *maindjimis* can descend along a rope, either male or female or mixed. So for all property." Similarly, "*maindjimis* are inherited down ropes, preferably always with a change of sex. *Ashins* and *yakats* are similarly inherited." Later Mead held the view that ropes required the alternation of sexes and asserted that sacred objects were always inherited in this fashion. It is equally plausible that these sacred objects, especially flutes, were transferred to descending generations via the mechanism of intergenerational exchange. A woman brought a flute to her marriage (or with her at marriage), but if she meant to elope it was her brother who held on to the flute and prevented her from taking it to bequeath to her son. Further, the son (according to Fortune's notes) actually received the flute during his initiation, during which his mother's brother was the central figure. These two facts at least tentatively suggest that the woman's brother was in some proprietary way associated with the flute and its transference to the next generation. The phrase "rope inheritance" by Fortune also suggests that inheritance through the rope was the rope metaphorically conceived: "The handing down of personal names, personal signal calls on slit-gong drums and initiatory bamboo flutes *in the two lines of a rope* was maintained, and second cousins were sometimes invited to initiate or to pierce the ears of third cousins in the way which was prescribed by their theory of the conduct of relations between themselves" [emphasis added]. Thus, according to Fortune, sacred flutes went "down the rope," but the rope had two interwoven strands and did not refer to a single strand of alternating sex. Perhaps the items passed from one strand to another and back again.

Mead noted another fact relevant here: "rope inheritance" ensured that important objects such as sacred flutes were passed on to one's own namesake in the second descending generation. Here again the identification between a man and his mother's father and a woman and her father's mother was central. The whole system operated so that objects would eventually reach these identificatory relatives. Mead wrote, "So the whole system may be regarded as passing [sacred flutes] down to one's namesake, or the equivalent." But one of the main functions of the intergenerational exchange system was to do precisely the same thing. This fact, along with Fortune's observations, suggests at least the possibility that these sacred objects were also a part of the intergenerational exchange and not formally inherited down lines of alternating sex.

There are no additional data on the inheritance of slitgongs, large sago storage pots, seed yams, and axes, so I can make no further suggestions about them. The issue of the inheritance of names is so ambiguous and the data so contradictory (they are inherited patrilineally, they are inherited down ropes, and so forth) that we can make little further sense here either. (I suspect, given the data on naming, that names were inherited patrilineally but that women had the right to bestow their clan's names on their sons, and these men then could pass them on as if they were patrilineal possessions. Thus in diagram 10, if 2 and 3 belonged to the same patrilineal group, then 2 could give one of the names to 5, 6 could give the same name to 8, and 7 could give it to her son, 10; or 8 could give it to his classificatory sister's son, also 10. All of this is very speculative. Another possibility is that there were two naming systems—a patrilineal one that was congruent with *maindjimi* names and another that was not.)

On the question of totemism I can give neither final answers nor even tentative suggestions. There are simply not enough detailed data, so I leave it as presented in earlier chapters.

One last item is relevant to "rope inheritance." Mead maintained that if a rope died out—that is, if there were no children of the sex opposite to that of the relevant parent—a same-sex child could inherit all possessions. Elsewhere, she noted that when a "rope" died, its land (this reference is the source of the inclusion of land in the list of things inherited down ropes) and *barets* go to "collateral lines." Just what kin composed these collateral lines is not clear.

My suggestion, then, is basically that formal structured inheritance of these objects was not by alternating sexes but was structured by the ideal marriage system and intergenerational exchange. That Mead recognized the close relationship is clear in the following passage from her notes:

If the ideal marriage scheme is followed, the same marriage will recur in the fourth descendant generation. However it is a simpler scheme to regard the whole society as based on ropes, with all descent except land, following this plan. So *ashins*, names, *maindjimis*, birds and plants [totemic emblems] are inherited in the ropes, and the economic arrangements for cutting, ear piercing, inheritance of skulls of enemies, rings, the personal property which is placed by the corpse, are all a form of reciprocity between ropes which culminates in the fourth generation in intermarriage, the forming of two strands again, and these two strands may but of course not necessarily reunite again after four generations or more.

It is probably making too much of a rough suggestion to emphasize Mead's shift from the ideal marriage system as the structural focus to the suggestion that it is simpler to see everything as structured by ropes, but it is certainly worth remarking upon. It is possible that Mead simply saw ropes as a more elegant way of describing an elaborate and complex set of relationships and transactions. Thus, the rope as descent conception might be a phenomenon in the head of the ethnographer that was not necessarily present in the minds of the Mundugumor. Again, a caution is necessary: this is a raw field note and not a finished idea, so one cannot rely heavily on it.

I have argued that rope *(geun)* was really a metaphor for the re-unification of the descendants of two intermarrying pairs of siblings and a metaphor for a complex set of transactions and relations that interwove people and groups and culminated in another sister-brother exchange marriage. Mead and Fortune also saw the whole phenomenon, regardless of what it is called, in terms of interweaving and bringing together. The whole point of the marriage in the fourth generation was to bring everyone and everything back together. Not only were the descendants of the first-generation siblings included in this, but also patrilineal groups were woven into the fabric as well. On her marriage a woman was supposed to bring with her a *maindjimi* (or other sacred object), which was eventually given to her son. Remember that *maindjimis* were also names of bush spirits that inhabited land owned by patrilineal groups, and thus these spirits themselves were associated with particular patrilineal groups. When the *maindjimi* flute came with the woman and went to her son, it was renamed to fit with the names of the bush spirits of the boy's clan. In this way patrilineal groups (and their land and bush) too were a small strand in the total interwoven system.

Much of the data presented contains a variety of contradictions and ambiguities, but I would like explicitly to mention only two of them. One is the inconsistent definition of the term "rope" in the notes, and the other is the problematic use of the concept of descent.

All the references to the term "rope" *(geun)* were given in chapter 4, but placed together they highlight the problem. In one place a rope is "either male or female or mixed"; elsewhere Mead described *kamain* as "a form of reciprocal amenities with distant brothers who belong to a straight male or a straight female rope." *Maindjimis* were "inherited down ropes, *preferably* always with a change of sex" [emphasis added]. In *Sex and Temperament* as well as in some raw field notes, Mead seems finally to have settled on the rope as a descent group based on alternating sex links. Fortune recognized the same descent lines of alternating sex but seems to have used the term "rope" to describe the whole complex. Finally, there is a great deal of confusion surrounding the compound terms described in detail in chapter 4, a basic confusion concerning the difference between rope *(geun)* and line, or descendants. Specifically, six terms were mentioned in the handwritten page of notes (which could have belonged to either Fortune or Mead). *Papakala* was translated as "line of grandfather," or *ungwasak* (Mead elsewhere translated this term as "rope of grandparent"); *papakalandi ke shemilu* was "sisters of *tumbunas*," or ancestors (Mead referred to these as ropes of grandparents' sisters); *shemi lukan geun* was "sisters of a half rope" (Mead had the same translation); *wiyak papakala* was "lines of grandfather and grandmother"; *ngu ke shemilu ke geun* meant line of a particular relative (exactly which one was not clear), but we know some sisters *(shemilu)* were involved; and finally, *owambo papa ke geun* was translated as "father's line and grandfather's line" (Mead's notes contain no translation of these last three terms). The confusion between rope as a form of descent and the general notion of a line of descendants from a particular person is reflected in two ways among the terms here. First, sometimes a phrase containing the word *geun* is translated as "rope" but in other places simply as "line," and the reverse is true—that is, phrases without *geun* are also translated as either "rope" or "line." [13] Second, the same phrase is translated in two ways.

These discrepancies indicate two significant points: that the ethnographers were not consistent in their understanding of *geun* and that they had a second major conceptual problem concerning the concept of descent. It is not surprising that the inconsistencies exist: the period of fieldwork was very short, and most of the work was conducted in pidgin rather than the indigenous language. Furthermore, formal and informal interviews were the primary contexts for data collection. Neither Mead nor Fortune monitored the use of the term *geun* in everyday conversation and surely missed the possible subtleties in its use. That the use of the concept of descent is problematic is also clear. The usage simply was not comparable with that of contemporary anthropology. Here it is important to recall the historical context of this work, for few of the seminal studies on the nature and structure of descent groups had been published (for example, Evans-Pritchard's *The Nuer* was first published in 1940, and Radcliffe-Brown and Forde's *African Systems of Kinship and Marriage* did not appear until 1950), and the anthropological delineation of the structure and nature of social groups was in its formative stages. I think Mead and Fortune were careless in the use of the concept, describing almost any kin tie between generations as descent. In this way they attributed a structural concreteness to the metaphorical phenomenon of ropes. The use of the term "rope" in the notes is some evidence, and further support exists for this assertion. Recall, for example, Mead's statement that "it is a simpler scheme to regard the whole society as based on ropes, *with all descent except land,* following this plan" [emphasis added]. Here descent is confused quite literally with inheritance, and although it would be unfair to take too seriously a raw field note that may have been a slip of the pen, later corrected, we cannot dismiss it either. Another example of the muddling of descent comes from Mead's book *Male and Female: A Study of the Sexes in a Changing World,* where she (1949:116) compounds errors when she says that "*lineages* are called ropes" [emphasis added].

There is additional if indirect evidence that indicates a confusion between descent and affect, structure and sentiment. Mead was a splendid ethnographic observer, and if she says that there was hostility between members of the same sex, close ties between father and daughter or between mother and son (each of whom helped the other significantly in a variety of ways), and that only people of the same sex who were connected through opposite sex relatives, such as mother's brother and sister's son, were friendly (see also my comments earlier), then it is probable that these sentiments were characteristic of the relationships. However, positive sentiment is analytically distinct from formal structure: patrilineal groups, although they were not especially significant in social organization, did manage to exist here and act in a somewhat corporate way despite the rivalry and competition.

The best indication that structure and sentiment were not clearly separated in Mead's analysis is revealed when we examine what these ropes would have been like as descent groups. First of all, they would not even have been real groups but lines of alternating sex: the "groups" never expanded horizontally down generations. In theory a man, all his daughters, all his daughters' sons, all his daughters' sons' daughters, and so on, should have been members of a "group," but they were not. Mead noted that "in social organization, each individual starts a *geun* so that one can speak of father's *geun*, father's sister's *geun*, father's brother's *geun* as all distinct." However, if father and father's brother had had the same mother, then they should have belonged to the same rope. Brothers of the same mother should structurally have been in the same rope, and if they were full brothers, they were members of the same patrilineal group as well. Sentiment—competition, rivalry, and so on—rather than formal structure separated them. Perhaps also they were distanced by the directionality of their exchange transactions, complicated by the fact that only the eldest entered into the "proper" rope exchange relations (we do not know what the younger siblings did or who scarified them, pierced their ears, and so on). It is even possible that a woman "helped" her father and a boy his mother because it was he or she who, in addition to being emotionally close, was the conduit through which the child would later engage in significant exchanges. With more data one might be able to argue, very speculatively, that the cooperation required to execute the exchanges fostered the positive affect, in contrast to the competition for resources that fostered the negative sentiments between same-sex (predominantly male) kin.

One further note here on why rope seems too anomalous to be a descent group. A woman was a member of her father's rope. Her son (at least the first-born) was the identificatory namesake as well as inheritor and rope perpetuator for her father. And yet Mead clearly states (1963:191) that her father and her brothers preferred her to have daughters (at least initially). More daughters minimized the disruption caused by male competition over rights to use female kin to acquire wives. In other words her father was more concerned with executing smooth exchanges (especially in regard to her earlier children) than in perpetuating his rope. Although such an attitude is certainly logically possible, it is in the least quite odd in the context of a descent group. If nothing else, it underscores the primacy of exchange and transactional phenomena over descent, however it is conceived.

MEAD AND THE MUNDUGUMOR | 6

Now that much of the data that can be gleaned from Mead's and to some extent Fortune's notes on the Mundugumor have been presented and an alternative interpretation of kinship and social organization has been advanced, what can be said of Mead and her work? A brief evaluation seems an appropriate and fitting way to conclude.

In setting the stage in chapter 1, I discussed several important factors that shaped the data available for this construction of Mundugumor society, including limitations on the data and on this project. One set of drawbacks concerned the nature of the fieldwork itself. Mead and Fortune were in the field for less than three months, they spoke only pidgin (and there were only a few fluent pidgin speakers in the village), the division of labor between them was too restrictive, and there are indications that they were not fully sharing data with each other. Fortune's notes are fragmented, disorganized, and practically unreadable. The theoretical paradigms within which they worked led them to ask only certain kinds of questions and neglect others. Mead's American cultural anthropological approach led her to assume that human culture was far more simple than it really is, that it could be encapsulated by particular themes or as "personality writ large," and she fell victim at least to oversimplification. The data presented and interpreted in these intervening chapters well illustrate how all these factors shaped the final product contained in this volume.

It is important too to recall that there are serious epistemological uncertainties as well as methodological dangers in constructing an ethnography from field notes belonging to someone else. Anthropologists, perhaps unknowngly, learn a context over time during fieldwork—a context into which observational data are put and within which such data are given meaning. The anthropologist gradually learns how to interpret fragments of behavior, associating and connecting this bit with that bit. This learned framework may very well not be a conscious one; it often remains unarticulated and unnoted by the ethnographer. It is certainly one that takes a considerable period to learn because it is built up out of multiple exposures to diverse events and utterances. Herdt (1981:127) expresses the problem this way: "This is the stupendous methodological problem besetting most ethnographic, especially symbolic, analyses: so much background information is needed to evaluate contextually fragments of individual behavior." Someone trying to use the notes of another has no access to this backdrop; observed fragments often do not assume relevance or meaning because they lack an appropriate context. We need also to note that this context requires a long learning period, and Mead simply did not have the time to build a rich one for the Mundugumor.

No one can write down every fact, detail, nuance, and context, and in using someone else's notes all that was not written is lost. The original anthropologist may perhaps be able to fill in from her or his memory, but another person cannot. Much information and rich detail are gone, and I think that the lack is a serious one in this ethnographic description. Another important problem is that the precise meanings of words used by the original ethnographer are not necessarily clear to later ones. Mead may have known what particular words meant and what she meant by them, but there is no guarantee that what I think they mean is what she thought they meant. What Mead observed she filtered through her own personality and culture before she recorded it, and in reading what she wrote I again filtered the data through my own personality and culture; thus, the end result is far removed from words spoken and activities accomplished on the Yuat River 60 years ago. All these difficulties and lacunae are apparent throughout the ethnographic chapters of this volume, and any evaluation of the reliability of the data contained herein must weigh them carefully.

Evaluating the reliability of any ethnographic text is a process that seems only recently to have found a place on anthropology's agenda. We are only beginning to recognize the need for and develop accepted ways of judging and evaluating ethnographic work. Should such evaluation be based on amount of detail, breadth of coverage, or "thickness"? Surely consistency and coherence are relevant factors, and I think these are amply demonstrated throughout this text. The ease with which the materials fit into a broad comparative context is also important. This concern with reliability and validity is one part of a broader range of issues about the need to become more conscious and critical of the data-gathering and analysis processes in anthropology. I am not suggesting a retreat to sterile quantification but greater willingness to examine the humanistic processes central to the discipline. In evaluating ethnographic materials we need not retreat to extremes—one extreme being the notion that we must mirror true reality, the other the notion that there is no true reality, only our vision of it. It is possible to judge the consistency, coherence, and sensitivity of an ethnographic account without necessarily evaluating how close to some objective, singular, ultimate (and probably unknown) reality it comes. As Weiner (1983:913) rightly argues,

ethnography is about interpretation—the weighing and sifting of observations, interviews, history, and myth, at a particular time and place, and by a particular person. The insight and validity of an ethnographic study depend on how perceptively the weighing and sifting are done. A reinterpretation or a refutation of an ethnographic account equally stands or falls by the same criteria.

This work, then, stands or falls on how perceptively the weighing and sifting were done by two people—Mead in the field and myself with her data. Although I must leave it to readers to judge the overall reliability and validity of the description presented in this volume, I think I can fairly evaluate Mead's sifting and weighing and perceiving.

Despite the many weaknesses and problems in this enterprise, upon reflection I cannot help but be somewhat astonished at the quality of the work Mead did in 1932. While it is possible to argue that she did not take notes on a particular topic, follow up on a specific question, gather enough genealogies, record quantitative data on subsistence, or examine symbolic constructions—the list of omissions is almost endless—the truth is that I was able to take her notes, supplemented by some of Fortune's, and write an ethnography from them. I do not claim that it is a complete or even a rich ethnography, but there is far more reliable information here than could be derived from the field notes of most anthropologists after less than three months in the field. It is a tribute to Mead's abilities as an ethnographer that anyone can do anything at all with her notes. That she, aided by Fortune, was able to gather as much data as she did in such a short time is a remarkable achievement. That it was possible for someone to use her field notes and construct an alternative explanation of social organization only serves to underscore further the excellence of her fieldwork and observational abilities. Although Mead may have been inclined to leap to premature conclusions, she was a gifted anthropologist given to sometimes brilliant insights.[1] Although the ethnographic description constructed here from her notes is somewhat less reliable (and certainly much more impoverished than an ethnography written by the actual fieldworker), it is predominantly so because my interpretation of the notes adds a second "weighing and sifting" (Weiner 1983:913).

The evaluation of Mead's work in its theoretical, historical, and political context may be on anthropology's agenda for some time to come, but some agreement is emerging on a few points.[2] One is especially relevant here: one of her greatest gifts was as a recorder of what Schwartz (1983:927) calls "everyday life—the middle matter of her books." Mead's observational abilities were remarkable, and her tireless approach to fieldwork and her rigorous recording methodology provide standards to strive for today. Her perceptions of the subtleties of behavior and its meanings were insightful and sometimes profound. Her greatest talent was seeing and recording what went on around her. No matter what further interpretations she made from her field materials, her initial incisive field perceptions are there to work with.

For those who read her work carefully her gift often manages to overcome some of the inherent weaknesses and strictures of the theoretical paradigm in which she worked. She was heavily influenced by Benedict and believed that cultures could be described as "personalities writ large," that one could discern dominant "themes" and "configurations" in every culture. Although she sometimes erred by emphasizing certain relatively simple themes or ideas rather than the full complexities, it is usually possible to find the other side, the complications she did not manage to incorporate into her theoretical paradigm, in either her notes or written publications. Shore (1983:936) notes the same for her work on Samoa: ". . . I suspect that the notion of cultural configuration—being worked out in its early phases by Benedict and being put to its first ethnographic test by Mead—had a crucial effect on simplifying Mead's observations so as to conform to a single dominant theme." Shore (1938:937) goes on to stress, however, that Mead's observations went beyond what fit into her paradigm: "Mead was, I think, a better observer than her theoretical predispositions should have permitted . . ." and later (1938:940) summarizes this idea by saying that "she observed more than her hypothesis should have permitted."

Although Shore is commenting on Mead's Samoan work, the characterization fits her work with the Mundugumor as well.[3] She saw and recorded rich and vast amounts of material that, when written up in *Sex and Temperament* (1963), was condensed and oversimplified as it filtered through her theoretical lens. For example, her

depiction of the Mundugumor is one of hostile, aggressive, and assertive people, but we know very well that there were meek and
gentle Mundugumor as well. Many of the contradictory data—or
data that did not fit precisely with this theme—while they do not
appear in the published work, are labeled deviant in some way. The
complexities of human behavior and culture can be found in her
work even if she failed to stress them or completely appreciate,
given the theoretical state of anthropology when she was writing,
the significance of her deviants.[4] Freeman (1983) does not adequately acknowledge this fact about Mead's Samoan work, but
Shore (1983) does: she interpreted her material in terms of a dominant theme but observed far more complexities than her theory
really allowed her.

I want to discuss two aspects of the Mundugumor material that
stand out in this context: the ethos of the society as Mead described
it and the theoretical importance of her recognition of the existence
of significant deviation from an ideal. A discussion of each of these
related topics illuminates not only important data and ideas for anthropology but also reveals, despite the weaknesses and problems,
Mead's strengths as an ethnographer.

ETHOS

Ethos is more difficult than other topics to discern from notes—
one's own or another's—partly because it is an abstraction and
partly because, to a much greater extent than most other phenomena we describe, it is heavily dependent on individual interpretation
and potentially ethnocentric contrast with Western ideology, categories, and assumptions. Furthermore, in this case it was also dependent on the ethnographer's mind and memory because while in
the field she recorded little specifically describing ethos. Why there
are so few notes on ethos and particularly on contrasts between men
and women in the entire corpus of materials must remain something of a puzzle here. Did Mead intend to conduct more detailed

research on her problem once she and Fortune had completed a more general ethnographic survey? Were the details so impressed on her memory that she did not need to write them down? Given the rigorous field methods she espoused and practiced, it seems more likely to me that the first possibility carries more weight than the second. Further, she left the Mundugumor, remember, at least partly because she believed that the society did not shed any more light than the Arapesh upon her field problem concerning the relationship between biological sex and individual temperament. It may have been that she quickly discerned that male and female ethos were so similar as to be essentially identical and turned her attention to other matters because there did not seem to be data here that added anything to what she had already gathered from Arapesh. I suspect also that she did not completely formulate her conception of Mundugumor ethos until after she had visited the Tchambuli or Chambri; it was the contrasts among the Arapesh, Mundugumor, and Tchambuli that generated the particular picture she painted in *Sex and Temperament.*

Much of what Mead wrote in *Sex and Temperament* about Mundugumor ethos is not in her notes but was in her own memory for she wrote the manuscript after the visit to the Chambri. If Mead had not written up at least part of her data, her perceptions of the people's behaviors and emotional proclivities would have been lost permanently. And because this kind of data is somewhat soft, word choice becomes especially critical: Does a particular piece of behavior reveal an assertive posture or an aggressive one? Is a person being submissive or cooperative? Here, then, for a variety of reasons, there is much room for interpretation and doubt.

General ethos, or the emotional and affective sense of a group, is one of the most noted aspects of Mead's work with the Mundugumor material. Her description of a group of aggressive (or perhaps simply assertive) individuals caught people's eye, was doubted, impressed. Although the actual notes Mead took in the field do not document incident after incident of violent, aggressive, or individualistic behavior on the part of both women and men, they detail many such events and do not indicate any alternative description of ethos. I divide my general remarks on Mundugumor ethos here into two categories: its general nature and the lack of differentiation along sex or gender lines.[5]

Mead's depiction of Mundugumor ethos was indeed striking. She describes them as "gay, hard, arrogant" (1963:167) and as "proud, harsh, and violent" (1963:233). "They were a fierce group of cannibals who occupied the best high ground along the riverbank. They preyed on their miserable swamp-dwelling neighbors ... " (1977:204) but always left a few of those neighbors alive to ensure their source of pottery (1963:171). They possessed an "aggressive individuality" (1963:183), a "ruthless individualism ... aggressive specific sexuality ..." (1963:190). They were "violent, competitive, aggressively sexed, jealous and ready to see and avenge insult, delighting in display, in action, in fighting" (1963:225). She also described them as charming if somewhat hypocritical:

These people have been charming in many ways; they are even postponing their quarrels until we leave, a point which we—scientifically, of course— do not appreciate. It takes adepts in hypocrisy to be sufficiently self-conscious to think of what a front they present to a white man. (1977:135).

Mead and Fortune left them "with gayer words and friendlier adieus than we have ever had from any primitive people" (Mead 1977:137).

It is easy for Westerners to misread this description: negative characteristics linger longer in our memories than the more positive ones. Mead emphasized what Westerners perceive as negative as a way of highlighting the contrasts between the Mundugumor and the Arapesh and Tchambuli. Although she stressed one aspect of their ethos—that they were harsh, aggressive, and so on—it crucial to note that she also said that they were gay and charming. It is easy to argue that her depiction of ethos is too one-sided and ignores the other side, the attenuated but nevertheless existing balance to the picture.

Is this description accurate? On one level it is not possible for anyone to say: it is Mead's intangible interpretation of what she sensed and perceived while in the field. Who defines and describes what Mundugumor reality was in 1932? However, all indications do point toward the perceptiveness of the balanced rather than the one-sided account. It is coherent and completely consistent with—and if not bolstered heavily, at least not contradicted by—Mead's field notes (from 1932 as well as some very significant observations on child rearing from 1971) and with Fortune's notes. Mission personnel working in the area basically agree; soccer matches in contemporary Biwat are considered dangerous by other villages, especially if the Mundugumor do not win, and a priest who worked among the Mundugumor for many years told me in 1973 that he thought Mead's description of ethos in *Sex and Temperament* was accurate and perceptive. Although his replacement in 1981 disagreed that the people he worked with were stubborn or unpleasant, he did note the reputation the Mundugumor had in the area for being aggressive and assertive people. Pamela Watson (personal communication), an anthropologist working with the people of Kinakatem in 1982, agrees with Mead's depiction of child rearing and the relatively assertive and unnurturing behavior of mothers toward their offspring. My own observations support Mead's description as well: during my fieldwork in Bun I often encountered people from downriver (indeed, some had intermarried in Bun), and my two-week visit to Kinakatem in 1981 generated nothing to contradict Mead's picture if the balanced view is taken without Mead's stress on the negative. And the Mundugumor I met certainly took a certain pride in their reputation for fierceness. An anecdote can provide some support for Mead's characterization. I was discussing the "old days" with a group of men in Kinakatem in 1981, and one man voluntarily reported, quite gleefully, that his recent ancestors had raided their Grass Country neighbors with impunity, the "miserable swamp-dwellers" to whom Mead referred. The man laughed mischievously and added, "And do you know what? Whenever they raided these people, they always left a few alive so that they'd have someone to make pots for them!" This comment, unprompted and unsolicited, came almost 50 years after Mead recorded the same thing. And it was related with charm, humor, pride, mischief, and a twinkling eye.

An issue related to Mead's depiction of ethos that anthropologists almost never discuss yet that has a profound impact on our field experiences and what we carry back from the field is how the anthropologist herself or himself reacts to the people and culture being studied. Cultural relativism dictates that we not judge, but how do we not react and feel? And should we not describe those feelings and reactions so that others can evaluate our results fairly and honestly? Some anthropologists are beginning to publish accounts of their feelings in the field—Kenneth Read especially comes to mind (Read 1965 and 1986)—but we are far from taking such things into account in evaluating the validity, reliability, or possible distortion in ethnographic interpretations. Mead makes it very clear in her autobiography (1972) that she did not like Mundugumor culture, particularly the way in which children were treated. In effect, she did not find the ethos very congenial to her own personality. Did her personal reaction affect the way in which she perceived what went on around her and the way she wrote up her ethnographic materials? How will we ever know? Although my own brief acquaintance with individual Mundugumor and my brief stay in the area are inadequate comparisons, I can only add here that I found the people warm, open, and generous with their time as well as their goods—as well as assertive and volatile. Indeed, if my reaction has any relevance here at all, I liked them very much. Perhaps the time has come to study seriously how the anthropologist's individual personality affects the fieldwork process, the data gathered, the analysis done, and the final interpretation presented.

Of course, the most striking aspect of Mead's discussion of Mundugumor ethos pertains to sex and gender. As a group women's ethos was not significantly different from men's. Women did not engage in the same activities as men, but both sexes were gay, hard, arrogant, aggressive, charming, individualistic, positively sexed,

and so on. Mead never wrote that women and men were undiffer-
entiated or that women and men were alike in all ways. According
to Mead, the women acted as we (by which she meant middle-class
white Americans in the first part of this century) expected men to
act: "in a fierce, initiating fashion" (1963:preface to the 1950 edition). Women were "actively masculine, virile, and without any of
the softening and mellowing characteristics that we are accustomed
to believe are inalienably womanly" (1963:165). Although I do not
necessarily agree with Mead's phrasings and with her 1930s characterization of North American gender ideology (she falls prey especially to describing ideology and ignoring the complexities of behavior, a not surprising error), based on my limited observations I
can only agree that her description and interpretation of Mundugumor—that male and female ethos are not significantly different or
at least not as different as Western "ideals" in the 1930s would have
them—is accurate. For example, Kinakatem women attended village meetings and spoke out at them in 1981 and were more than
present and visible. An anecdote illustrates and indicates the extent
to which Mead was insightful about gender ethos. When I visited
the Mundugumor in 1981, I first took a walk through all four river
villages. I began upriver, in Biwat proper. It was Sunday, and the
people, now heavily Catholic, were relaxing. Organized sport has
become important in Papua New Guinea, and the Mundugumor are
no different in their love of soccer, basketball, and other sports.
Many young people were playing basketball on this day, a commonplace scene in contemporary Papua New Guinea. What was not
commonplace was this: the teams in Biwat were composed of both
men and women, and the women playing were indeed just as assertive—in basketball language, they had just as much "hustle"—as
the men (see fig. 13).

Mead's description of Mundugumor ethos is, on one level, not
verifiable. The description relies more heavily on her own memory,
constructs, and interpretation than it does on concrete field observations codified forever in written field notes. However, all the evidence that can be mustered at this point verifies that she showed

Figure 13. Coed basketball, 1981. Photograph by N. McDowell.

good insight in her depictions if not her emphases. There is no evidence to doubt that Mundugumor men and women were more similar to each other in emotional configuration than North American men and women were during the 1930s and that both men and women of Kinakatem were more assertive than typical North American women when Mead published *Sex and Temperament* in 1935.[6]

VARIATION AND CONTRADICTION

That Mead saw more than her paradigm allowed is true in the area of what she called deviation. She expected to find dominant themes and configurations that were expressed psychologically (predominantly in personality but also to a lesser extent in cognition) but also socially and culturally. Child-rearing practices enculturated people into the patterns and ideals appropriate to and relevant for the group. One of the main problems faced by this theoretical paradigm was that of variation: What happened when people did not fit the pattern? Why were they anomalous? How did the society handle the ambiguity? This problem of deviation was, in Kuhn's terms (1962), one of the puzzles that the paradigm had to recognize as central and relevant (although perhaps this puzzle later became an anomaly). Mead's work to a large extent addressed itself to the main issue of the paradigm—how cultures got themselves into the hearts and minds of people through socialization—but her gift at observation forced her to come to terms at least on one level with exceptions, deviations, anomalies, and things that just plain did not fit. In describing ethos, for example, she elaborates (1963) at length on people who were *not* the ideal type in order to show how deviation was handled by the society.

In a simple way and on an individual level Mead appreciated that no two people were quite alike. Personality, individual experience, all the distinctive or idiosyncratic traits of individuals were of central concern to her (but see Gewertz 1984). In this way Mead recognized not only temperamental and behavioral deviants but also approached the broader topic of intragroup variation as well. But Mead's analysis of deviance was more complex: she contended that without deviation from the cultural norms and rules Mundugumor society could not have existed. Here she was far ahead of her time, and even many who came after her falsely conceptualized the problem in terms of "real behavior" versus "cultural ideals." If everyone had followed the rules or fulfilled the ethos-ideal, the result would have been chaos:

Although the . . . ideal is that every man should be a lion, fighting proudly for his share and surrounded by several equally violent lionesses, in actual practice there are a fair number of sheep in the society, men to whom pride, violence, and competitiveness do not appeal. Because of these men a certain number of rules are kept, and so are passed on to the next generation; some families of sisters are equally divided among brothers, the dead are mourned for, children are fed. When the proud polygynist quarrels with the son whose sister he is about to use in exchange for a wife for himself, the son can take refuge with one of these milder men. The atmosphere of struggle and conflict would become unbearable and actually impossible to maintain if it were not for them, for each man would have only an army of one to put in the field. Instead of complicating the social life by taking up positions that are confusing and unintelligible, as do the misfits among the Arapesh, they actually make possible the violent competitive life that is really so uncongenial to them (1963:226–27).

Mead's point here is that not only were there temperamental deviants, but that the society could not have existed without them. On this point she showed an awareness of a higher-level set of systematic relationships than that of a simple model of rules and behavior here. Her analysis of behavior and deviations from the rules (e.g., marriage "rules") showed similar insight. Critics of Mead who argue that the Mundugumor society could not have existed as Mead described it, with its endless rivalries and aggressive and violent individualism, fail to understand one of her most significant points: if these rules and ideals had been fulfilled by all, there indeed could have been no society; those she labeled deviants were an essential element in perpetuating the system.

Even if one looks only at the social structure and its rules and ignores the issues of temperament and personality, the same principle holds: Mead stressed and intended to emphasize in her monograph that perhaps a time existed when the Mundugumor were able to marry correctly, follow the "rope" rules, and so on, but that they certainly could do so no longer. Although Mead couched her explanation in an evolutionary context and believed that the society had changed, had degenerated, the essential point remained: ideals simply could not be followed.

If Mead had been writing in the 1980s instead of the 1930s, theoretical advances in anthropology would have helped solve some of the dilemmas here, especially the theoretical recognition that cultural structures contain within them variations and contradictions of themselves. Cultures are not perfectly logical and internally consistent, nor are ideal rules and behavior necessarily related in any simple and direct fashion.[7] She was hampered by the theoretical paradigm she espoused: she looked for the simple rule, ideal, or personality type and then tried to explain variation and contradiction as deviations. But despite the extent to which her theory affected the quality of her ethnographic analysis and interpretation, the fact remains that Mead *saw* and *recorded* phenomena that did not fit the pattern and explained, at least in the case of the Mundugumor, how these deviants were an essential part of the sociocultural system as a whole. One could, if so inclined, go though *Sex and Temperament* and reanalyze the material Mead presented there in more modern theoretical terms without much difficulty. Instead of discussing deviants from the ideal or norm, one would focus on variation and contradiction and on how differences on the psychological, social, and cultural levels all helped create the system as a whole so that it could continue to function, provide meaning and coherence in people's lives, and structure their experiences. That it is possible to do so is due to Mead's special talents as an observer and ethnographer.

NOTES

CHAPTER 1: INTRODUCTION

1. Mead spelled the name of this village in different ways. In her publications (e.g., 1963), the spelling was *Kenakatem*, but current spelling and pronunciation are much closer to the spelling I use here. Fortune (e.g., 1947b) spelled the group name *Mondugumor*, but for the same reasons I use *Mundugumor* here.

2. There remains some doubt about these dates and the actual length of the field trip. In Mead's *Letters from the Field* (1977:130), one letter from Kinakatem is dated a hazy "September," but the fact that there is no specific numerical date (as most other entries have) indicates some question, perhaps a dating after the fact or simply a general time period. I use the dates October 4 and December 18 because when Mead began to plan a monograph on the Mundugumor and organize her notes, these are the dates she herself used. In her notes there are no entries dated earlier than October 6 (Fortune's notes are by and large undated).

3. See, for example, Mead 1934, 1961, 1963, 1970, 1977, and 1978 as well as the discussion to follow.

4. Portions of this section of this chapter were included in McDowell 1983a. See also Gorecki 1989.

5. Swiss and German scholars have taken a broader perspective for some time, and I think it no accident that the first Wenner-Gren Symposium on the Sepik region was initiated and hosted in Basel by these scholars in 1984.

Papers prepared for this conference by Hauser-Schaublin, Schindlbeck, Schuster and Schuster, Stanek, Wassmann, and Weiss are illustrative.

6. See, especially, Tuzin 1976 and 1980, Gewertz 1983, Métraux 1978, Mead 1978, and Bateson 1978.

7. See, for example, Bateson 1932 and 1936 and Thurnwald 1916.

8. The name of this village has been spelled variously, but this is the official government spelling. It sounds more like *Akurang* to me, but here I adopt the official spelling. Mead and Fortune spelled it in various ways, including *Akerang*.

The correct spelling of village names is a difficult issue; throughout this volume I have adopted the spellings established in 1968 by the Department of District Administration in its *Village Directory* (Territory of Papua and New Guinea 1968) for most.

9. In her rough drafts Mead left spaces for references to be filled in later; I am leaving the parentheses as she had them, but I am adding in brackets the references I think she intended to cite.

10. There is an ever-growing literature in anthropology on the ways in which the sex of the fieldworker affects the nature of data and analysis. I am convinced that a significant part of Freeman's disagreement (1938) with Mead's depiction of Samoa is the result of the fact that male and female fieldworkers have access to different kinds of data as well as different orientations if not interests. See McDowell 1984b.

11. She also at that time wrote to me while I was in the field and asked me to record some myths if possible and if the people remembered any. I was preparing to leave the field then and did not manage to record anything especially reliable, only stories from a Mundugumor man and woman who lived in upriver Bun most of their adult lives.

12. One must wonder, then, why I have written it this way. I did so largely because of the promise I made to Mead before her death: if she herself did not finish the monograph, I would write up the data for her. I felt—and continue to feel—a certain obligation to present the material in at least somewhat the manner that she herself would have.

13. Many of the facts and interpretations of both Fortune and Mead have, of course, appeared in print. Mead's *Sex and Temperament* (1963), in particular, contains a wealth of information on the Mundugumor; see also Mead 1934, 1949, 1961, 1970, 1977, and 1978, and Fortune 1947a and 1947b.

14. In earlier versions of this book I included such a section myself but deleted it for a variety of reasons. Anthropologists who want to peruse Mead's entire corpus of material, not all of which is included somewhere in this volume, are free to do so at the Library of Congress.

15. Portions of this section were included in McDowell 1983b.

16. In notes to herself and staff Mead wondered if indeed she had copies of all of Fortune's notes because they seemed so few, but the pages were numbered consecutively, and Fortune seemed to have concurred that she had a complete set.

17. According to Mead's file of correspondence, she did share many of the linguistic notes with a prominent linguist of the Sepik, Don Laycock. Furthermore, for those interested in the Mundugumor or Biwat language, these notes are available in the Library of Congress.

18. Of course I could not be successful in doing this. I have taught *Sex and Temperament* numerous times and know it well; it surely constitutes a framework in my own mind by which I interpreted—at least partly—the field notes.

19. Mead (1978) is incorrect in asserting that the Bun and the Mundugumor have different origins; I think the linguistic data and cultural data clearly substantiate that they were and continue to be closely related.

20. For information on the Bun, see, for example, McDowell 1975, 1976, 1977, 1978a, 1978b, 1979, 1980a, and 1984a.

CHAPTER 2: THE MUNDUGUMOR IN CONTEXT

1. This is, I suspect, one of the weaknesses of Mead's Samoan ethnography, a characteristic of Mead that Freeman (1983) makes much of. See also McDowell 1984b.

2. I do not believe that Mead visited any of these neighboring villages herself. Thus, the information she has about them can come from only two possible sources: the Mundugumor themselves and visitors from other villages among the Mundugumor.

3. A *baret* is a portion of river or stream that has been cut off from the main flow of water, somewhat like an ox-bow lake.

4. The process was not always successful. One man constructed a new *baret* correctly, but his first catch was meager, and he believed that the small distribution offended someone because he could later find no fish at all. He was convinced that the offended person had taken a fish from the *baret* and bewitched it. He left these vengeful instructions with his kin: "'When I die, take a little earth from the edge of the *baret*, place it on my corpse. As I rot, it will rot, and then no one will ever be able to get fish out of that *baret* again.'"

5. The genealogies I recorded in 1981 indicate that Mead may have missed some residents of Kinakatem and that the population was actually

larger than she recorded. Her possible miscalculation can be attributed to the dispersed settlement pattern; my suspicion is that in Mead's reckoning some hamlets were associated with other localities.

6. A *luluai* was an appointed native official, ostensibly the head of a village.

7. Parts of this chapter were originally included in McDowell 1983a; see also Gorecki 1989.

8. This area was referred to as the "Grass Country" by Mead, Fortune, and others. It was mostly grass- and swampland. It comprised the Grass Census Division during the Australian administration.

9. Pamela Swadling (personal communication) has reservations about Mead's speculation on the origin of these shells. Perhaps Mead meant another island?

10. "Half-caste" (pidgin *hapkast*) is a term used to describe someone with parents from two different groups or from areas with two separate sociocultural identities. On the Yuat River it often refers to someone with parents from two different villages.

11. The arguments of Godelier and Modjeska are far more sophisticated than I present here; I am significantly simplifying their complexities to highlight aspects of the Mundugumor system and place that system in an areal context. Both authors are concerned with process rather than typology and merely construct heuristic opposites and contrasts. Readers interested in these issues are urged to consult the original sources, especially Godelier 1982 and 1986 and Modjeska 1982.

12. It is interesting to speculate on the extent to which the absence of large pig herds may have been associated with the differential development of political systems in Melanesia. See also Godelier 1982 and Modjeska 1982.

13. Omblean described a good woman as one who was "generous with food, betel, and tobacco, isn't stubborn and retentive of her property, doesn't [insult people], and smiles at other people's children." Mead also recorded the following description of a good woman from Omblean in 1938:

Women shouldn't talk like men. A good woman will take care of her husband. She won't wander around. She won't ask for all kinds of things, [such as] another person's betel. Tobacco, too, she won't request from another. She will listen to her husband. If a man makes advances toward her, she won't like it, and she will tell her husband. This kind of woman we like. . . .

And here is how he described a bad woman: "She'll always be asking for things from other people. She will always be asking for everything, she won't know how to get it herself. She'll ask for things, betel, tobacco, and joke around a lot."

14. Fortune's notes contain two versions of this event. One has details such as names of people and hamlets; this more general version is clearly Fortune's interpretation of the other one. It was handwritten in narrative form. See Fortune 1947b for the published version.

15. One must question whether Fortune's interpretation here, that they "accept the loss" because there was no existing enmity, is the correct one. It seems to me equally likely that they did not want to risk further deaths by attacking villages who were possibly superior in strength.

16. Enemy bodies were eaten, but one's own people were not. One reason Mead thought that Dowaning and Andafugan were separating from the other river villages was that river folks had eaten victims from these villages, indicating noncommunity.

17. Fortune clearly wrote "was told" here, indicating that the Kinakatem leader went to Akuran and was told there of the deaths of the potters, implying that the people in Akuran did not know who killed their impending visitors. It seems odd to me that after being allies and coconspirators in this affair the people in Akuran did not know what the Kinakatem people had done, but perhaps it was kept from them because they were the potential hosts of the potters and should have tried to prevent any injury to them. Another aspect open to speculation is Branda's seeming neutrality throughout this entire series of events. Fortune does not comment on it.

18. See Fortune 1947b for the details. Mead records different details for this third case; she identifies the women as co-wives quarrelling about insults received from others. Mead's notes indicate that the woman paddled not to Anduar but to Saparu, also a downriver village.

19. Who gave this assurance is not reported, but it is an interesting question. If neither Alemi nor Mongova did, one must question the motive of the person who did: Did he think he was strong enough to ensure the visitors' safety in the face of hostility from the two leading men? Was he attempting to establish himself as a third influential man? Were the people of Akuran aware that he was in no position to protect them?

20. This is the only reference in all the notes to people from downriver, and enemies at that, coming to acquire food. Grass Country villagers occasionally did so.

21. Older informants in Bun told me that they heard from their ancestors tales of Bun raiding Biwat, but they were uncertain of the details.

22. Nowhere does either Mead or Fortune specify just what these homicidal decorations are. They perhaps refer to the possession, decoration, and display of enemy skulls; see note 23.

23. Mead noted elsewhere that a "cannibal feast" could also occur at the beginning as well as the termination of a raiding party, but the obvious question here would be, Whom did they eat? I think that here she was careless with the phrase "cannibal feast" and meant that perhaps a feast of some sort preceded a raid.

24. In the same note referred to earlier Mead also recorded that this ceremony could occur at the beginning or ending of a raid, but it makes no sense to hold it before a successful raid because there was no spirit of a slain enemy to banish. Such an event could have been designed to send the spirit of a slain kinsperson away, however, but it is mentioned nowhere in any of the notes on death and burial in general.

25. In the next chapter a similar ceremony celebrating the launching of a war canoe is described. Similar rituals pertain in Bun as well, but it is not clear to me whether the purposes were comparable.

26. Neither Mead nor Fortune hints at why a captive would be sold to another village rather than just dispatched by his or her captors. My speculation is that the captive had kinship ties with some of the captors, and they felt restrained in simply killing him or her.

27. I use the masculine pronoun in this context because it is unlikely that female children killed captives. Although they were initiated (see chapter 3), they did not participate directly in warfare and raiding.

28. I think it is clear that Fortune's use of the word "friend" here does not fit with current English connotations of that word. I suspect that it is a gloss for the pidgin word *pren*, which can also be translated as exchange partner—a far more likely person in this context. See chapter 4 for additional comments on the meaning of *pren*.

29. There is a contradiction in Mead's notes as to who took possession of the enemy skull. In one place she wrote that the men who took part in the raid decorated the skull and gave it to the man who provided the feast to celebrate the successful vengeance killing for his kinsperson. Elsewhere, she recorded that the killer kept it before passing it on via the inheritance pattern described here. I think the contradiction is a surface one only. If a man's brother was killed, that man would in all likelihood take part in the vengeance raid and thus would be one of the killers.

30. Mead's inconsistency about who can and cannot wear homicidal decorations (and what they were) is puzzling as well as frustrating. My guess is that one could not claim a homicide or the right to wear any decorations for it if it was only the killing of a captive but that if later on (as Mead elsewhere says) a man killed an enemy who was not a captive, he could then claim the privileges of a successful killer.

31. Along with this note Mead added the following in parenthesis: "Note:

a pig's skull is so treated in the repudiation ceremony when told to vomit up a pig." This cryptic remark is impossible to interpret. There are no other references to a repudiation ceremony. Perhaps it refers to the *yakat* initiation ceremony, in which pigs provided the main theme (see chapter 3), but this is only a guess.

32. It was a commonplace among American cultural anthropologists of the 1930s to refer to the people they had studied as "my people," and indeed this practice continues to some degree today. It suggests an arrogance somewhat at odds with Boasian cultural relativism.

33. Today there is a reawakened interest in traditional carving among men in these villages, and innovative as well as traditional work is being done.

34. In 1932 Mead recorded this observation about gender and group behavior:

Groups which contain [both] men and women are watchful, spaced, alert, nervous, continual shifting of positions. . . . Groups which contain only women and adolescent boys and children are jolly. Note that all jesting so far seen [November 7] has been seen when an elder one of one sex was with a group of adolescents, not in a mixed group of adults.

35. Given the traditional attitude toward children, it is difficult to be sure whether this is change or continuity.

36. He ostensibly died in a quarrel about a woman rather than in the line of duty, but Mead was skeptical about informants' knowledge of the actual event.

37. Omblean had died by the time of my visit in 1981.

38. The boat was eventually purchased but ran into trouble on its first run. I am indebted to Pamela Watson, of the University of Queensland, for this information.

39. People in Bun, for example, noted with some dismay the lack of adequate land in Mundugumor. They had ample land and noted the pressures on their neighbors with some anxiety.

40. Records from Angoram's Health Centre indicate that Mundugumor women were not heavy users of contraceptive methods and family planning. In 1981 three women from Biwat and one from Kinakatem were active attenders of the family planning clinic; five women from Biwat, one from Branda, and two from Akuran had by 1981 stopped attending. These are small numbers, especially if one considers the possibility that the Biwat women were not native Mundugumor but associated with the school or mission (as workers or wives of workers). I am indebted to Dr. Patricia Townsend for sharing these data on family planning clinic attendance.

41. I assume that these figures include both mission personnel and school personnel.

42. Crocodiles have become relatively rare on the main course of the river apparently for two reasons. One is the obvious fact that people have been killing them for their skins, but also they seem to have moved into the inland areas as a result of the noise from outboard motors.

43. There is still no school in Bun, and the only upriver school is further upriver, in Sipisipi. It was not built until, I think, about 1976.

44. Indeed, in looking at photographs taken by Mead and Fortune, I was sometimes amazed at the similarity between their photographs and ones I took in 1981. The similarity was due primarily to the architectural style and the use of bush materials such as sago thatch and sago rib walls. In recent pictures people are dressed differently, and various items of introduction— such as clotheslines, pots, and so forth—are in evidence. From the river the village of Kinakatem looks very much as it did 50 years ago (see figures). Also, as Mead noted, the villages had grown together; their boundaries almost touched. The settlement pattern, however, still indicated some distancing from neighbors: it almost seemed as if within each "village" there were separable compounds composed of man, wife or wives, and children, isolatable and identifiable units. This was especially true in Biwat, less so in Akuran.

45. One important informant during my two-week stay was a man who was a participant in the Gavien resettlement scheme near Angoram. He returned to his home village on occasion because, he said, he was hungry, and the rubber plantation in Gavien was not yet adequate for his subsistence. He processed sago while he was home.

CHAPTER 3: RELIGION

1. There are few additional data on what Mead called "seer dreaming" or who these seers are.

2. Mead uses the masculine pronoun in this example, as she did in most examples; in this case I think that it is possible that only men approached their associated spirits in this way, and therefore I follow Mead's convention. But note that old women were the main participants in approaching water spirits; thus, it is always possible that women did so as well in this context. If so, Mead's use of the masculine pronoun serves to mask a significant ethnographic fact. For this reason, if for no other, use of the "customary masculine" is undesirable in anthropology.

3. The same procedure for disposing of the body was followed in Bun. The old woman who described it to me in 1974 said that it was without a doubt one of the first customs the people had abandoned when Europeans came—and they were glad to do so.

4. It is not at all clear whether women could be actual sorcerers—that is, the people who manipulated the physical leavings and invoked the supernatural means. Women frequently began the process by taking dirt to an outside sorcerer.

5. It is very tempting to argue that these axes—upriver, downriver, and bush—constitute major directionalities in Mundugumor thought. They are also relevant, for example, in trading considerations, warfare alliances, and perhaps other arenas. That the Mundugumor thought others used different sorcery methods and that they themselves seemed to use the methods of bush peoples is highly suggestive of their sense of identity and differentiation from others.

6. This model was possibly similar to the one constructed for initiation ceremonies.

7. As is true of all stories of events told to but not witnessed by ethnographers, there is the possibility of distortion and exaggeration in this tale. But even if the precise events are not accurately described as they occurred, the attitudes are certainly clear.

8. The distinction between using natural and supernatural means is, of course, a Western one, one that probably would not have been espoused by the Mundugumor in 1932.

9. I never heard of such a method in Bun.

10. It is not clear in the notes whether all instances of "spitting" involved ginger or merely "spitting nothing" (i.e., only saliva).

11. That the performers of the ritual are not in any close relationship to the owner of the canoe seems odd, and I suspect that Mead and Fortune erred here. A similar ceremony is performed in Bun between the canoe owner and his cross-cousins for the launching of any new canoe. My guess is that the two sides of the Mundugumor ritual are mother's brother and sister's son; one is the owner.

12. See the next section on initiation for the few details available on crocodile mothers.

13. In 1932 Mead did note that downriver in Anduar "there is a ceremony in which the wives of the elder brothers beat their husbands' younger brothers. [The Mundugumor] shudder at such a practice."

14. "Group" may not be the correct word here, for the nature of Mundugumor "groups" is vague and confusing in the notes. See chapter 4.

15. I was talking mostly with male informants and therefore have a defi-

nite male perspective here. I had to ask these men what women did; they did not volunteer that women had their own facility.

16. Unfortunately, all these 1981 informants were male. Women were included in the group and were listening, but they did not speak on this topic. I had the sense that they would have corrected the men and added their opinion if they had wanted to, but of course I cannot be sure.

17. In Mead's original notes she also has the boy's *wareun* accompanying him into the model. What relative Mead was identifying here is difficult to discern; I suspect, as I argue in the next chapter, that she confused *wareun* (a distant trading partner) with *kamain* (a special exchange relative). If anyone accompanied the boy, it would be a *kamain*, not a distant trading partner.

18. In another place in the notes Mead says that the fire was designed to "cook" the boys, but the meaning is not clear. Does the crocodile cook them before eating them?

19. In 1981 informants said that boys indeed were afraid during this initiation and had to be reassured by their mother's brothers. The scarification also caused many to cry. In the text Mead recorded from Afima in 1938, his general fear during the initial phases of this ritual is more than clear.

20. I am reminded here (as elsewhere) of Keesing's call (1985) for anthropologists to avoid overinterpretation and deep symbolic meaning where perhaps there is none.

21. He intended to get only one pig, but because of a mix-up in shooting, he ended up with two.

22. I suspect that for the performance Mead and Fortune witnessed a house was set up in the village for the ceremony, the preparations, and so forth. If the ritual had been performed in its entirety, including the seclusion of initiates, it would probably have been in the bush.

23. Note the casualness with which this "initiation" was treated. The boy accidentally saw a ritual object he should not have seen; the error was dealt with by treating the incident as if it had been an initiation. The incident ended with the standard feast releasing the initiate from food taboos.

24. See Mead 1934:234 for a photograph of a dancer wearing a cassowary headdress.

25. This is the only reference in the notes to a "big woman."

26. The directionality of the pig is questionable here. Informants in 1981 argued that the mother's brother was supposed to compensate his sister's son for the lost blood, and therefore the senior relative gave to the junior. But they also mentioned that rings were involved as payment here too, and no one was quite certain who really gave what to whom. Was the real moth-

er's brother compensated for his support? For the details of exchanges between these two relatives, see chapter 4.

27. There is a discrepancy in the notes about the instrument used for cutting. In one place Mead noted that pig teeth, not crocodile teeth, were used in the *yakat*; however, in Omblean's text of his own *yakat* initiation, he claimed that crocodile teeth were used.

28. For photographs of various Mundugumor masks, see Mead 1934:239.

29. Why they say this to the *ashin* rather than the *baika* is a puzzle. This ceremony took place before the *ashin* initiation commissioned by Mead and Fortune, and it is unlikely that these initiates were being released from food taboos imposed at another *ashin* ceremony.

30. The only other incident recorded in Fortune but not in Mead is difficult to decipher, and many of the events in Mead's version are simply absent from Fortune's abbreviated text.

31. I would spell it *Fwonbarame*, and *Bilishoi* I would spell *Verushoi*, but I retain Mead's spellings here and elsewhere for consistency.

32. I assume, although it is not clear, that "friend" here (pidgin *pren*) is really *kamain* (see chapter 4). In the Bun version and the version I recorded in Kinakatem in 1981, *kamain* is explicit.

33. The meaning of the term "rope" in this context is unclear. Mead meant it to indicate a kind of kinship connection that was passed from father to daughter to daughter's son and so on (see chapters 4 and 5).

34. I would change the spelling of the husband to *Sambiertuma* but keep Mead's spelling for consistency.

35. The pidgin phrase here is *em i lait nogut tru*, and it is possible that my translation of it should be "malevolently" rather than "brilliantly."

CHAPTER 4: KINSHIP AND MARRIAGE

1. Mead's spelling of kin terms is somewhat troublesome. In 1981 I spelled the following terms differently: M—*ome*; F—*ungwang*; elder B—*uyea*; younger B—*kakaiyea*; Z—*shemi* or *same*; elder Z—*unyang*; younger Z—*kakaniang*; B—*aveut*; S—*fwa*; MM, FM—*uyak*.

2. In one note Mead wrote that the term *weyak* also included mother's mother's brother. But he was included anyway if the term was extended to all males of the grandparents' generation.

3. This note suggests that an alternation of sex was not necessary; that is, here we have a man presumably calling his father's father by the term for

brother and this grandfather's mother's brother by the term for father. It is an odd note in another way: if ego was identifying with grandfather and taking his terms, why refer to mother's brother as father and not mother's brother *(gumi)?*

4. Despite writing in her notes about the conceptual boundary between close and classificatory relatives, Mead never actually identifies or specifies precisely where that line is. That she does not do so is revealing: it probably could not be done precisely. Given the flexibility of the system and the ways in which kin terms in general were used, it is unlikely that the distinction was ever perfectly clear and unequivocal.

5. Informants today claim that the postpartum sex taboo has diminished considerably and that women are having children too close together.

6. In one note Mead states that both women and men knew of a drug that acted as a contraceptive for young women by preventing menstruation and, thus, pregnancy.

7. It is also interesting to speculate on who these "informants" were for the data on infanticide. Presumably they were not the parents of the newborn, and to a significant extent—at least in the cases of successful infanticide—Mead relied on seemingly hearsay evidence (the successful adoptions may have been described by those who witnessed the adoption or perhaps were the adoptive parents). Of course, this problem of hearsay is common to all ethnographies.

8. Mead wrote that dry-breasted women and women who had not conceived sometimes adopted babies and let the infants "stimulate dry breasts, [while at the] same time [they drank] coconut milk, and [breast] milk comes, not enough but plenty."

9. Mead noted that the woman "drank a lot of coconut milk, which in native belief made her breasts flow again, and nursed the child who is plump and well-grown when compared with her [twin] sister."

10. Mead thought it worth noting that the woman's daughter showed no outward jealousy and seemed to feel affection for everyone around. She contrasted this behavior with that of another child who screamed with rage whenever his mother suckled his younger sister.

11. The reasons women preferred sons over daughters are never made clear. Sons did not seem to provide any more material support to their aging mothers than did daughters. Mead believed that a woman and her son were members of the same descent group—the rope—but as I hope is clear in chapter 5, this is not a likely reason. Women used their sons in their seemingly unending battles with their husbands, as men used their daughters. Mead believed that there were few close ties between people of the same

sex among the Mundugumor, but I am not as convinced as she was on this point.

12. It was precisely this kind of behavior that provided a model for play among children.

13. There are contradictory notes on the content of the relationship between distant brothers. In one note Mead wrote that there was physical sex play between them. They could

emerge from the bush handling each other's penises and asserting that the other one's wife and he had just [had sexual relations]. The other contradicts and affirms that *he* [is the one]. This can be done in the sight of all men, not when two people are alone.

Earlier, however, Mead had recorded the following: "No regular homosexuality known, no sodomy, no pairs, grabbing penises as group horseplay." Mead never comments on the contradiction.

14. Mead (1970:26–27) made a point that such relationships were a central theme throughout the Sepik:

Congruent with the presence of moieties is the system of ceremonial friendships and rites which depends . . . upon closely identifying individuals who stand in a real or classificatory brother-in-law relationship of symmetrical opposition to each other. Hereditary relationships of this sort, in which the two individuals perform ceremonial exchanges and other acts similar to those which occur between affinal relatives and between a man and his maternal kndred, are to be found . . . among the Mundigumor. . . .

15. Mead thought that this system might have been imported from the Banaro. She goes on to speculate on the possibility of the original system being an "eight class system with endogamy of generation, exogamy of clan" but makes more of the fact that few rules were followed and that the system had completely collapsed. Her speculation on a subsection system here derived from the rather tenuous proposition that the *kamain* relationship introduced a dual division.

16. Men were not allowed to delouse women or their male affines. Women, however, did delouse their female affines as well as other women. The notes are not clear whether women could delouse men. Lice were caught and then bitten (but not eaten) or crushed with a thumbnail.

17. The nature of Mundugumor totemism is unclear in general. At times the patrilineal clans seem to be totemic, but at other times the ropes seem

to be the referent category for totemic affiliation. This question is discussed somewhat more in the section on ropes but never resolved.

18. Whether comparable age was an issue as well is unclear. Men often married women younger than themselves, but how often women married younger men is not clear. One might surmise that the practice of the levirate would lead older women to marry younger men, but there are no indications in the notes.

19. In 1981 informants translated *maikua* for me as "road"; it seemed to have no kinship connotations whatsoever.

20. In preparing her ideas for publication Mead noted that Vedder (1923) described a naming system among the Bergama somewhat similar to the rope system of the Mundugumor.

21. Both Mead and Fortune sometimes spelled the word *ngung, ngeung,* or *nggung. Geun* seems phonetically better to me.

22. In 1981 I asked informants to list kin terms. Among those they listed were *uyak paparap,* which they translated as *tumbuna bilong tumbuna* (female), and *ungwasak paparakap,* which they translated as *tumbuna bilong tumbuna* (male).

23. This is an interesting passage. Mead indicates here that mothers are "represented as" doing something, thus indicating that she is reporting informants' statements or images and not their behavior.

24. Mead never explicitly explains "split rope." See my alternative interpretation of ropes in chapter 5.

CHAPTER 5: KINSHIP, EXCHANGE, AND ROPES

1. Portions of this section were included in McDowell, 1990.

2. There was probably a gradation in the acceptability of nonexchange. The data (presented mostly in chapter 4) seem to indicate that exchange almost always occurred within the village, less often with another Mundugumor village, and least often with "foreigners," such as Grass Country residents. The closer the potential affines were, the more compelling exchange became. There were obvious practical reasons for this state of affairs—it was easier to get away with something with distant people, less easy with one's neighbors—but I suspect that other considerations were also at work. In Bun exchange and reciprocity are central means for establishing one's humanity and autonomy, and although I cannot assert that the same is true for the Mundugumor (the data are simply lacking), I suspect that it is. Refusing to reciprocate, whether in a marital exchange or any other transaction, demonstrated a belief not only in one's own superiority but also

in the other's inferiority and subhuman nature. See McDowell 1980a for a discussion of this phenomenon in Bun.

3. Sometimes other combinations were relevant, such as mother's brother–sister's daughter or father's sister–brother's son.

4. Again, I am tempted to fill in here with analysis relevant for Bun but perhaps not Mundugumor. In Bun these transactions are the way in which people define themselves as human, both as autonomous individuals and social persons. Autonomy is, I suspect, a seminal issue throughout Melanesia (see McDowell 1980a, 1984a). Exchange allows for both separation and connectedness and is thus almost a natural means for expressing and possibly resolving problems of autonomy and self.

5. The role of the *kamain* in this entire complex is not at all clear. Mead played with the idea that it introduced social organizational complexities such as dual structures, but there are simply not enough data to be certain. See McDowell 1976 and 1980a for a discussion of how the *kamain* relationship pertains to transactions in Bun.

6. In discussing the complexities of the "atom of kinship" among the Mundugumor, even Lévi-Strauss (1976:88–90) was required to incorporate female actors. He found that he especially needed to include father's sister as well as mother's brother; furthermore, he found it necessary to distinguish the sex of the child (and not assume male or generic). This indicates a twofold significance: first, that women were important social actors among the Mundugumor, just as Mead described in *Sex and Temperament*, and, second, that the opposition between male and female (and, I suggest, between these two kinds of intergenerational exchanges) was important in the conceptual system or culture.

7. Although Lévi-Strauss (1967:35; originally published in 1945) carefully distinguishes between what he calls the system of attitudes and a system of terminology, he fails to take into account the possibility that there could be divisions or differences and shadings within either system. This is one of the major problems with his analysis of Mundugumor kinship (1976; originally published 1973). He also relies on a misunderstanding of the nature of and motivation behind a person "feeding" the child of her or his opposite-sex sibling. Despite these problems and others (such as his reliance on rope as a form of descent), his analysis is fascinating and suggestive. However, an adequate discussion of it would involve relatively esoteric debates on the nature of kinship and is outside the scope of this book.

8. It is interesting to note again the potential structural equivalence between a man and his actual sister here.

9. Indeed, some anthropologists would argue that because both were classified in the same category we should not try to distinguish them at all, for

doing so violates the native categories of the culture under study. An *un-yenya* is an *unyena*. The Mundugumor data, at least as recorded by Mead, would seem to belie this interpretation. For example, although first and second cross- and parallel cousins were lumped with siblings, the Mundu-gumor clearly distinguished among these various relatives at least in terms of their "closeness"—they were not all the same even if they were called the same terminologically.

10. It is interesting to note here that in upriver Bun the phrase "the rope is broken" refers to a marital exchange that did not work out—that is, only one of the two marriages took place.

11. I do not mean to imply that all elements of a cultural structure must integrate together neatly and perfectly. It is likely that all cultures contain potential contradictions. However, in this case it seems odd that the reunit-ing of ropes cannot be done if brother-sister exchange also occurs.

12. I think that Mead was sloppy in this context, but then it is likely that she would have straightened out inheritance patterns if she and Fortune had remained longer in this field site. There is some evidence that she rec-ognized this when she began to sort her materials for publication: in 1973 she wondered in a note to herself whether there might be "two sorts of *geun*" inheritance or whether perhaps "just a parental preference" was in-volved.

13. In 1981 I noted these terms and translations: *ungwasak paparakap* (male), which meant "*tumbuna bilong tumbuna*," and *uyak paparap* (fe-male), which meant "*tumbuna bilong tumbuna*." I think these terms indi-cate that the phrases Mead and Fortune recorded that included the term *papakala* and so on probably did not refer to ropes at all but simply lines of descendants.

CHAPTER 6: MEAD AND THE MUNDUGUMOR

1. See also McDowell 1980b and especially Shore 1983, Schwartz 1983, and Weiner 1983.

2. The agreement is certainly not total. The primary dissent comes from Freeman (1983); see later discussion as well as his replies to reviews of his book (e.g., Freeman 1984a and 1984b).

3. See also Schwartz 1983 on Manus and Gewertz 1981 and 1984 for the Chambri or Tchambuli. See also McDowell 1984b.

4. It is also very important to note that Mead's data are still available for others to analyze with new and more complex theoretical paradigms. Her

notes and papers are deposited and available in the U.S. Library of Congress for other anthropologists and scholars to use.

5. Some of the information and interpretation included here and below was originally in McDowell 1983b.

6. As Gewertz (1984) aptly argues, Mead inappropriately used Western categories and ideology to describe these differences, and I am guilty of the same here. The contrasts did exist, however, as did others (such as the central one—differing concepts of the individual—suggested by Gewertz)

7. It is interesting to note here that if Mead and others had only incorporated more early 20th-century psychology into their paradigm, we might have come to this recognition sooner. If culture is personality "writ large," then endopsychic conflicts and contradictions might have translated into the cultural realm as well.

REFERENCES

Ardener, Shirley, ed.
  1975   Perceiving Women. New York: John Wiley & Sons.
Bateson, Gregory
  1932   Social Structure of the Iatmul Peoples of the Sepik. Oceania
         2:245–91, 401–53.
  1936   Naven. Cambridge: Cambridge University Press.
  1978   Towards a Theory of Cultural Coherence: Comment. Anthropo-
         logical Quarterly 51:77–78.
Benedict, Ruth
  1934   Patterns of Culture. Boston: Houghton Mifflin.
Bohannan, Paul, and Mark Glazer, eds.
  1973   High Points in Anthropology. New York: Alfred A. Knopf.
Douglas, Mary
  1952   Alternate Generations Among the Lele of Kasai, South-West
         Congo. Africa 22:59–65.
  1966   Purity and Danger. New York: Pantheon Books.
Evans-Pritchard, E. E.
  1940   The Nuer. New York: Oxford University Press.
Fortune, Reo
  1932a Sorcerers of Dobu. London: Routledge.
  1932b Omaha Secret Societies. Columbia University Contributions to
         Anthropology, Vol. 14. New York: Columbia University Press.

1935 Manus Religion. Philadelphia: American Philosophical Society.

1939 Arapesh Warfare. American Anthropologist 41:22–41.

1942 Arapesh. Publications of the American Ethnological Society, Vol. 19. New York: Augustin.

1943 Arapesh Maternity. Nature 152:164.

1947a The Rules of Relationship Behavior in One Variety of Primitive Warfare. Man 47:108–10.

1947b Law and Force in Papuan Societies. American Anthropologist 49:244–59.

Fox, Robin

1967 Kinship and Marriage. Baltimore: Penguin Books.

Frazer, Douglas

1955 Mundugumor Sculpture. Man 55:16–20.

Freeman, Derek

1983 Margaret Mead and Samoa: The Making and Unmaking of an Anthropological Myth. Cambridge: Harvard University Press.

1984a 'O Rose thou art sick!' A Rejoinder to Weiner, Schwartz, Holmes, Shore, and Silverman. American Anthropologist 86:400–405.

1984b Response to Ala'ilima, Wendt, McDowell. Pacific Studies 7:140–96.

Gewertz, Deborah

1981 An Historical Reconsideration of Female Dominance Among the Chambri of Papua New Guinea. American Ethnologist 8:94–106.

1983 Sepik River Societies: A Historical Ethnography of the Chambri and Their Neighbors. New Haven: Yale University Press.

1984 The Tchambuli View of Persons: A Critique of Individualism in the Works of Mead and Chodorow. American Anthropologist 86:615–29.

Godelier, Maurice

1982 Social Hierarchies Among the Baruya of New Guinea. *In* Inequality in New Guinea Highlands Societies. Andrew Strathern, ed., pp. 3–34. Cambridge: Cambridge University Press.

1986 The Making of Great Men. Cambridge: Cambridge University Press.

Goodenough, Ward Hunt

1949 Premarital Freedom in Truk: Theory and Practice. American Anthropologist 51:615–20.

Gorecki, P. P., ed.

1989 A Crack in the Spine: Prehistory of the Upper Yuat and Lower Jimi Region, Papua New Guinea. Townsville, Australia: James Cook University of North Queensland.

Harrison, Simon
  1982 Yams and the Symbolic Representation of Time in a Sepik River
       Village. Oceania 52:141–62.
Hauser-Schaublin, Brigitta
  1984 In the Swamps and on the Hills: Traditional Settlement Patterns
       and House Structures in the Middle Sepik. Paper prepared for
       Wenner-Gren Symposium no. 95, "Sepik Research Today," Basel,
       Switzerland.
Herdt, Gilbert
  1981 Guardians of the Flutes. New York: Columbia University Press.
Howard, Jane
  1984 Margaret Mead: A Life. New York: Simon and Schuster.
Keesing, Roger
  1981 Cultural Anthropology: A Contemporary Perspective. New York:
       Holt, Rinehart and Winston.
  1985 Conventional Metaphors and Cultural Metaphysics: The Prob-
       lematic of Cultural Translation. Journal of Anthropological Re-
       search 41:201–17.
Kelly, Raymond
  1977 Etoro Social Structure. Ann Arbor: University of Michigan Press.
Kroeber, Alfred, and Clyde Kluckhohn
  1952 Culture: A Critical Review of Concepts and Definitions. New York:
       Vintage Books.
Kuhn, Thomas
  1962 The Structure of Scientific Revolutions. Chicago: University of
       Chicago Press.
Laycock, Donald
  1973 Sepik Languages: Checklist and Preliminary Classification. Pa-
       cific Linguistics, series B, no. 25. Canberra: Linguistic Circle of
       Canberra.
Lévi-Strauss, Claude
  1967 Structural Analysis in Linguistics and in Anthropology. In Struc-
       tural Anthropology. pp. 29–53. Garden City, New York: Anchor
       Books.
  1976 Reflections on the Atom of Kinship. In Structural Anthropology,
       Vol. II. pp. 82–112. New York: Basic Books. (Original French ver-
       sion 1973.)
Maslow, A. H., and J. J. Honigman
  1970 Synergy: Some Notes of Ruth Benedict. American Anthropologist
       72:320–33.

McDowell, Nancy

1975 Kinship and the Concept of Shame in a New Guinea Village. Ph.D. dissertation, Department of Anthropology, Cornell University.

1976 Kinship and Exchange: The *Kamain* Relationship in a Yuat River Village. Oceania 47:36–48.

1977 The Meaning of "Rope" in a Yuat River Village. Ethnology 16:175–83.

1978a The Struggle to Be Human: Exchange and Politics in Bun. Anthropological Quarterly 51:16–25.

1978b The Flexibility of Sister Exchange: Case Studies. Oceania 48:207–31.

1979 The Significance of Cultural Context: A Note on Food Taboos in Bun. Journal of Anthropological Research 35:231–37.

1980a It's Not Who You Are But How You Give That Counts: The Role of Exchange in a Melanesian Society. American Ethnologist 7:58–70.

1980b The Oceanic Ethnography of Margaret Mead. American Anthropologist 82:278–302.

1983a Trade and Power in the Middle Yuat Region. Paper read at the Annual Meeting of the American Anthropological Association, Chicago.

1983b An Evaluation of the Work of Margaret Mead: The Mundugumor. Paper read at Barnard College Symposium on an Evaluation of the Work of Margaret Mead, April 8, 1983.

1984a Complementarity: The Relationship between Male and Female in the East Sepik Village of Bun, Papua New Guinea. *In* Rethinking Women's Roles: Perspectives from the Pacific. Denise O'Brien and Sharon Tiffany, eds. pp. 32–52. Berkeley: University of California Press.

1984b Review of Derek Freeman's Margaret Mead and Samoa: The Making and Unmaking of an Anthropological Myth. Pacific Studies 7:99–140.

1990 Intergenerational Exchange in Diachronic Context: A Melanesian Example. Anthropos 85:393–401.

Mead, Margaret

1928 Coming of Age in Samoa. New York: William Morrow.

1930 Social Organization of Manua. Bulletin no. 76. Honolulu: Bishop Museum.

1932 The Changing Culture of an Indian Tribe. New York: Columbia University Press.

1934 Tamberans and Tumbuans in New Guinea. Natural History 34:234–46.

1937 Cooperation and Competition Among Primitive Peoples (ed.). New York: McGraw Hill.

1949 Male and Female: A Study of the Sexes in a Changing World. New York: William Morrow.

1959 Preface. *In* Patterns of Culture, by Ruth Benedict. pp. vii–x. Boston: Houghton Mifflin.

1961 Cultural Determinants of Sexual Behavior. *In* Sex and Internal Secretions. William C. Young, pp. 1433–79. Baltimore: Williams and Wilkins Co.

1963 Sex and Temperament in Three Primitive Societies. New York: William Morrow (1st ed. 1935).

1968 The Mountain Arapesh. Vol. 5, The Record of Unabelin with Rorschach Analyses. Garden City, N.Y.: The Natural History Press. (1st ed., New York: American Museum of Natural History, 1949).

1970 The Mountain Arapesh. Vol. 2. Arts and Supernaturalism. Garden City, N.Y. The Natural History Press (1st ed., New York: American Museum of Natural History, 1938, 1940).

1971 The Mountain Arapesh. Vol. 3, Stream of Events in Alitoa. Garden City, N.Y.: The Natural History Press (1st ed., New York: American Museum of Natural History, 1947).

1972 Blackberry Winter: My Earlier Years. New York: William Morrow.

1977 Letters from the Field: 1925–1975. New York: Harper and Row.

1978 The Sepik as a Culture Area: Comment. Anthropological Quarterly 51:69–75.

Meigs, Anna

1984 Food, Sex, and Pollution: A New Guinea Religion. New Brunswick, N.J.: Rutgers University Press.

Métraux, Rhoda

1978 Introduction. Anthropological Quarterly 51:1–2.

Mitchell, William

1978a The Bamboo Fire. New York: Norton.

1978b On Keeping Equal: Polity and Reciprocity Among the New Guinea Wape. Anthropological Quarterly 51:5–15.

Modjeska, Nicholas

1982 Production and Inequality: Perspectives from Central New Guinea. *In* Inequality in New Guinea Highlands Societies. Andrew Strathern, ed. pp. 50–108. Cambridge: Cambridge University Press.

Oliver, Douglas

1955 A Solomon Island Society. Cambridge: Harvard University Press.

Radcliffe-Brown, A. R., and C. D. Forde, eds.

1950 African Systems of Kinship and Marriage. London: Oxford University Press.

Read, Kenneth

1965 The High Valley. New York: Charles Scribner's Sons.

1986 Return to the High Valley. Berkeley: University of California Press.

Reiter, Rayna, ed.

1975 Toward an Anthropology of Women. New York: Monthly Review Press.

Rosaldo, Michelle, and Louise Lamphere, eds.

1974 Woman, Culture, and Society. Palo Alto: Stanford University Press.

Sahlins, Marshall

1963 Poor Man, Rich Man, Big-Man, Chief: Political Types in Melanesia and Polynesia. Comparative Studies in Society and History 5:285–303.

Scaglion, Richard, and R. G. Condon

1979 Abelam Yam Beliefs and Sociorhythmicity. Journal of Biosocial Science 11:17–25.

Schieffelin, Edward

1976 The Sorrow of the Lonely and the Burning of the Dancers. New York: St. Martin's Press.

Schindlbeck, Markus

1984 Tradition and Change in Kwanga Villages. Paper prepared for Wenner-Gren Symposium no. 95, "Sepik Research Today," Basel, Switzerland.

Schuster, Meinhard, and Gisela Schuster

1984 Aspects of the Aibom Concept of History and Aibom Genealogy as History. Paper prepared for Wenner-Gren Symposium no. 95, "Sepik Research Today," Basel, Switzerland.

Schwartz, Theodore

1963 Systems of Areal Integration. Anthropological Forum 1:56–97.

1983 Anthropology: A Quaint Science. American Anthropologist 85:919–29.

Shore, Bradd

1983 Paradox Regained: Freeman's Margaret Mead and Samoa. American Anthropologist 85:935–44.

Stanek, Milan
1984 Social Structure of the Iatmul People of the Sepik River, East Sepik Province, Papua New Guinea. Paper prepared for Wenner-Gren Symposium no. 95, "Sepik Research Today," Basel, Switzerland.

Stocking, George
1968 Race, Culture, and Evolution. New York: The Free Press.

Territory of Papua and New Guinea (T.P.N.G.)
1968 Village Directory. Port Moresby: Department of District Administration.

Thurnwald, Richard
1916 Banaro Society: Social Organization and Kinship System of a Tribe in the Interior of New Guinea. Memoirs of the American Anthropological Association, no. 3.

Tuzin, Donald
1972 Yam Symbolism in the Sepik: An Interpretative Account. Southwestern Journal of Anthropology 28:230–54.
1976 The Ilahita Arapesh: Dimensions of Unity. Berkeley: University of California Press.
1980 The Voice of the Tambaran: Truth and Illusion in Ilahita Arapesh Religion. Berkeley: University of California Press.

Tylor, Edward B.
1883 Primitive Culture. New York: Henry Holt and Company.

Vedder, H.
1923 Die Bergama. Hamburg: L. Friederichsen and Co.

Voget, Fred W.
1975 A History of Ethnology. New York: Holt, Rinehart, and Winston.

de Waal Malefijt, Annemarie
1974 Images of Man: A History of Anthropological Thought. New York: Alfred A. Knopf.

Wassman, Jurg
1984 The Nyaura Concept of Space and Time. Paper prepared for Wenner-Gren Symposium no. 95, "Sepik Research Today," Basel, Switzerland.

Weiner, Annette
1983 Ethnographic Determinism: Samoa and the Margaret Mead Controversy. American Anthropologist 85:909–19.

Weiss, Florence
1984 The Child's Role in the Economic System of a Village Community

in Papua New Guinea. Paper prepared for Wenner- Gren Symposium no. 95, "Sepik Research Today," Basel, Switzerland.

Williams, F. E.

1932 Sex Affiliation and Its Implications. Journal of the Royal Anthropological Institute 62:51–81.

1933 Physiological Paternity in the Morehead District, Papua. Man 33:123–24.

1934 Exchange Marriage and Exogamy. Man 34:110.

1940–41 Natives of Lake Kutubu, Papua. Oceania 11:121–57, 260–94, 374–401; 12:49–74, 134–54.

INDEX

*Index prepared by
Andrew L. Christenson*